Late Gothic to
High Renaissance Painters

THE LIVES OF THE PAINTERS
by John Canaday

FOR *KATHERINE*

Contents

Contents

Contents

Preface to
The Lives of the Painters

This book is a history of painting from the end of the Middle Ages to the eve of the twentieth century—from Giotto's revolution to Cézanne's—told in the form of several hundred biographies strung together on a historical cord. By way of its index it can also double as a reference encyclopedia, since each biography is self-contained, whether within a brief paragraph or a long essay.

If the book is an acceptable history, I am glad. If it is a helpful encyclopedia, so much to the good. But what I most hope is that these biographies will enlarge the reader's enjoyment of painting, and I like to think that this is a book that can be picked up and opened anywhere for a bit of pleasurable reading from time to time. It was written in somewhat that way: the biographies were composed not in chronological sequence, but according to my interest from day to day and were collated en route.

The question may be asked why a history of painting should be told in the form of linked biographies. There are good arguments to support the contention that knowledge of a painter's life and personality should not be allowed to intrude upon our response to his paintings, since paintings are objects with independent existences. This is a principle upon which I used to insist and with which I still agree in the cases of living artists. We have our own firsthand experience of our times as a basis for putting the work of our contemporaries in context. But even the greatest art of the past can be fully understood only if we can see it in the context of the society in which it was conceived as well as in its timelessness.

Preface

If we accept the truism that art is not produced in a vacuum (and we must), it follows that artists' lives tell us about the air they breathed, how it differed from one part of the world to another, and how it changed from one century to another —all of which explains the changing forms that in their succession make up the history of art.

Some of these biographies may seem too long or too short as measures of the painters' worth. No such proportion has been observed. A minor painter may have had an interesting life or a life that, as in the case of one very dull Spaniard, Francisco Pacheco, affords the best opportunity for describing the climate in which painters better than he were working. In an instance or two I have included artists not because they were important but simply because I like them. This personal indulgence accounts for the presence of, for one, the minor Florentine mannerist Bernardo Buontalenti. I hope there are no omissions except those explicable by the truth that a book can't go on forever.

Cézanne's birth year, which was 1839, has been adopted, with a few self-explanatory exceptions, as the boundary date for artists included in this story. The story ends with the triumph of impressionism—shared by Cézanne—and the rift between nineteenth- and twentieth-century painting, which Cézanne initiated. Cézanne's fellow post-impressionists, as they have come to be called (Vincent van Gogh, Seurat, and Gauguin) were all younger than he and thus are ruled out by date. In any case their biographies would have had to begin yet another volume in this already very long book, and we would have had to go on to a shift in fundamental premises corresponding to the radical change in the concept of creative art represented by Cézanne's descendants, Picasso among them.

The list of acknowledgements that usually concludes an author's preface would in this book have to include the hundreds of museums and private collections in Europe and America that have given me for many years the opportunity to see paintings, and then the hundreds of historians whose work over the centuries has supplied the factual material that has been given yet another winnowing here. Some special debts to other winnowers, and researchers, are acknowledged in the course of the text. The general debt, shared by every art historian who has followed him, goes back to Giorgio Vasari, the father of us all, whose biography appears on pages 284-86. But I should mention that Rudolf and Margot Wittkower's book on the character and conduct of artists, "Born Under Saturn," was particularly helpful not only as a guide through Vasari but as a summary of references to other early histories.

Inevitably, a major source was the work of that great and delightful man, the late Erwin Panofsky, and I want to say here that I treasure our friendship of more than twenty-five years. He was wonderfully generous and patient with me as a writer who could not aspire to his kind of scholarship; on my part, as a writer, I once complained to him that he was a difficult scholar to crib from because he expressed everything so perfectly that to rephrase anything he had written was to butcher it.

Essays on several of the artists have appeared in somewhat different form in *Horizon* magazine. Permission for the use of this material is gratefully acknowledged.

I cannot conclude without thanking Robert E. Farlow, who wanted this book written and gave me the chance to write it.

JOHN CANADAY

New York

GIOTTO, DUCCIO, AND THE END OF THE MIDDLE AGES IN ITALY

The history of painting can be followed, in a limping fashion, from prehistoric times, but the history of painters begins in medieval Italy. Until then (in spite of exceptions here and there, especially in ancient Greece, which was an exception to everything) the names of artists were thought hardly more worth remembering than the names of stonemasons and other craftsmen. Similarly, the suggestion that the lives and personalities of artists could be of any interest in connection with their painting would have seemed as absurd as the idea would seem today that the life and personality of the man who hangs your wallpaper would be worth recording for the benefit of your grandchildren. The history of painting in the Western world, of painting as an art expressing the individualities of its creators, came fully into its own only with the Renaissance, when each man became important as a self-contained and responsible unit in a world of multiple choices. In late-thirteenth-century Italy (still, by arbitrary definition, a medieval time), when the painter became an explorer and an inventor and a personality rather than an anonymous workman, the history of painting as we know it began.

THE BEGINNINGS

Less than fifteen years after Cimabue's death, Dante, in three famous lines from the "Purgatorio," cited him as one of many examples of the transcience of human glory:

> In painting Cimabue thought to hold
> The field; now hath Giotto all the cry,
> So that the other's fame is less extoll'd.

But chronologically Cimabue must be allowed first on stage. A great artist, he firmly occupies his position as the patriarch of Italian painting, and it is his misfortune that his brilliant performance as a curtain raiser is certain to be lost on an audience getting settled in its seats and waiting for the appearance of the stars in the first big scenes.

Cimabue was probably born about 1240—certainly no later than 1250—and died about 1302, dates deduced from the earliest and latest records of commissions he executed. In his half of the thirteenth century, Italian painters had revivified the Byzantine tradition (they called it the "Greek style"), but the tradition was at a crossroads. Courtly painters followed a set of conventions so rigidly studied that one artist's work might be differentiated from another's only by the most subtle nuances. But beneath the surface of these conventions, painting as we think of it—painting as the expression of emotion or personal convictions—was struggling for release. There was a provincial as well as a courtly Byzantinism, which sacrificed the elegance of the more formal style to greater naturalness and intensified dramatic expression in an effort to satisfy a yearning to bring the heavenly subjects within the realm of understandable human feeling. Everything was ready for a revolutionary genius.

Cimabue was not quite that genius, but he did harmonize the elegance of the traditional hieratic style with the contradictory elements of a new realism. His *Madonna Enthroned with Angels,* from the Church of Santa Trinità in Florence and now in the Uffizi, is his most majestic achievement. His very late works show a failing power; the expressive vitality that makes him a precursor of Giotto falters, and he becomes not much more than a formula painter. But when he died he was still the great painter of Italy. He had only begun to be rivaled by the young Giotto.

Dante could have added a second name to Giotto's, that of Duccio di Buoninsegna. Between the two of them, Giotto and Duccio fulfilled Cimabue's promise, in two directions. Duccio set a direction that was followed over several generations; Giotto set one that was not really questioned for a matter of six centuries, when it was challenged by Cézanne, the father of the revolution called modern art.

If the most decisive moment in the history of Western painting had to be pinpointed to one day and one place, it could be the day in Padua more than six and a half centuries ago when Giotto di Bondone rinsed out his brushes and took a last look around at the cycle of frescoes he had just completed for a chapel intended to salvage the soul of a usurer—or, at the very least, to amend his earthly reputation. The year might just possibly have been as early as 1306, or as late as 1312. Giotto would have been in his early forties, since 1267 seems to be the most probable date of his birth. He died in 1337.

The donor of the chapel was Enrico degli Scrovegni, the son of a man whose evil reputation led Dante to consign him to the seventh circle of hell. Pelted by fiery earth, steamed by hot vapors, "their grief gushing from their eyes," the "Inferno" tells us, notorious usurers were identified by the coats of arms on the moneybags hung around their necks as the badges of their sin.

If Enrico was haunted by some such vision of old Scrovegni's damnation, he must have been comforted by Giotto's record of his plea for clemency toward his father's soul. In the lower section of the fresco on the chapel's entrance wall, where the Last Judgment is pictured, Giotto makes clear that the building is a placative gift. Enrico is shown offering it, in the form of a model, to three haloed emissaries of the Lord. He kneels before them with one hand supporting the model (most of the weight is held on the shoulder of an attendant priest), while his other hand is raised reverently and with awe, hesitantly, toward a saintly hand extended in acceptance and on the point of touching his.

It is a grave and touching scene typical of the dramatic power in Giotto's selection of revelatory attitudes. The saints are nobly erect, their heads slightly inclined toward the supplicant with a combination of majesty and compassionate recognition that befits their role as couriers between the earthly realm and the celestial one they have attained, while Enrico kneels in full humility without loss of dignity.

Today it is hard for us to realize how revolutionary painting of this kind was. We cannot see it in its innovational context. At a time when painters had mastered only a few repetitious formulas for facial expressions, Giotto made of Enrico's head not only a portrait that we are safe in accepting as an accurate one but a full revelation of a complex emotional state. Enrico is at the moment of realization, the awesome moment when his fears for his temerity, his fears that his gift might be rejected, are about to be dissipated by the joy of learning that it is acceptable. Yet we feel that in this joy, too, he will remain reverently self-contained.

Giotto was able to depict this scene with all its psychological interplay despite the technical difficulties besetting an artist who was still feeling his way toward the representation of forms of monumental character in combinations and from angles of vision that painters had never before presented realistically. His technical failures are as obvious to us—after centuries of perfected drawing and a century of photography's deadly accuracy in the reproduction of the visual world—as they are unimportant. We see that Enrico's far hand and wrist seem to grow from his near arm; that his near leg looks as if it had been amputated at the point where the knee rests on the ground; that there is no room behind the model of the chapel for the lower body of the nearest saint. There are other awkwardnesses, including the inaccurate perspective of the miniature building.

These are technical shortcomings of a kind that remained unmastered for another hundred years, but they are only technical, and in Giotto's century they were part of an advance in representational accuracy that was as astounding as his mastery of psychological interrelationships. We find Boccaccio giving his opinion of Giotto through one of the characters in his stories, who says that Giotto could paint the natural world so accurately that you might mistake his paintings of objects for the objects themselves.

Even if we accept the exaggeration in this comment, it helps us understand Giotto as an innovator. There was nothing he would not try, nothing that he would not dare. He abandoned the safe conventions of a limited catalogue of formulas for drawing and cast his figures in the dramatic compositions that revolutionized not only the techniques but the whole spirit of painting. If ever a soul was granted the privilege of ransom from hell, this soul must have been Scrovegni's, for the history of painting holds no nobler monument than these frescoes—not even Michelangelo's cycle on the ceiling of the Sistine Chapel.

The Scrovegni Chapel—more commonly called the Arena Chapel because it was built on the site of an ancient Roman arena—was consecrated on March 16, 1305, and presumably Giotto began work on the frescoes shortly thereafter. The building itself is without architectural distinction, even though Giotto designed it. Little more than a shedlike structure of brick about 68 feet long, it is roofed by a barrel vault, illuminated from one side by six long narrow windows, and terminated by an apse of routine character. But the side walls are lined with Giotto's thirty-eight scenes from the lives of Joachim and Anna, the Virgin, and Christ. The incidents in the story, of course, had been portrayed hundreds of times. But Giotto recast them in an interpretation that raised painting to the supreme position among the arts. Henceforth it was to be the medium for the most profound expression of human aspiration, of the sustaining hope that life on earth is a purposeful affair, subject to divine authority and divine mercy.

Such breadth and depth of human affirmation had always been, primarily, the function of architecture. The temples of the ancient world and the cathedrals of the Middle Ages had summarized man's ideas about himself and his gods, with sculpture as a powerful corollary and painting as a decorative and a didactic addition. But with Giotto all this changed—not because he set out to change it, but because as a painter he became the instrument of change. The fact that the Arena Chapel is little more than a shell providing walls for the frescoes becomes symbolic. And so does the fact that in 1334 Giotto was appointed head of the cathedral workshop in Florence—the first painter to receive an honor that was, in addition, a major civic responsibility. For although he was also an architect and a sculptor, Giotto was first of all a painter. The great age of painting had begun.

Painting became, as it had never been before, the summarizing art, and remained so—despite the creations of such architects as Brunelleschi and of such sculptors as Donatello —until Michelangelo completed his ceiling in the Sistine Chapel in 1512. The two centuries bounded by the supreme pictorial cycles of Giotto and Michelangelo produced the only others that can stand in their company—Masaccio's in Florence, cut short by his death; Piero della Francesca's in Arezzo; and, usually included, Raphael's in the Vatican. In the different temper of the North there are the great achievements of the Van Eycks' *Ghent Altarpiece* and Grünewald's *Isenheim Altarpiece,* as well as a staggering quantity of individual paintings, both North and South, that explore the world, the mind, and the spirit in pictures that are lesser only because their physical dimensions preclude the wider statement of the cycles.

In the centuries that followed, sculpture and architecture resumed larger importance in the shifting balance of the trinity of the arts. But Giotto set painting on a course that it followed, albeit with a thousand variations, until the radical innovations of the twentieth century—initiated at the end of the nineteenth by Cézanne. There is, in truth, a parallel between Giotto and Cézanne as innovators. Cézanne is the link between the tradition of Giotto and the disruptive force of cubism, just as Giotto is the link between the Middle Ages and the revolutionary developments of the Renaissance.

We have no reason to believe that Giotto thought of his art as revolutionary: it was revolutionary in the natural course of things. He reoriented the painter's way of representing the world, but this reorientation, as filtered through his genius, was the inevitable expression of a change in the way people thought and felt about the world. As the age of mystical faith waned, Giotto changed painting from an art of symbols into an art of passion. He tied painting to the earth—to the look of the world and to the emotions of people in the world—and in doing so he released it to explore in a multiplicity of directions the vast range of the human spirit and intelligence.

Giotto was a practical man who made a great deal of money and managed his affairs well, but he was not the moneygrubber or the shady financial manipulator that some fanciful biographers have made him out. (Nor was he the man indifferent to money and totally dedicated to his art that others have imagined.) He owned land and lent money at interest like any other good prosperous Florentine, but there is no indication that he was anything but an honest man, as well as a successful one. He was famous and admired for extraordinary gifts beyond those of hand and eye at a time when artists held a rather low position in the social scale.

The fact that Giotto was a Florentine may account for the high esteem in which he was held, for it was Florence that was to discover the artist as a man of God-given talents and feelings who could honor princes and popes with his friendship. Thus Giotto might in a double sense be considered the first Renaissance artist. (Two hundred years after Giotto, Michelangelo was to acquire the epithet "The Divine" during his lifetime.)

The sources of Giotto's art are the subject of constant

scholarly detective work. Cimabue is the link between conventional Byzantinism and Giotto's drastic revolution, and Giotto has been called, not on the soundest basis in the world, Cimabue's pupil. Giotto may or may not have had a major hand in the famous cycle of frescoes in the Basilica of San Francesco in Assisi, and most of his later frescoes have suffered badly from repainting. The Arena Chapel remains his unquestioned and unviolated masterwork, and from it we may trace backward to various probable sources—classical sculpture and the sculpture of the Pisanos in Italy included —but any sources are ultimately negligible in comparison with the individuality of Giotto's genius.

There is no way to understand Giotto without visiting the Arena Chapel. Photography and reduction in size somehow produce a heavy outline that flattens the roundness of the figures; the camera tends to make Giotto's full volumes seem merely bulky, and the pearly colors lose both their strength and their subtlety. Nor can individual scenes from the cycle give any impression of the majestic progression of the story from one section to the next along the chapel walls, with each incident conceived in its own appropriate emotional air as a unit in a—the word is inevitable—symphony. The story is told with such tenderness and passion that we are moved as human beings, whatever our religion. The Virgin as she mourns her dead Son is a woman suffering the anguish of her own loss, but beyond that she is the universalized expression of an emotion that each of us can share. Giotto's technical realism—his revolutionary advance in the approximation of the natural look of people and objects— would be pointless if it did not serve this greater realism. We are involved as vicarious participants in a human drama elevated to a noble scale that purifies us through pity, if not through terror.

This was the nature of Giotto's revolution—that he re-established a recognition of the capacity for grandeur in human emotion. His technical revolution was only the necessary adjunct to this achievement. He is sometimes called the medieval climacteric because of the power of his narration of the Christian story. He is usually called the first Renaissance artist because in humanizing that story he opened a tradition of reference to nature. He is both of these. And he is also a great artist in the classical tradition, which ennobles man in his physical being as a vessel of the intellect and the spirit.

If we can say all this with truth of a single artist, we are saying that his art is beyond time and place. We are saying that Giotto's art is universal.

Over the rest of his century, Giotto's innovations were only partially absorbed by other painters, and those who tried to imitate him most closely ended by imitating him most superficially. The following painters—the Giotteschi—were of that kind, with the exception of one who, as noted, reacted against Giotto. One painter is included who, possibly, contributed to Giotto's development.

Taddeo Gaddi (*c.* 1300-*c.* 1366) was the most important of the Giottesque painters. He worked for more than twenty years directly with Giotto, but as an independent painter he was fond of more complex, livelier pictures, with a strong story-telling quality and plenty of realistic detail. His *Life of the Virgin*, a series of frescoes in a chapel of Santa Croce in Florence, displays his talents as a designer and sprightly raconteur. Like other Florentines who admired Giotto but could not reach his level, he came under Sienese influence. The son of an artist, Gaddo Gaddi, he was the father of another, Agnolo Gaddi. Agnolo, active between 1369 and 1396, is the last Florentine who can be called Giottesque without stretching the point too far. His descent from Giotto is apparent in his thinned-down versions of Giotto's forms, but his essential dedication is to elegance, elaboration, and decorative detail — all antithetical to Giotto's basic monumentality and intensity.

Bernardo Daddi was one of the most important—and most attractive—of the Florentine followers of Giotto. He was active from about 1320 to 1350. Apparently a busy, successful artist, he was among the founders of St. Luke's Guild, by which the painters came into their own, having been fobbed off, until then, with membership in the guild of doctors and apothecaries. Daddi's Giottesque style was modified by an exceptional love of bright color, and also a taste for the complexities of Gothic line (considerable modifications, these), and he is thought to have been influenced by association with the Sienese Ambrogio Lorenzetti.

Founder of the early school of Verona (his birthplace), Altichiero (*c.* 1330-1395) also worked in Padua, where Giotto's frescoes impressed him indelibly. Deftly enough, he followed Giotto's compositional principles, but with more grace than force. Giotto's passionate drama is reduced in Altichiero to attractively staged anecdotes. Still, to be attractive is something.

Andrea di Cione, called Orcagna, succeeded Giotto as the most eminent Florentine artist, and is certainly the most interesting Florentine of the second half of the fourteenth century. His style is often called reactionary and anti-Giottesque, since he returned to flat, linear composition, even while retaining Giotto's firm modeling. Orcagna, more likely, was engaged in no academic reaction but found that this manner was more adaptable to expression of the mystical-moral intensity generated by the plague of 1348, which had decimated the population. But those of his frescoes that have not been destroyed are in such pitiful condition that he can hardly be evaluated as a painter. Also a sculptor and architect, he was one of a family of artists that included his brothers Nardo and Jacopo di Cione. Orcagna was born about 1308 and died sometime after 1368.

The disappearance and mutilation of Pietro Cavallini's works have reduced him to a shadowy figure. It seems almost certain that he was dissatisfied with the Byzantine formula and tried, under the influence of Roman sculpture, for the monumental form that Giotto later achieved. Born about 1250 in Rome, where he did important work, he is inevitably called the father of the Roman school. He died in 1330. The extent of his contribution to Giotto's development has been the subject of much scholarly speculation.

By the neatest coincidence, Giotto's Arena Chapel frescoes were created all but simultaneously with a parallel cycle of paintings on the same themes, also innovations but in a different sense. Between 1308 and 1311, Duccio di Buoninsegna was at work on an altarpiece for the Siena Cathedral, and it is quite possible (depending upon what dates you accept for Giotto's cycle) that there were months when the two painters were at work on their masterpieces at the same time. Geographically they were not far apart; today you can make an excursion to Siena from Florence by bus within a single day if you are a sturdy tourist. But the cities were widely separated in terms having nothing to do with mileage. Siena was (and still thinks of itself as) the aristocratic heart of central Italy, while Florence was a bustling, ambitious, adventurous town. Sienese intellectualism was elegant and conservative without being stodgy; Florentine thought was virile and adventurous without being coarse.

Duccio and Giotto reflect the personalities of their cities. The brilliance of Duccio's accomplishment seems less revolutionary than Giotto's because Duccio, as a Sienese, made his innovations within the limits of medieval style; yet Duccio was the fountainhead of a school of late-medieval painting—graceful, aristocratic, highly refined, sometimes sophisticated and often intense to the point of neurasthenia—that flourished in Siena while Giotto's revolution was spreading around it. And by way of later Sienese painters, echoes of Duccio's influence were carried northward to affect an international style that in turn contributed to the final miracle of medieval art—Netherlandish painting of the fifteenth century.

Giotto's power and Duccio's refinement, Giotto's humanistic clarity and Duccio's mystical tenderness, brought both artists to expressions so complete that if one of them had never existed it would certainly seem to us that the other, whether Duccio or Giotto, was the natural, the inevitable, the only possible and unapproachable master painter for that particular moment—a thought that could be a bit chastening to the art historian. For anyone who is accustomed to thinking of the late Middle Ages in terms of a waning celestial dream, Duccio's altarpiece is more to be expected than Giotto's chapel. The main panel of the altarpiece shows the Madonna as the Queen of Heaven, enthroned with the heavenly Prince on her lap, while saints and angels crowd around as an adoring court. Sumptuously attired, Duccio's Madonna is monumental not only in actual dimensions (standing, the figure might be 8 or 9 feet tall) but in what must be called spiritual scale. She is the true Queen of Heaven, and of aristocratic Siena also. Dozens of other Italian cities claim the Madonna as their patron, but the Sienese have never had any doubt that Siena is her own preference. The citizens have called Duccio's courtly scene the *Maestà*, or "Majesty," ever since the altarpiece was carried through the streets in triumph from Duccio's workshop to the Cathedral. This was on June 9, 1311, and it was cause for a citywide celebration.

A contemporary account of the occasion tells us: "On the day when it was brought to the Cathedral, the shops were shut and the Bishop decreed a solemn procession of a large and devout company of priests and friars, accompanied by the nine Signori and by all the officers of the Commune and all the populace; and one by one all the most worthy persons approached the picture with lighted candles in their hands and behind them came the women and children in devout attitudes. And they accompanied the said picture to the Cathedral, marching in procession round the Campo, as is the custom, while the bells sounded the Gloria, in homage to so noble a painting as this is. And they remained all day praying and gave many alms to poor persons, praying to God and to his Mother, who is our patroness and with her infinite mercy defends us from every adversity and evil and preserves us from the hands of traitors and enemies of Siena."

At that time the altarpiece, about 14 feet wide, consisted of a large group of paintings. Thirteen smaller subjects were included on the predella beneath the main panel, and sixteen small panels rose above it. The back of the altarpiece was also divided into numerous panels, with twenty-six pictures relating the story of the Passion and other smaller panels providing niches for a further congress of saints who had not been included in the immediate presence of the Madonna. All this was held within a base and frame so elaborately carved, pinnacled, and gilded that the altarpiece must have glittered like a heavenly mansion. It was in effect a miniature architectural fantasy, in harmony with the Cathedral of Siena, which remains the most luxuriantly ornamental medieval structure in Italy.

Duccio's glorious structure was taken down from its place on the high altar in 1505; its architectural frame was discarded, and it was placed in one of the chapels. Some two hundred and fifty years later the main section, with its Virgin and Child in front and its twenty-six scenes on the back, was sawed into seven parts; the back and front were pried apart, and the parts reassembled to make two separate paintings, which were hung elsewhere in the Cathedral. In 1878 the sadly butchered and dismembered work was once again moved, this time to the cramped little Cathedral museum, where it remains today. Some of the panels have been lost; a few have found their way to museums or private collections in various places about the world. The spiritual entity of the altarpiece has been violated along with the violation of its physical being. Today we are denied any sense of the *Maestà* as a religious object, as the visual and spiritual focus of the Cathedral, illuminated by candles and transforming the Cathedral itself into the throne room of Paradise. But we are lucky to have it at all.

Long used to accurate representation, we cannot imagine the overpowering impression of physical presence that Duccio's Madonna must have created six and a half centuries ago. Its reality was all the more vivid because the division between the physical world and the spiritual world was less drastic than it is now. The transcendent image and the human representation of the Madonna merged as a single identity, and thus Duccio's Queen of Heaven must have seemed invested with a true life, a warm life, for the special reason that he introduced human tenderness into what had been a tradition of aloofness. He humanized the Byzantine tradition without diminishing its imperative and aristocratic elegance.

In the panels on the reverse of the *Maestà*, Duccio perfected Byzantine narrative techniques. With the brilliant dramatic sense of a superb director he staged his scenes with maximum economy; he was a master of the telling gesture, the revealing attitude; he could play a figure or a group of figures against another to reveal the essence of an encounter.

But his actors, somehow, never lose their consciousness that they are performing at court, and since the court is a celestial one, they crystallize supernatural moments forever within their few square inches of color and line. The final difference between Duccio and Giotto is that where Giotto reveals the grandeur of human passion, Duccio seems to regard passions as inconsequential in the face of divine miracle. It is not necessary to take sides, but one ardent pro-Sienese critic has put the difference in another way, saying that where Duccio's Madonna is a queen, Giotto's is a peasant.

Duccio himself was neither an aristocrat nor a mystic. Not a great deal is known about his life, but there are records —in those incredible centuries-old documents preserved in the files of Italian cities—of heavy fines and large bills for wine. Some of the fines are heavy enough to have been exacted for political transgressions, the offense taken most seriously by the courts. There are also records showing that, in spite of the large sums he received for the *Maestà*, Duccio was forced to go into debt, and he seems to have ended his life in bankruptcy. Nowhere in surviving records is he celebrated by his intellectual contemporaries as an important man. He remains the typical medieval artist. Siena was not yet ready to recognize him as Florence recognized Giotto. His *Maestà*, celebrated as it was, was revered primarily as a votive object. Its aesthetic qualities may have been admired, but only as adjuncts to its spiritual references, and Duccio was not thought of as a creator, but only as an exceptionally skilled manual intermediary in the translation of a heavenly subject into visual terms.

Duccio was about ten years older than Giotto, having been born about 1255. Accordingly he would have been about forty-three when he began the great altarpiece, about forty-seven when he completed it, and about sixty-four when he died in 1319.

THE SIENESE TRADITION

Giotto's revolution was too great to be assimilated overnight. It proved, in fact, too great to be assimilated during the century and more that elapsed before the appearance of a genius named Masaccio, who assimilated and expanded it. But in the meanwhile, if the revolution could not be assimilated, neither could it be ignored, and nobody—at least no Florentine painter, and few elsewhere—wanted to ignore it. Giotto's followers were sometimes charming, sometimes merely awkward. None approximated his expressive power.

Duccio's revolution was another matter. His innovations, less drastic than Giotto's, were immediately comprehensible within the technical tradition of Byzantine painting and, more important, within the emotional refinements of Gothic sensibilities. Hence Duccio found immediate followers of merit. Perhaps part of the explanation is simply fortuitous circumstance: Siena happened to birth some worthy talents to follow Duccio during a century when Florence produced none who could stand close to Giotto.

Whatever the reason, Sienese painting flourished, and even the Giottesque Florentines adopted some Sienese mannerisms (while the Sienese grafted onto their styles whatever served them best in Giotto's). As an aristocratic, elegant, and sensitive expression of the late-medieval spirit, Sienese painting flowered during the fourteenth century. As an aristocratic, elegant, and effete school that cut itself off from the Renaissance, it faded during the fifteenth. Of all major schools, Sienese painting is probably the least well known to a wide public, but it is also one of the most vehemently defended and lovingly cultivated of all schools by a group of ardently united admirers.

Simone Martini, a generation younger than Duccio, succeeded him as the leading Sienese painter, and next to Duccio he is probably the finest artist that the school produced. The "probably" is introduced here as a tactical precaution, since each member of the small body of fans who have attached themselves so passionately to Sienese painting has his own hierarchy and will defend it to the death.

Simone is even, in some judgments, the painter who, surpassing Duccio, achieved the supreme expression of Sienese genius. In one category of this genius no one denies him the crown: not only in Sienese art but in all Western art he is the greatest master of pure line as an expressive device—unless (another tactical precaution) he must share that position with a later Florentine, Botticelli.

Simone was the only Sienese except Duccio to have remained altogether Sienese while working within a vigorously living tradition. Even the best of his successors, before Sienese painting died entirely, must be enjoyed as one may enjoy the special fragrance and the slightly morbid discolorations of a fading blossom—gentle forms of the death throe, whose symptoms in Sienese painting were nostalgia, hypersensitivity, and exquisitely cultivated anemia. No other school of painting ever died a lingering death so entrancingly.

It was Giotto's revolution that eventually killed Sienese art, but Simone worked during the years when this revolution was still being absorbed bit by bit rather than fully assimilated and enlarged. He was the one painter, in or out of Siena, who successfully harmonized some of Giotto's new power with the sophistications and delicacies of the waning Byzantine decorative tradition. His figures take on greater weight and volume because of his exposure to Giotto, and occupy more logically a deeper space than Duccio's. He made his own advances in color harmonies and in color as an expressive instrument without sacrificing the medieval use of color as a sumptuous ornamental addition to drawing. But however progressive he was, however alert and receptive to the world beyond Siena's walls, he was always first of all Sienese. His final masterpiece, an *Annunciation* painted in 1333 for the Cathedral in Siena but now in the Uffizi in Florence, is Sienese through and through, with its princely flaming Gabriel and its neurasthenic young princess of a Virgin.

Born in Siena about 1284, Simone Martini was a man of the world and exceptional among Sienese as a traveler. We know nothing about his early work. He emerges for us full-fledged and already eminent in 1315 (he would have been only thirty-one) when he signed and dated his great fresco of the *Maestà* on an end wall of the main chamber of the Palazzo Pubblico. Fresco had not been a popular medium in Siena, and Simone seems not to have been altogether a master of it, since the color deteriorated so badly that much of the fresco has been repainted within the boundaries of Simone's drawing. But otherwise this *Maestà* is his, and the Madonna surrounded by her celestial court remains the only one that rivals Duccio's *Maestà* as the Sienese Queen of Heaven.

Simone's *Maestà* must have been greatly admired, extending his renown outside Siena. Just after its completion he received a summons from the Angevin court of Naples, where he was so successful that he was knighted. From Naples Simone went to Pisa in 1319 (the work he did there is lost) and the next year to Orvieto, in both cases on Dominican commissions. He was back in Siena in 1321-22—he was now in his mid-thirties—where he repaired some damages to the *Maestà*, did another Madonna, now lost, for the same Palazzo Pubblico, and other works—also lost. When he was about forty he married the sister of an artist who was his frequent collaborator, Lippo Memmi.

In and out of Siena over the following years, Simone traveled to Assisi and Florence, which meant renewed contact with Giotto's frescoes in both cities, and then received an impressive call to the papal court at Avignon. He went there, probably in 1340, and was followed by his wife and brother, Donato. He was in his mid-fifties, and died in Avignon four years later, in July, 1344, without seeing Siena again.

Simone must have been happy in Avignon. There is little record of his activities, but we do know that he painted frescoes in the Cathedral and that Petrarch was a good enough friend to refer to him as *"il mio Simone"* and to mention him in his sonnets. Simone painted a miniature portrait of Petrarch's romantic love, Laura, that is unquestionably lost, although various implausible works have been optimistically identified with it from time to time.

Simone was the only truly international Italian painter of his century, and his influence, spreading from Avignon, was a powerful one on the late-Gothic manner called the International Style. But as for the temper of his art, Simone might never have left home. His *Annunciation* and Duccio's *Maestà* are the two supreme Sienese monuments in any final judgment. The *Annunciation* is a glittering affair where the angel Gabriel alights in a flutter of iridescent robes whose linear convolutions, twisting and spiraling upward against the burnished gold background, show that he has just alighted. The Virgin recoils in shock just before the moment of comprehension; her angular, almost broken posture contrasts with the sinuous, graceful attitude of Gabriel.

There is little that can be connected with Giotto's formal revolution here, and nothing at all that can be connected with his humanization of the holy story. Everything is antirealistic, and by an unsympathetic standard the painting could be seen as an opulent, theatrical synthesis of stylish affectations brilliantly assembled. But the scene is electric with a sense of miracle, and filled everywhere with mystical tenderness. It is wonderfully and wholly Sienese.

For a visitor to Siena today, the paintings of the brothers Pietro and Ambrogio Lorenzetti seem a bit out of key, a disruptive intrusion by the world on Siena's tradition of aristocratic mysticism. The Lorenzetti are always called the painters who brought Sienese art down to earth, and so they did—but it did not stay there. After they died, Sienese art reverted to an otherworldliness that proved too comfortable to abandon even during the next century when the Renaissance flourished nearby in Florence—Siena's more vigorous and, to the Sienese way of thinking, rather vulgar neighbor.

The art of the Lorenzetti is a reminder that in the first half of the fourteenth century Siena was an alert and powerful city-state, wealthy, and as progressive as any other. If its artists chose tradition before innovation in case of a showdown, it was because the tradition itself was still living and growing. The symptoms that this growth might be turning inward were not apparent or not disturbing. But the Lorenzetti were more adventurous than other Sienese artists. They pop up like brilliant country boys among courtiers, and are easier to think of as Florentines somewhat affected by Sienese grace than as Sienese whose native heritage was transformed by the Florentine Giotto's revolution.

One of the brothers, Pietro, may eventually be proved to have been a student of Giotto's; both were his students at least by example, and they exceeded their Florentine contemporaries in the progress they made toward discovering the systems of perspective that the Florentines were to perfect in the next century. Pietro's *Birth of the Virgin* (in the Opera del Duomo in Siena) has become the standard example of the thirteenth century's preliminary victory in the conquest of space. We look directly into a vaulted room, and in spite of some technical inaccuracies the illusion is so strong that we can hardly establish in our vision the flat plane of the actual picture surface. It has simply been painted out, and within the pictorial space thus created the figures stand logically, each displacing its own volume and existing in perfectly reasonable relationship to the others. Refined and elaborated, this scheme of static interior space explicitly defined by perspective served painters in Italy and in the North for another hundred and fifty years.

The Lorenzetti were essentially secular painters even in their religious pictures, which naturally, at that time, made up the bulk of any artist's work. They tried to humanize the ethereal, long-faced, almond-eyed Sienese Madonna to make her a proper sister to Giotto's human mothers, but the hybrid is not always successful from our point of view. Some Lorenzetti Madonnas are disturbingly pig-eyed, heavy-faced and squat-bodied. Their awkwardness disturbs for the very reason that the effort to bring the Queen of Heaven down to earth has been so successful: if these Madonnas were not so real, their awkwardness would not be so bothersome.

The translation of visual experience into painted forms was always more important to the Lorenzetti than imagination or the symbolical conventions. Ambrogio brought painting down to earth in a quite literal sense in his frescoed *Allegories of Good and Bad Government* in the Palazzo Pubblico. To show the effects of good government in the country, he painted the rolling hills around Siena with fields under cultivation, with oxen and plowmen—everything quite obviously observed directly from life and reproduced with reference to life. Painted in 1337 or 1339, this was the first landscape of its kind since Roman times, and since there is not much chance that Ambrogio could have seen any ancient Roman painting (though he was probably acquainted with Roman sculpture), it represents an astonishingly independent kind of painterly vision rather than the revival of one legitimized by antiquity.

As part of a *renaissance avortée,* the art of antiquity was receiving at that moment a degree of sympathetic attention that anticipated its reflowering in the Renaissance proper. Like Renaissance artists, the Lorenzetti found in classical art a confirmation of their rediscovery of the visual world. Ambrogio's figure of Peace in the *Allegory of Good Government* is a barefoot goddess clad in a white robe, and although she may be the most curiously formed goddess in the history of painting, with a thick torso like an overstuffed sack, she is at worst an ambitious failure, and only in comparison with goddesses painted later. As a classical figure painted in the 1330's she is revolutionary not only because the body is revealed sculpturally in the classical way, by the fall and clinging of drapery, but because, even more experimentally for a painter, it is half seen through a gauzy fabric.

Ambrogio did not quite have the temerity to paint his goddess of peace nude. If he had, she would probably have been painted out in the period of reaction that followed the Black Death. Years earlier, he had sketched a classical statue of Venus that had been unearthed in Siena during the construction of water pipes for a new fountain in the town's central square (the Fonte Gaia). The citizens established this Venus on a pedestal in an honorable position in front of the Palazzo Pubblico, a rather daring recognition of a pagan goddess in a medieval city. But the goddess herself was in a way a victim of the plague: in 1357 the statue was taken down and destroyed, probably on moral grounds because of her nudity. The Black Death had carried off half the urban population, and the survivors were divided between a return to piety (as if the plague, like the Flood, had been a punishment for sin) and a cultivation of licentious pleasure (witness Boccaccio) stimulated by an acute consciousness of the hazardous brevity of life.

Pietro and Ambrogio Lorenzetti were probably victims of the Black Death in 1348, since all records of either brother cease abruptly just before that year. The records are sparse enough in any case. Pietro's birth year is set by deduction as 1280, since he received payment for a painting from the government of Siena on February 25, 1306, and under regulations then existing could not have received it directly before the age of twenty-five. He could not have been much more than twenty-five, since the document refers to him as Petruccio—the diminutive of Pietro, which would have been used only for a very young man. By these birth and death dates Pietro would have reached the ripe age of sixty-eight by the year of the plague. Ambrogio? He was probably younger, since Pietro's name came first when the brothers signed a painting jointly.

In 1321, when Pietro would have been about forty, the brothers were perhaps not too prosperous: there is a writ of seizure, of that date, allowing creditors to repossess a suit of clothes belonging to Ambrogio. The clothes had been left in the house of one Nuto Vermigli in Florence—proof of one of several stays in Florence, where (as well as in Assisi) the brothers must have studied Giotto's frescoes. But in 1341 Pietro was prosperous enough to have to pay a special tax levied on the wealthiest citizens of Siena. There are no anecdotes that allow a reconstruction of the brothers' personalities.

The Lorenzetti are, altogether, a thorny problem for art scholars, so thorny that a third artist, "Ugolino-Lorenzetti," was invented by Bernard Berenson to take care of a group of works formerly attributed to Pietro. The mythical Ugolino since then has acquired other puzzling anonymous works. Ugolino is a convenient receptacle, and was perhaps a real person with a name of his own, but he is a rather weak brother to Pietro and Ambrogio.

Siena's decline from power through a combination of social and political lassitude and corruption was complete by the end of the fourteenth century—to the year. In 1399 the city ceded itself to Gian Galeazzo Visconti of Milan—not reluctantly but with a great celebration. The boy who was to become Siena's greatest painter in her acquiescent decay— Stefano di Giovanni, born in 1392 and called Sassetta—was seven years old at the time.

Siena's fall was not entirely a debacle; there was still money enough, with recurrent periods of prosperity, for good living. (There were also intervals of religious revivalism.) Nevertheless, Siena was reduced from a position of prestige vigorously defended to one of subservience accepted in relaxation, and this change is reflected in the character of Sassetta's art, sometimes as a mood of rather pleasurable melancholy. Sassetta inherited almost intact the great tradition of Sienese refinement from Duccio and Simone Martini, but, expectably, he applied it with more charm than strength. The physical stature of the characters who enact his religious dramas seems drastically reduced: they are doll-like, inhabiting doll-like houses or moving within doll-scaled models of delightfully invented landscapes. And even though they are exquisitely formed and gracefully articulated, like small versions of extraordinarily lovely human beings, their capacity for spiritual experience seems correspondingly reduced. The mystical passion of Duccio and Simone Martini becomes a tender yearning.

But Sassetta was a superbly skillful artist. A dramatic raconteur, he was a master of expressive gesture and arrangement. As a colorist he had no superior within the limitations he deliberately chose, the limitations of late-medieval sprightliness, grace, and elegance. Chronologically Sassetta is a fifteenth-century painter; he was still working in a medieval spirit while the Renaissance blazed away just on the other side of a few hills, in Florence. This is difficult to remember—and there is perhaps not much point in remembering it, since Siena and its artists seem to have been determined to forget it at the time. Sassetta had a perfectly sound knowledge of perspective and anatomy, the twin passions of his Florentine colleagues, but he regarded them as auxiliary advantages that could be employed in the continuation of a traditional style, rather than as the foundations of a new mode of expression.

Sassetta's life was quite uneventful. He kept busy in Siena, traveling very little, and when he died in 1450 he had created a body of work that, not too badly decimated by time, is the delight of connoisseurs.

Giovanni di Paolo was born in Siena about 1403, lived in Siena always, and died there in 1483. He was staggeringly productive during his long life, and just as staggeringly uneven in the quality of his work. He ranges from careless to meticulous, from beautiful to ugly, not only from picture to picture but often within a single picture. But it makes no difference. His inventiveness, his independence, his unexpectedness, and the bizarre meters of his painted poetic narratives make him an artist so arresting and so special when

he is at his best that his name is something of a password
among people who have discovered him.

That anyone should have to discover him seems unnatural, since museums are full of his work and his reputation is firmly established. But he is seldom mentioned in
general histories of art for the very reasons that distinguish
him as an artist. If you are following the story of art in his
century, you are involved in an account of the sequence of
explorations that began with Masaccio and went straight
through Leonardo to culminate in Raphael and Michelangelo. Giovanni di Paolo rejected these explorations in a
way that was extreme even for a Sienese. He was so far to one
side of the main current that the historian is obliged to make
an interruptive detour, with the result that he is usually
passed up while many minor artists who rode the current
are widely known. He was not even the kind of isolated
revolutionary, ahead of his time, who requires historical attention from the other direction. He was neither reactionary
nor stagnant in his isolation: his exceptional position is that
he was an aggressively original artist without being at all a
revolutionary one.

Very little is known of him as a person, and if his life
included any exceptional events they were not recorded, or
the records have been lost. Even the legendary anecdotes are
lacking that are usually fabricated around an artist who
worked in an eccentric style. There are voluminous records
of the dates of his various commissions, but these do not
make a very interesting story. Nor is it fascinating to learn
that he was a pupil of the Sienese master Paolo di Giovanni
Fei. Only a specialist can take much interest in the early
influence of Gentile da Fabriano on Giovanni di Paolo, or
in the fact that through the tradition of Sassetta he is connectible with the late-Gothic International Style. And there,
even the professional historian's interest is likely to end. The

rest is the paintings, and these are not to every taste. They happen to be much to the taste of this particular writer, as may already have become evident.

Giovanni di Paolo was as divorced from the measured rhythms of the Renaissance and its fascination with order and logic as a painter could possibly be. Perspective, which for Renaissance artists meant the control of space, for Giovanni would have been only an intolerable fetter to imagination. For its geometrical system he substituted an irrational chopping of lines (in the rectangular divisions of fields and meadows in landscapes that are seen from an impossible point high in the air) that is often compared with the broken planes of cubism. Instead of investigating the way figures become smaller and smaller with distance, Giovanni will show in the foreground of a picture the young St. John the Baptist setting off for the wilderness and then, in an area that logically should be miles away, show him again at the same size vigorously entering a chasm between two cliffs that should tower above him but that he could easily peer over.

These violations of logical relationships can never be mistaken for the artist's ignorance of perspective or his incompetence in applying the rules. For one thing, the violations are too drastic to be unintentional. But primarily this is obviously the kind of artist whose poetic vitality is simply incompatible with science and erudition. He sets the world to his own scale and shifts that scale at will.

If Giovanni di Paolo had been a writing poet instead of a painting poet, he would have observed no conventional forms and might have been the first practitioner of free verse. But it would not have been an unordered verse dependent upon suggestion and association. Giovanni's forms are always clean-edged; everything is implacably defined in its irrationality; there is no dreamy fuzziness; fantasies are presented with an absolute conviction as if they were the literal truth.

The result is that the narratives—as in a lively sequence of predella panels telling the life of St. John the Baptist, the majority of them now in the Art Institute of Chicago—are absolutely clear. The story is told with all the vividness and speed that we demand of a good thriller; yet everything takes place in a never-never setting where architecture that could never have been built has been built in a world that could never have been created by any conceivable geological development, one created so convincingly, however, that the entire geological process as known to scientists is thrown into question. If there is an identifiable reference to real nature in any of his pictures, it is to the chalk mounds near Siena— themselves geological freaks that give you the impression, when you suddenly find yourself traveling through them, that you are the victim of planetary displacement.

On Giovanni's extraordinary stages the actors are totally convincing in their roles although they have the puny scale, the wiry look, the angular thinness, of marionettes, with the same broken joints between otherwise inflexible members. These oddly anatomized manikins may have at the same time the physical tension of rubber bands stretched to the break- ing point. But Giovanni can also be languid. He can be fiery, or tender. He has his limitations, but they are inherent in his uniqueness. He is never profound, but that is the price of his intensity. He is never a philosopher, but that is the price of his visionary genius. If that reasonable, watchful, and suc- cessful courtier Raphael knew Giovanni di Paolo's work, surely he could not abide it. But for Giovanni that would have been an even exchange.

If a young provincial notary had not encountered an illiterate peasant girl to produce an illegitimate child who turned out to be a genius, the title of the complete man of the Renaissance might have gone to Francesco di Giorgio Martini rather than to the product of that encounter, Leonardo da Vinci. Francesco di Giorgio (the surname Martini is usually omitted, not quite correctly but conveniently) was Leonardo's senior by thirteen years, having been born in 1439, and died seventeen years earlier than Leonardo, in 1502. Like Leonardo he was an architect, a military and civil engineer, a sculptor, a mathematician, a writer on science and art theory, and, still like Leonardo, a painter who virtually abandoned painting for his other activities. Patrons quarreled with one another in their efforts to obtain his services in these multiple capacities, whose range is typified by the distance between the practicality of the city waterworks of Siena, which he engineered, and the ethereal sweetness of the Virgins he painted.

The trouble is that while his activities are attested by historical record, physical evidence of them today is largely conjectural. One is certain that he was an architectural designer, but not quite certain that he designed the important buildings attributed to him. Only two paintings are authenticated as his by record, although a body of about sixty are generally assigned to him on the basis of style. Four existing sculptures can be given to him without question.

As a painter, Francesco di Giorgio had a documented partnership with his brother-in-law, Neroccio de' Landi (1447-1500). Between them they represent the best of Sienese painting in the second half of the fifteenth century before its complete absorption by outside influences. Neroccio's hypersensitive Madonnas, blonde, pale, and neurasthenic, would look as if they could be blown off their panels with a whiff of breath except that they are held there by his precisely contoured lines. Francesco's Virgins, as well as the characters from mythology that he also painted, are only slightly more robust sisters to Neroccio's. In spite of his excursions to more progressive Italian capitals as an engineer, Francesco remained thoroughly Sienese as a painter, dedicated to a gentle, brooding mysticism in his Christian subjects and to decorative lyrical grace when he recounted mythological tales.

If Francesco di Giorgio is comparable to any painter outside Siena, he is closest to Botticelli, and it is possible to read into Francesco's Madonnas some of the same foreboding quality that in Botticelli is rather presumptively seen as a prophecy of Florence's troubles. In Francesco, the moodiness could be interpreted as a nostalgia for Sienese greatness in realization of her decline. His sculpture is clearly influenced by Verrocchio.

Francesco di Giorgio met Leonardo da Vinci on a trip to Milan in 1490, admired him, and won his respect in return. Along with Leonardo, Alberti, and Piero della Francesca, he was among the most influential Renaissance artists, and Dürer, outside Italy, seems to have known and studied his writings. But his painting reflects little of his advanced and adventurous thought. In spite of a generous use of classical architectural motifs that link him with the Renaissance revival of antiquity, the mood of his painting affirms that Siena preferred to pretend, up to the very end of the fifteenth century, that the century had not yet arrived.

Sienese painting, in truth, simply skipped the century. After 1500, foreign influences triumphed. But the painting, then, was only nominally Sienese.

For those who feel there is no such thing as an uninteresting Sienese painter or painting, another half-dozen artists must be included here.

Lippo Memmi was a skilled artist whose misfortune has been that he must constantly bear immediate comparison with Simone Martini. He co-signed the great *Annunciation* in the Uffizi with Simone and probably did the figures of saints at either side of the main panel. His chief work is a *Maestà* in the Palazzo del Popolo of San Gimignano that closely follows Simone's in Siena. Active by 1317, Lippo Memmi died in 1356.

Sano di Pietro (1406-1481), probably the single most prolific painter of the Sienese school, was a pupil of Sassetta's and occasionally approximated that master's charm, by imitation. Even for conservative Siena, however, Sano was an unprogressive artist. He early developed his own variation of an old-fashioned formula—gentle Madonnas with plenty of gold and pure bright color, decorative in a saccharine way. He was content to repeat the formula indefinitely and, for us, tiresomely, although now and then, among the repetitive mass of his work, one runs into a painting of great charm.

Domenico di Bartolo Ghezzi (*c.* 1400-*c.* 1449) (the Ghezzi is usually omitted) was the only Sienese painter of his generation to be stirred by the innovations of Masaccio in Florence. He attempted to infuse the Sienese tradition with some of the classical grandeur of the early Renaissance, and hence, although a native Sienese, always seems somewhat foreign to the school. He also worked in Perugia, and had more influence abroad than he had at home, where his only major follower was Vecchietta.

Lorenzo di Pietro, called Vecchietta, was a pupil of Sassetta's and combined this master's blond coloring and delicate sentiment with the grander scale and classical references of Domenico di Bartolo. Vecchietta, born about 1412, was a sculptor, architect, and engineer, as well as a painter. He was of a melancholy temperament, according to accounts of the time. There is always about his rather uneventful career, and his painting, an air of unfulfilled potential; he is the kind of artist who leaves you with the feeling that he managed to produce only the minor works from what was meant to have been a major contribution. He died in 1480.

Born in Borgo San Sepolcro about 1435, Matteo di Giovanni (also called Matteo da Siena) became a pupil of Piero della Francesca. He adopted Siena as his home (after what he thought would be only a visit) and developed a semi-Florentine, semi-Sienese, manner. He is one of the few artists, with Domenico di Bartolo at their head, who represent the Renaissance in conservative Siena, insofar as it is represented at all. He died in Siena in 1495.

Bernardino Fungai lived from 1460 to 1516. Although he was a pupil of Giovanni di Paolo, he was an eclectic who drew from any convenient source, Sienese or other. He was a poor assimilator, however, and coming at the end of the school's last days, he is representative of the ultimate dissolution of Sienese painting.

The leading Sienese mannerist, Domenico Beccafumi was an artist of almost intolerable affectation, although it is possible, sometimes, to imagine that in his paintings the Sienese tradition of acute sensitivity was given a degenerated expression. More to his credit are the inlaid pavements of the Siena Cathedral and his many sculptures on that flowery edifice. His drawings, too, are of great attraction. Like so many mannerists, he drew with stylishness of a kind that tells best at small scale and when offered in an informal spirit. In his large, ambitious paintings he is like a charming master of light conversation whose assignment exceeds his abilities when he is put on the speaker's platform.

Beccafumi, who was born about 1486, took his name from the owner of the estate where his father, a peasant, worked. This patron discovered the boy's talent and, adopting him as a protégé, sent him to Siena to study. Beccafumi's real name was Mecarino, sometimes given as Meccherino or Mecuccio. He died in 1551.

THE INTERNATIONAL STYLE

In following Sienese painting to its conclusion, we have by-passed the International Style except in incidental references. This postscript may be bypassed in its turn by the hasty reader, but for a conscientious one may fill in a gap.

The term "International Style" is something of a catchall applied to the work of painters in any country who at the end of the fourteenth century and into the first part of the fifteenth shared certain characteristics attributable to the mutual impact of Italian adventurousness and the persistent Gothic traditions of the North. The painters sometimes did, sometimes did not, know one another's work. Certainly they were not banded together as a school with a program and a set of standards. The International Style is something that we have perceived historically, not something that a group of artists was, at the time, consciously practicing.

Predominantly the spirit of the style was courtly, reflecting the manner of life of the nobility at the end of the Middle Ages—a life of sophisticated indulgence and, upon occasion, graceful intellectualism, carried on in resplendent costumes. Religious subject matter was (almost as if habitually) the rule in picturemaking, but the mystical passion of the Middle Ages was reduced to fashionable pageantry or intimate narrative, presented in decorative terms. There was at the same time great interest in realistic detail, as if to fill the void left by the evaporation of deep religious feeling.

Often called the most important of the Italian artists whose late-Gothic sensitivities connect them with the International Style, Gentile da Fabriano cultivated the fine ornamental detail and the tender mood typical of the Northerners, but he could not help hybridizing delicacy with a typically Italian propensity for solid form: he often seems to be subjecting a talent for monumental compositions to the restrictions of a manner based on manuscript illumination.

Gentile was a native of Umbria, wellborn if not quite a patrician. He is easy to imagine as a person of the same courtliness that he gave to the ladies and gentlemen who move with ceremonial grace in his pictures. With his aristocratic manner, which was certainly fundamental to his painting if not to his person, and his poetic sensibility, expressed in a conservative tradition, he would have made a good Sienese. He worked in that city and exerted a strong influence there, as he did in Orvieto, Brescia, Rome (where he was called by Pope Martin V in 1419), and his native city, Fabriano, where he was born about 1370. He had gone to Venice in 1408 to execute frescoes, now destroyed, in the Doges' Palace, and during his six-year stay may have become acquainted with the young Jacopo Bellini, whom he possibly took with him to Florence as his apprentice. Florence was the city to which he was most closely attached. For good or ill, he barely missed the Renaissance: the forceful Florentine realism seems always ready to break through his stylized surface. He died in 1427 at the age of about fifty-seven in Rome, where he was at work on frescoes in St. John Lateran.

Pisanello, whose name indicates the city where he was born about 1395, apparently worked with Gentile da Fabriano in Venice, and was called in to complete Gentile's murals (now destroyed) in St. John Lateran in Rome. His work took him all over Italy, but Verona became his home base. He died in 1455.

Any evaluation of Pisanello's art must begin with the words "delightful" and "vivacious" and go on from there through all their synonyms and superlatives, although they would not apply to his drawings of hanged men and would not indicate the acute observation that makes all his drawings, especially those of animals, a harmonious combination of high style, accurate record, and consistent response to the visual world as an elegant theatrical spectacle. His air of fashion makes him a late but consummate representative of the International Style at its most engaging, but as one of the great draftsmen of any time he is outside the boundaries of any school.

In one medium Pisanello is of unique importance. The foremost portrait medalist of his day, he not only founded a school but set a standard for the design of medals and coins that is still valid but is seldom approached. His first medal, of John VIII Palaeologus, was made at Ferrara in 1438, and his subsequent ones are a roster of great names: Gonzaga, Visconti, Sforza, Este, and Malatesta are among them.

The climactic painters of the International Style were Pol de Limbourg and his brothers Herman and Jehanequin, Franco-Flemish miniaturists who flourished in the early fifteenth century and whose *Très Riches Heures du Duc de Berry* (Chantilly, Musée Condé) is probably, and justifiably, the most precious illuminated manuscript in the world. Its glories are concentrated on the twelve pages where the occupations of the months are illustrated—a standard medieval theme, but presented in anything but a standard manner. The tiny pictures are unprecedented in the acuteness of their observation of commonplace particulars in fields, farmyards, vineyards, and interiors, whether simple or palatial. The interpretations of the seasons—the feeling for the verdant delight of spring, the cold of winter and, by contrast, the cheeriness of a good fire where you can warm your toes—are so original as conceptions of man inhabiting nature that they can be called the fountainhead of Western landscape painting, which treats nature as something more than a topographical accessory.

In one way the International Style is specifically related to the flowering of Netherlandish genius in the fifteenth century: both made a new reference to the factual details of the everyday world. Both, too, continued the Gothicisms of the North, but here there was a difference. For the artists of the International Style the medieval tradition was a charming remnant. For the Netherlandish masters, whom we are now ready to see, it was a revitalized force.

2

THE
FIFTEENTH CENTURY
IN THE NORTH

For anyone trying to tell the history of art as a continuous story, the fifteenth century always appears as a slight embarrassment. Up until then the story can be followed along a reasonably straight path, but with the year 1400 the narrator comes upon a bifurcation. The stylistic and ideational split between the art of Italy and that of the North may not be as wide as it seems, but it is nevertheless too wide to straddle gracefully.

During this fantastic century, when painters of genius were born by the dozen, the Renaissance flared up and spread like a grass fire in Italy while a triumvirate of Flemish artists brought medieval painting to its apogee. The birth dates of these three—the Master of Flémalle, Jan van Eyck, and Rogier van der Weyden—occurred within a period of less than twenty years and can be averaged out to the year 1388. This is the same year, granting a few uncertainties, as the average birth date of Donatello, Masaccio, and Brunelleschi, the epochal Florentine triumvirate of sculptor-painter-architect. Yet, as the initiators of Renaissance art, the Italians divided the Age of Faith from modern times, and it is easier to think of them as men who followed the Flemish masters by a century than as their contemporaries. In spite of re-evaluations and indisputable demonstrations that northern and southern Europe in the fifteenth century were closely allied intellectually, we still have to combat a tendency to regard the art of the North as a beautiful medieval tag end, a last gasp rather than a consummation.

The term "Renaissance" is a bit of a misnomer, or at least an exaggeration. Art and learning hardly needed to be reborn, especially in the North, where they had been flourishing for centuries. "Redirection" would be a better term than "Renaissance" for what happened in Quattrocento Italy, except as "Renaissance" can apply to the resuscitation of the forms of classical antiquity. "Renaissance" as an established label suggesting that Italy brought a dead world to life again has had a great deal to do with the persistence of an old idea that once placed even the Gothic cathedral, that most luminous expression of logic and revelation, within something mis-called the Dark Ages.

In this book we will make the usual division, telling the story of the medieval culmination in the North first. But it should be remembered that if the art of the North seems to have remained Gothic in spirit during the first seventy-five years of the Renaissance adventure, this was not a matter of ignorance or incapacity on the part of the artists. It was a matter of stylistic choice, and the fifteenth century in the North was a century of triumph, just as it was in Italy.

The triumph of Flemish genius came in part as the result of a French disaster—the Battle of Agincourt in 1415. Until then the most alert and talented young Netherlandish artists had been lured away from home by Paris, Bourges, and Dijon, the seats of the great schools of manuscript illumination and of the wealthiest feudal patrons. But with Agincourt, and Philip the Good's withdrawal of his sumptuous court from Burgundy to Flanders shortly thereafter, expatriation lost its point. The best commissions could be found at home.

This geographical shift would have been of no importance had it not involved more than the simple transplantation of the centers of production. What was important was that the expression of talent was redirected in response to locale, and the locale was now bourgeois rather than princely. In France the artists had naturally been drawn into the hyperrefined brilliance and sweet sophistications of that courtly manner called the International Style. But now, in addition to serving a weakened aristocracy, they found patrons among the bankers and merchants who had become the true rulers of the wealthiest society in Europe. A degree of healthy homeliness became a tolerable ingredient of painting in this tough-minded, practical society.

Yet the new society was not homely. It was bourgeois, but it was not provincial. Representatives of the great banking and merchandising firms went back and forth across all Europe, and foreign houses maintained their commercial ambassadors in the Low Countries. This was cosmopolitanism of a new kind, and was so conducive to growth, variety, and experiment that any suspicion of provincialism might attach more fittingly to the preciously cultivated closed society of the feudal courts. The Virgin, as the Queen of Heaven, had become in the International Style an entrancing chatelaine in a princely court. The events leading up to her coronation took on much the air of a series of vignettes summarizing the high spots of an unusually brilliant social season. For the audience of the International Style this conception was perfect, but for the new audience of burghers the role had to be recast and the action placed in a new setting. Which leads us immediately to the mysterious genius known as the Master of Flémalle.

The painter called the Master of Flémalle (*c.* 1378-1444), or sometimes the Master of the Mousetrap, or sometimes the Master of Mérode, who was perhaps identical with the painter Robert Campin, obviously presents the greatest problem for the biographer, since nothing really is known about him, or about Robert Campin, as a person. As an artist he is known by a body of work that varies in its listing from one scholar's study to the next, but he is most closely identified with the *Mérode Altarpiece,* now in the Metropolitan Museum, which is a key painting in the genesis of the Flemish miracle of the fifteenth century.

The *Mérode Altarpiece,* a triptych, shows in its central panel an Annunciation placed not in a palatial setting but in an intimate bourgeois domestic interior, and in this representation the Master of Flémalle effected the transformation of the Virgin from a star of the international set into a girl of the people. The picture was probably completed about ten years after the Battle of Agincourt—that is, around 1425. The Virgin's house is filled with all the possessions dear to a good burgher's heart. The artist's obvious primary interest is in the things of this world, and his first delight is in displaying his technical mastery in the reproduction of the shapes and textures of objects. The event is miraculous on the face of it, but even the presence of an angel in broad daylight among the accouterments of daily living is not sufficient to give the air of miracle to this charming inventory of household effects. "Charming" remains a legitimate adjective: what the new staging has lost in elegance it has not quite gained in passion. But that is a matter of opinion. In the many

and contradictory studies on this master, he is as often credited with the intensification of spirituality as he is tasked
with an obsessive interest in realistic detail for its own sake.

Technically, the Master of Flémalle is the father of
Flemish painting in his development of a method that allowed the most minute description of detail to be coupled
with luminous depth of color. He and his follower or colleague Jan van Eyck are often called the inventors of oil
painting. This is not quite true. Certainly their technique
involved the use of tempera underpainting and of micro-
scopically fine layers of glazing incorporating oil, but the
meticulousness of Flemish painting has nothing to do with
the fatty richness and vigorous application associated with oil
technique today.

The Master of Flémalle, in his acutely detailed representation of objects, initiated a trend in realism that characterized Flemish painting for scores of years thereafter. He
also exemplifies at its apogee the use of symbols as a form of
literary exposition. The sweet domestic interior of his *Annunciation* includes lilies in a jug symbolizing Mary's purity;
their white petals enclose a golden heart representing Christ
in her womb; a polished vessel hanging in its niche symbolizes
Mary as "the vessel most clean." An extinguished candle on
the table, its wick still smoking, symbolizes the Divine Light;
its extinction at the moment of the Annunciation means that
God, in the person of man, has become flesh.

By investing every object in a picture with symbolic
meaning, the Master of Flémalle spoke to his contemporaries
in a language not intelligible to our century. He supplied by
association the emotional context that the twentieth century
expects an artist to create through form and color. Much of
the symbolism was clear to anybody at the time, but since
much of it is abstruse, and surely was, even to his contemporaries, the Master of Flémalle may have been a very learned

man. Certainly his fascination with the world for its own sake, as a visual phenomenon, allies him with the shift in attitude that determined the character of the Renaissance— an increasing faith in tangible values at the expense of mystical ones. But this only half accounts for the nature of his expression and not for what is most important about it. By investing these tangible values with spiritual associations he remained true to the medieval conception of the world as the visible manifestation of the power and mystery of God. It is this union between mere optical fact and supreme faith in a power beyond man that transforms Flemish painting of the century from a form of realism that is in itself almost a miracle of pure skill, into an art where skill becomes, as it must in great art, only the means to an expressive end.

The art of Jan van Eyck, with its balanced, reserved, and dignified realism, is generally considered the summary expression of Flemish genius. He is by any standard and without any legitimate question the supreme technician among realists, combining ultimate mastery in the detailed rendition of forms and textures with an understanding, and equal mastery, of light as the unifying element of the visible world. He understood, apparently without benefit of theory, the principle of aerial perspective by which the appearance of objects in the distance is affected by the veil of atmosphere between them and the eye. And he has never been excelled, and perhaps not equaled, unless by Vermeer two centuries later, in the painting of natural light as it enters the closed space of a room and, in the most subtle gradations of tone and color, binds every object within the room, down to the last thread of a carpet, into harmonious union.

Traditionally, Jan (as well as his older brother Hubert) was born at "Eyck" (Maaseyck), but nothing is known about his life, except by conjecture and uneasy deduction, until, in about 1422, he was appointed painter and *varlet de chambre* to John of Bavaria, the unconsecrated bishop of Liège, in The Hague. He is referred to at that time as a "master painter," and he might thus have been born as early as 1380, and almost certainly no later than 1390. As he became increasingly famous his life was, naturally, increasingly documented, but there is little to be known about him as a personality except as we may construct a portrait from his career and his art.

It is never safe to synthesize a personality from an artist's style, but everything about Jan van Eyck's way of painting coincides with documented facts to give a picture of an industrious, sensible, intelligent, cultivated, dependable man. In 1425 he became painter and *varlet de chambre* to Philip the Good, duke of Burgundy, and from then on his life supplies an early example of the artist in a position well above that of supercraftsman—his characteristic status until the Renaissance. Philip the Good stood as godfather to one of Van Eyck's ten children, and ten years after the artist's death the Duke by special grant enabled one daughter, Lyevine, to enter the convent of her choice.

Philip was obviously more than a generous patron who favored an underling. Well in advance of those Renaissance princes who cultivated artists like Raphael and Michelangelo, Philip accepted Jan van Eyck as a respected friend, and once wrote that he "would never find a man equally to his liking nor so outstanding in his art and science." This was a new kind of artist, the artist as intellectual, the master of other arts and of learning—an initiation of the universal genius personified by Leonardo da Vinci.

Philip the Good also employed Van Eyck as a confidential emissary. In 1427 he sent him to Spain to help negotiate his marriage with Isabella, daughter of James II, count of

Urgel. The negotiations failed, for reasons unknown, and in the following year Van Eyck was sent to the Portuguese court, where, with better luck, a marriage was arranged with another Isabella, the eldest daughter of King John I. During this time Van Eyck was not only court painter but also an independent artist serving the wealthy bourgeoisie. A good burgher himself, he set himself up in Bruges in about 1430, and there, approaching the age of fifty, he purchased a handsome house where he lived until his death in 1441, when he was between fifty-one and sixty-one years old.

Jan the artist seems to have been little affected by the princeliness of his associations with the court. He remained the solid citizen of a new mercantile society, and was not too proud to accept commissions for coloring and gilding statues, in the tradition of the artist as craftsman rather than creator. His steadiness and solidity and practicality might imply a baldly mundane art, and there are spots in his painting that, out of context, could seem to be just that. But the new society in its exploratory vigor did something more than demand of its artists a concern with tangible rather than mystical values: it made innovators of them.

In the famous altarpiece that is in Ghent's Cathedral of St. Bavo, Jan's Adam and Eve, only a bit under life size, were daring as the first large nudes in Northern panel painting and are startling even today in their explicit description of two individuals whose acceptance of public undress is remarkable for its placidity. There is hardly any effort toward idealization beyond the selection of well-formed models. (The Adam, at least, must have been posed by an individual whose appearance was closely reproduced.) It has been argued that this literalism is not a failure in imagination but rather a form of piety. Since God created man in his own image, the artist would have been presumptuous if he had beautified the normal appearance of the human form, as though suggesting improvements to the Creator.

An equally valid argument is that the craftsmanship of realism, at the level attained by Van Eyck, is a form of genius in itself. By perfecting the technical methods employed by the Master of Flémalle, he found the means to imitate the appearance of anything—from the hard sheen of polished metal to the soft texture of a curl of hair. As far as can be determined, he seems to have alternated microscopic layers of tempera and of glazes of oil; that is, he alternated opaque with transparent color. Detail by detail, a Van Eyck is a series of staggering technical exercises in the reproduction of the colors and textures and shapes of mundane objects. As such, it is an inexhaustible source of astonishment. But taken as a whole Van Eyck is something more, a declaration that the world is not a series of accidents or a random collection of objects but a meaningful unity—the habitat of ordinary men, yes, but so perfectly ordered that it must exist only as the manifestation of some ultimate logic, whether earthly or divine.

Painting of this kind had never been seen before, and for that matter nothing quite like it has been seen since. The paint and the objects represented by it do not have a separate existence; they are fused into a new identity in which reality and illusion are inseparable. The artist acts as a microscope, revealing objects with a minute precision that is beyond the capabilities of the normal eye. But in unifying every incredibly fine detail into an entity, he explores the universe in two directions: microcosm and macrocosm exist as one.

Jan van Eyck's fame was international. (Giovanni Arnolfini, a Lucchese merchant representing Italian interests in Bruges, commissioned him to do the famous double portrait, now in the National Gallery in London, of himself and his wife, Jeanne.) Giorgio Vasari, who included Jan in his collection of biographies, credited him with knowledge of alchemy. Jan was perhaps a chemist of sorts; the "secret" of oil painting as he practiced it could have been an oil medium refined to a purity and fluidity beyond any known until that time. But he was an alchemist in a figurative sense. No other painter has been quite as skillful at transforming the base metal of routine visual experience into pure gold.

Hubert van Eyck, (*c.* 1370-1426?), the half-legendary elder brother of Jan, may best be left, for the purposes of this book, to the scholarly circles where his identity and his work are meticulously analyzed with contradictory results. Some scholars deny his existence. There are no signed and dated works. It is probably safe to say—at least, the statement is always risked—that Hubert began the twenty-panel polyptych commissioned by a burgher for a chapel in the Cathedral of St. Bavo. The *Ghent Altarpiece*, begun in 1425, a year before Hubert's presumed death date, was finished in 1432. During that span of seven years, Jan completed the work, executing the major part—if not, indeed, the whole—of this greatest monument of Flemish painting.

At about the same time that Jan van Eyck was completing the *Ghent Altarpiece*, Rogier van der Weyden, the third in the triumvirate of founding fathers of the early Flemish school, was at work on the only painting that can rival it as the greatest and the most influential work in early Netherlandish art. Rogier's *Descent from the Cross* (Prado) became known within a few years all over Europe through copies, and for generations it affected painting, graphic arts, and sculpture at all levels, sometimes because the artists knew the original and sometimes because its motifs became so widely adopted that even folk artists who might never have heard of Rogier were producing naïve variations of the figures that he invested with such passion and elegance.

"Passion and elegance" immediately declares Rogier's departure from the rather placid and (at least superficially) mundane character cultivated by his colleagues. Rogier deliberately rejected the objective realism of Jan van Eyck and re-examined the outmoded manner of the Master of Flémalle for its undeveloped expressive potential. He wanted to combine the consistency of Van Eyck, that harmonious fusion of every element of a painting, with linear pattern as an abstraction of emotion—a goal that makes him the protomodern painter of his century in the North.

Passion and elegance, on the face of it, make uneasy companions. The greater the elegance, the more likely it is to act as an inhibiting shell, giving pleasure but rejecting the full expression of passion as a tasteless excessive indulgence. Or, the more intense the passion, the more likely it is to break up a polished surface and disrupt a graceful pattern, since the niceties of taste become inconsequential before the force of emotion. In art, elegance usually wins out, since an elegant manner is something that can be learned whereas the capacity for passionate expression is God-given, and not given to everyone. Rogier van der Weyden is paramount among the very few painters who have touched the apogee of passion and of elegance without conflict, contradiction, paradox, or compromise.

To some historians the contrast between Rogier and Jan van Eyck has made Rogier "anti-Eyckian." It is true that Rogier rejected the literalism that had produced Jan's great Adam and Eve. If the accurate simulation of visual phenomena is the key to Jan's style, the use of line as a structural and expressive device is the key to Rogier's. For Jan, line hardly exists. He may respond to the folds of a robe or the ruffled edge of a headdress and make the most of a pattern that is offered ready for use, but he is not an inventor of line. Line for Jan was an incidental if inevitable optical fact—the visual boundary of an object in nature seen from a certain viewpoint. In painting, this boundary takes the form of a separation between one area of color and the next, and though such separation may qualify as line in the most inclusive sense of the word, it does not constitute a manipulated, artist-created line. Any concept of line except as a natural visual boundary would be opposed to Jan's concept of volumes in space, since (as artists know) pure line exists on a plane, and linear emphasis demands as a corollary some flattening of the third dimension.

Rogier was a master designer of line; he never rejected inventive artifice when it could add a fillip to a decorative conception without weakening the expressive impact. His compositions are unified by the steady, slowly eddying and winding flow of line across the picture, paralleling the emotional current traveling from figure to figure.

Rogier was not one of those geniuses whose thought and art, like Leonardo's, rise from inexplicable sources so basic to the powers of expression that any dependence on recognizable antecedents becomes unimportant. And nothing in his meditative, carefully organized, and meticulously executed paintings has that quality of autonomous revelation that is called "inspired." Everything that is known about Rogier led Erwin Panofsky to say that he "represents, perhaps even more paradigmatically than Jan van Eyck, the novel type of bourgeois genius." He lived quietly, applying himself as industriously to his work as if he had been a master carpenter instead of a celebrated public figure. He married in his middle twenties and for the remaining forty years of his life maintained the respectable position of a devoted husband and father and a good citizen generous in his charities and solicitous for the welfare of the community. The one exceptional event in his life was his pilgrimage to Italy in the Holy Year of 1450. Born in 1399 or 1400, and hence some ten years younger than Van Eyck, he died on June 18, 1464, twenty-three years after Jan.

His quiet life had been full of honors. He was successful from the first, and by the time he was thirty-five the honors, as well as material rewards, had accumulated impressively. There is a record of his investing a considerable sum in Tournai securities on October 20, 1435, and it was probably at about the same time that the city fathers of Brussels endowed him with the title of City Painter, an honor significantly following upon the completion of *The Descent from the Cross* and apparently created for Rogier, since there is no previous record of such a post. For that matter there is no record of Rogier's appointment, and the date 1435 is presumptive. But there is no uncertainty about a verifying resolution put on record the following year, declaring that the position of City Painter, a lifetime appointment, should remain empty after Rogier's death. If the fathers were guessing that Rogier's pre-eminence was of a kind never likely to be rivaled, they were not far wrong.

We have, much diluted, Rogier's self-portrait. In a series of murals for the Brussels Town Hall, he included himself among the spectators of a miracle. The originals were destroyed by fire during the French siege two and a half centuries later, but a tapestry copy, with whatever inevitable modifications, still shows us a face alert, searching, both inquisitive and analytical, not quite skeptical, in which the keen gaze of the eyes is balanced by the sensuality of a handsome mouth.

Petrus (real name, Pieter) Christus, who frequently signed his painting XPI, the Greek abbreviation for the name of Christ, became a master painter in Bruges in 1444. From this first known date in his life his birth year, by deduction, must have been between 1410 and 1415, or thereabouts. He died in 1472 or 1473. Beyond these dates, not a great deal is known about his life, and his works provide apparently inexhaustible, because ultimately unresolvable, problems for scholars.

Petrus Christus may or may not have served at one time as an apprentice to Jan van Eyck. His art reflects this master's, as well as Rogier van der Weyden's, although in fusing the two reduced both to a sometimes almost commonplace simplicity. The precision of Jan's delineation is somewhat softened; its complexities are ironed out. And Rogier's heroic intensity becomes ordinary mournfulness.

There are compensations, however. In the eyes of his admirers, Petrus Christus's simplification of Eyckian space establishes him as a master of volumetric unities suggestive of an orderly and perfectly integrated world, while in bringing Rogier's passion down to earth he imbues his personages with an appealing air of introspection. Being an early Netherlandish painter of stature he was, of course, a superb technician. But many people, including this writer, find difficulty in regarding Petrus Christus as anything more than a country cousin to genius.

Born in Haarlem about 1415, Dirc Bouts probably came early to Louvain. In 1447/48 he married a daughter of a prominent family, Catherine van der Bruggen, who bore the enchanting nickname of "Catherine with the Money." A respected citizen, he certainly remained in Louvain until he died in 1475, about sixty years old.

Bouts seems to have formed an early friendship with Petrus Christus, who was almost his exact contemporary, and, like Christus, he drew heavily upon Jan van Eyck and Rogier van der Weyden. His sources were both the originals and Christus's innovational variations, which he is usually given credit for having perfected.

Bouts's "devitalized" figures, sometimes so stiff and motionless as to appear clumsy, have been compared by Erwin Panofsky to "sign posts on the road into depth," placed as they are at intervals from foreground to deep background to mark the progressive recession of his pictorial stage. Thus Bouts anticipated, although surely without formulating for himself any such approach, a concept of landscape perfected by Nicolas Poussin two hundred years later, by which natural forms are synthesized into essentially abstract spatial arrangements.

But if Bouts's human beings seem to be set forever in rigid, depersonalized attitudes where all drama is avoided, their very immobility accentuates an inner life perceptible in their faces. With hardly the slightest change of expression even during scenes of violence, these people regard us or one another from heavy-lidded eyes that protect their secrets from us and from one another. Their reluctance—or refusal —to share their emotional responses is not a matter of aristocratic reserve. Rather they seem neurotically isolated, introspective, indifferent to human attachments. One may wonder to what degree this Boutsian reserve reflects the artist's interpretation of his subjects and to what degree it is only the result of a manner of representation in the work of a painter who cared very little about the problems of drawing the figure. Bouts endows the individuals in his portraits and portrait drawings (some of the most beautiful in all early Netherlandish art) with this same air of pensive removal, which could hardly have been universal among the prosperous burghers who sat for him. But no matter. There it is.

As the painter of the *Portinari Altarpiece*, Hugo van der Goes is one of the three major Northern stars, with Jan van Eyck and Rogier van der Weyden, in the dazzling galaxy that stretched between Italy and the Netherlands in the fifteenth century. And as a painter afflicted with mental illness, he offers a case history that is fascinating in its correlation of genius with insanity, but frustrating because its documentation, remarkably complete during the final stage, is nonexistent earlier.

Nothing at all is known about Hugo van der Goes's parentage, his childhood, his youth, or the period of his twenties. His birth date is deduced as no earlier than 1435, perhaps as late as 1440. As far as any records are concerned, he might not have existed until 1467, when he was admitted as a free master of the painters' guild in Ghent. He was immediately and spectacularly successful. Within a few years he was famous. In addition to private commissions he was given important public ones in both Ghent and Bruges, and in 1474 he became dean of the guild, an indication that he was esteemed as highly by his fellow artists as by the princes and international financiers who were his patrons.

And yet, in spite of the records of his success, Hugo remains unrevealed as a person during those years. Nothing that we know of his history prepares us for the suddenness of his decision to abandon the world. In 1475, when he was at most barely forty, he entered the Roode Kloster, a priory near Brussels, and died there only seven years later, in 1482. The history of those seven years includes the painting of the *Portinari Altarpiece* and a series of attacks of acute depression terminating in a severe breakdown with suicidal mania the year before his death.

His last days, spent in spiritual agony, are recounted by one of the monks, Gaspar Ofhuys, in a document remarkable for its combination of straightforward clinical observation and offensive post-mortem backbiting disguised as pious moralizing. As a *donatus* who had given all his worldly goods to the order—and these goods must have been considerable—

Hugo held a status somewhere between that of lay brother and monk. He was allowed privileges within the monastery that were denied the lay brothers, and also some worldly privileges that were denied the monks. He received whatever visitors he pleased and continued his work as a painter. Brother Gaspar does not manage to conceal his envy when he writes that Hugo "while he was with us became more acquainted with the pomp of the world than with the ways of doing penitence and humbling himself," and reports that Hugo was visited by "persons of high rank, and even by His Serene Highness, the Archduke Maximilian."* On such occasions fine wines were allowed at the guest's table, and Ofhuys, half as diagnostician and half as gossip, suggests that Hugo himself might have partaken too liberally of the wine and thus encouraged the growth of malevolent biles that resulted in his sickness. Ofhuys also hints that it only served Hugo right when God "in His great mercy sent him this chastening affliction which, indeed, humbled him mightily." In the last months of his life Hugo exiled himself from the refectory and ate with the lay brothers.

The picture of Hugo as a sybaritic ecclesiastic does not jibe with his despair for the salvation of his soul in heaven and his despair that he might leave his painting unperfected on earth. Nor can it be fitted into the pattern of the mad genius popularized by romanticism—the great painter whose hand is guided by an irrational force called inspiration. Hugo's derangement had nothing to do with violence and hallucination. "Throughout his illness he never once tried to harm anyone but himself," Ofhuys reports. For all his sanctimoniousness, Ofhuys was as good a diagnostician as the century afforded. As the *infirmarius* of the monastery he had a certain amount of medical knowledge, and his account,

* The translations of Ofhuys are from "Born Under Saturn," Rudolf and Margot Wittkower, New York, 1963.

when it is limited to the description of Hugo's symptoms, is that of an observant but puzzled physician. He could explain the symptoms neither as the result of possession by an evil spirit nor as a "frenzy of the brain" produced by "noxious juices" within the body of the victim.

"In truth, what it was that ailed him only God can tell," Ofhuys concluded. And while that conclusion must always hold to a large extent, psychiatrists and art historians in combination can modify it by an examination of the clinical record and the *Portinari Altarpiece* together. Even knowing as little as we do about the rest of his life, we can recognize Hugo at forty as a personality so torn by conflicting impulses and convictions that he found his life inexplicable and intolerable. He was as devout as Fra Angelico, but he was incapable of Fra Angelico's beatific reconciliation of faith and reason.

In the twelfth century, or even in his own if he had entered a monastery as a boy, Hugo might have been a mystic. As it was, he could not deny everything that his rational intelligence told him about the world and everything that his brilliant success had taught him about the relation of the world to his art. He could not truly withdraw from the world without sacrificing his life as an artist, which was unthinkable. His dilemma was related to Ofhuys' objection that "he had developed a rather high opinion of himself due to the many honors, visits and compliments which were paid to him." But pride was not his trouble. His trouble was that true humility, the pious depersonalization that he held sincerely as his ideal, was totally incompatible with fame, and increasing fame was unavoidable as long as he remained not only an artist but an artist who was involved, even when he entered the monastery, with the creation of his masterwork. Psychiatrists would find that Hugo's breakdown was his way of escape from his dilemma.

Hugo may have begun the *Portinari Altarpiece* as early as 1474, completing it about 1476. It was commissioned by Tommaso Portinari, who represented the Medici banking interests in Bruges, and not long after completion it went to Florence (where it remains, in the Uffizi). It made Hugo as famous in Italy as he was at home, and was so much admired by Florentine artists that it is as important in the history of Italian painting as it is in the North. It made its effect through a realism that the Italians found staggering. In their admiration they were both right and wrong.

In their book "Born Under Saturn," Rudolf and Margot Wittkower point out that "modern students have not noticed that in his interpretations of the Holy Stories [Hugo] was profoundly indebted to the teaching of Thomas à Kempis. . . . Here he found such admonitions as 'Keep company with the humble and simple, with the devout and virtuous. . . . Unfailing peace is with the humble. . . . Better surely is the humble peasant who serves God than the proud philosopher who studies the course of heaven. . . .'"

This apostrophe must have haunted an artist who kept company not with the humble but with the great, not always with the devout and virtuous but with men like Tommaso Portinari. It is also a key to the nature of Hugo's realism. The most famous portion of the *Portinari Altarpiece* is the group of three shepherds in the central panel of the *Adoration*—gnarled, weatherbeaten men, one of them a young oaf, snaggle-toothed and coarse-haired, staring in amazed half-comprehension at the miracle of the Child.

Hugo's realism of surface—everything is recorded down to the last whisker, the last pockmark, in a shepherd's face—had been equaled by other artists, but had not been directed toward quite the same goal. His shepherds are conceived as states of mind, not as appropriately costumed actors posed in reverent attitudes. Their whole meaning is spiritual, and their superbly descriptive surfaces are as powerful as they are only because Hugo's realism, if it can be called that, comes from within. Preoccupied with the fate of his own soul, Hugo recognized the portion of spirit in other human beings too, and he realized that the painter must reveal more than he sees. Through the medium of what he sees, he must reveal all that he can perceive.

Hugo's nominal realism blinds most modern eyes (as it did Renaissance eyes) to his extraordinary departures from convention in ways that anticipate twentieth-century devices. It is easy to admire the *Portinari Altarpiece* as an unusually sumptuous fifteenth-century panel painting, constructed according to the customary formula of a large central panel flanked by twin wings showing the donors and their patron saints, and filled with wonderfully described textures—hair, velvets, furs, flowers and leaves, wood, and the like—appropriately bound together in an architectural setting unified with landscape. In view of its date, one might be surprised that Hugo reverted to the earlier device of representing figures at varying scales according to the degree of their importance, and might even feel that the tiny angels, in their different groups, the adoring shepherds at a larger scale off to one side, the Virgin and St. Joseph large and isolated, and the diminutive Christ child lying most isolated of all upon an eventless patch of earth, give the composition an unconventional choppiness at a time when painters had learned to create harmonious units in logical relationships.

But the point is that Hugo denied the validity of realistically logical composition just at the moment of its triumph. He deliberately reverted to contradictory scale not as an indication of relative importance but as a means of creating an air of unreality. He placed his Adoration within a conventionally perspected architecture—but within that space employed half a dozen contradictory perspectives. Taking an extreme position, we could argue that he anticipated the cubist idea of simultaneous vision from any number of angles, but his purpose had nothing to do with such a technical experiment. By the violation and reorganization of the laws of vision (while each detail seems to be seen through a supranaturally precise objective eye) he turned the usual *tableau vivant* of the Adoration into the miracle that he wanted it to be. And within this scene where the best of the earth is fused with the mystery of divinity, Hugo incorporated an iconographic scheme as complicated as any that can be found in painting. The *Portinari Altarpiece* is a final synthesis of faith, intellectualism, technical genius, and mystical sensibility so wonderful that the word "synthesis" in reference to it is a profanation.

The ultimate contradiction in Hugo van der Goes is that his agonized and disrupted spirituality should receive such powerful expression through means so analytical. Admittedly this contradiction is inherent in most great religious painting, but Hugo represents an extreme of both spiritual vision and painstaking factualness. Although he achieved their fusion into an inseparable whole in his painting, their conflict in his life cost him his sanity.

Hans Memling is one painter who gives the lie, so far as it can be given, to the argument that an artist cannot amount to much if his vision is not in some way original. Unless we accept an inherent sweetness and gentleness as his special genius, we are at a loss to discover any distinctive quality in his work. He borrowed—or adapted—his compositions and his symbolism wholesale from Rogier van der Weyden, and took what he wanted from Jan van Eyck and Hugo van der Goes. Of course he could not have chosen much better sources. And if we must recognize that he distilled away all passion, grandeur, and mystery from the art of the great men, we cannot, for all that, consider his own art merely a residue. It is always imbued with a compensating, if rather mundane, tenderness, and seldom offends by pretending to offer anything more. His technique is flawless, and even in some comparatively large paintings he holds to a miniaturist's approach that is harmonious with the reduced spiritual scale of his conceptions. He was in no way progressive or exploratory: his style, not advanced when he started out, changed hardly at all during the forty or so years of his career.

As a portraitist Memling was a faithful, and exquisite, delineator of features. His sitters, one and all, men and women, seem to share his own unquestioning acceptance of an earth and heaven undisturbed by either suffering or ecstasy. If there are often suggestions of individual character beneath this uniform placidity, it is not because Memling sought to reveal character, but because certain sets of features, like those of some stranger glimpsed on the street, suggest character of one kind or another—with how much truth is another question.

In attributing an inherent sweetness and gentleness of nature to Memling as we have done, we are of course falling into the trap of making the same kind of guess, deducing his character not from a glimpse of his face on the street but from the consistent character of his work. Not much is known about Memling's life, but what is known does not support any picture of him as an unworldly man, although he may have been a very good one.

Memling was born near Frankfurt, about 1435 or 1440, but he was put on record as a new citizen of Bruges on January 30, 1465. Two years later he became a member of the painters' guild there. His popularity was international: English, German, and Spanish patrons commissioned work from him, and even Italian ones—"even," because he worked during the century when great painters seemed crowded shoulder to shoulder in Italian streets. Memling's art apparently held for his contemporaries the same appeal that it holds for a mass public now. He is more easily appreciated by most people than are his contemporaries whose art was more complicated, subtle, and profound.

Memling earned a great deal of money. He was one of the wealthy citizens who, not quite of their own volition, lent money to the city of Bruges to help defray the costs of Maximilian I's war with France. This was in 1480, when he would have been in his early forties; at the same time he was investing in real estate. He was married, had three sons, and was eulogized upon his death in 1494, at the age of about sixty, as "the best painter in all Christendom."

Born in Oudewater about 1460, and a member of the painters' guild in Bruges by 1484, Gerard David succeeded Hans Memling as the leading painter of the city, and became the last great one in its tradition. In the city's decline, its artists looked backward to the founders of this tradition, the Master of Flémalle and Jan van Eyck, with a new sense of historical pride. It is easy to see, or to imagine, a nostalgic spirit in the sober, gently melancholy art of Gerard David. There is no need to imagine his return to Eyckian space, however: it is apparent in his monumental compositions of Madonnas with saints, although the air that fills this space has become softer, the light more diaphanous, and the forms existing in the new rarefied ambience more dulcet.

Among a group of painters who merely imitated the early masters to satisfy a lively market, David stands alone in having extracted from the tenets of the founders nourishment for an independently expressive style. He has much of the exquisiteness of any late development, the purely aesthetic subtleties of a failing tradition that must compensate for the forcefulness of first growth. The sensitive languor of decay may be only a few steps from this position, but David never took them.

In the pellucid landscapes revealed through arches or windows behind the thrones of his pensive Madonnas, David's world, for all its explicit detail, is only half real, not doubly real as it is in the landscapes of Van Eyck. But everywhere David is his own man. If his art is archaistic in some measure, as a tribute to the past, it is an art grown out of his own understanding rather than a mere recitation by rote of his predecessors' virtues.

Tremendously productive, successful, and respected, Gerard David was four times head of the painters' guild. He died in 1523, in his early forties.

Gerard David found an exquisite and altogether delightful follower in Joachim Patinir (c. 1485-1524), the kind of painter who, considered a secondary master in a great school, demonstrates by the excellence of his painting how strong that school must be if he is not placed in its first rank. Patinir learned from the backgrounds of David's religious paintings just how sweetly harmonious and just how wonderfully pellucid the forms of nature bathed in air can be, and he reversed the usual relationship to make the religious subject incidental to landscape. His enchanting scenes bask in blue-green light, and his gentle little people inhabit them gracefully. The Rest on the Flight to Egypt was his favorite subject; he shows the Holy Family enjoying immaculate picnics in spots so lovely that it seems a shame the fugitives must ever leave them. Patinir is an early master of the imaginary landscape.

The wonderful century that was given its character in the North by the sane, luminous realism of Jan van Eyck and the intellectual passion of Rogier van der Weyden came to its end with a most unexpected and curious terminal picture, a phantasmagoria called *The Garden of Delights,* painted about 1500 by an artist who maddeningly resists explanation.

He signed some of his work "Jheronimus Bosch," taking his surname from his small home town of 's Hertogenbosch, where he worked all his life. Jeroen Anthoniszoon was probably his real name. He died, or at least ceases to be mentioned by any records, in 1516. His birth date is estimated as 1450. He is known to have been a member in good standing of what Erwin Panofsky calls the "furiously respectable" Confraternity of Our Lady in 's Hertogenbosch for the thirty years from 1486 to 1516. And that is just about all we know of Hieronymus Bosch except what can be deduced by decoding, or trying to decode, the most wildly complicated iconography ever left behind for unraveling in a single painting.

There is no chance, short of some miraculously lucky documentary find, that Bosch's personality can ever be reconstructed on any basis but wild surmise. The surmises so far have included a theory that in his quiet little home town this respected member of the Confraternity of Our Lady was *sub rosa* a member of a heretical religious sect and a practitioner of the Black Mass. He has been the subject of post-mortem Freudian psychoanalysis based on the sexual symbolism of his pictorial fantasies, which would be rich Freudian material indeed if they were pure inventions comparable to dreams. At another extreme, Bosch could be interpreted as a quiet little man whose apparent fantasies were in fact only illustrations of popular symbols drawn from current folklore, proverbs, legends, and instructive moral allegories (all of these familiar to his contemporaries no matter how bizarre they seem to us, who have forgotten them) compounded with orthodox Christian theology and centering upon an obsession with the pleasurable seductions and terrible punishments of original sin.

Sin, torture, scatology, and perversion have never been pictured with such grace and delicacy, or with moral purpose so nearly indistinguishable from morbid fascination, as in Bosch's masterpiece, which significantly goes by two titles, the one used nearly as often as the other: *The Garden of Lust* and *The Garden of Delights*. This painting is the center panel of a triptych now in the Prado, in which the first panel shows the creation of Adam and Eve, marked for the Fall, and the third, the horrors of hell, to which, in their frailty, they consigned their descendants.

Armies of slender, dainty girls and lissome youths, all deliciously pale and naked, inhabit the pink, blue, and green Garden of Delights where animal, vegetable, and mineral forms have been multiply hybridized into weird growths and monuments. There is no question but that all the activities here are concerned with fornication; if it is not going on (with two lovers entrapped and pinched within a gigantic oyster shell, as one variant) it is always in prospect. Everything is at once lovely and ghastly. A single detail, of a fresh, sweetly tinted bouquet of flowers protruding from the anus of a crouching figure, can be isolated as a summary of the mixture—but in description it sounds at once less startling and more unpleasant than it is in Bosch's representation.

The garden radiates from a central pool (the Fountain of Life?) where a cavalcade of creatures parades in a circle. One of them seems to be part pig and part antelope, modified by genes connectible only with a strawberry and a warty cucumber. Others seem to be products of mixed unions between giraffes, camels, and unicorns. Jellyfish and cacti have interbred with macaws and mice. A huge flower, something like a dahlia, holds within its petals a monstrous red-veined bladder, a balloon where lovers embrace. What is this form, ambulating through hell on spindly legs that support a pair of ears and, projecting from between these ears like a phallus, the knife that might have severed them from some giant's head? And how are we to interpret a sinner crucified across the strings of a harp, the symbol of celestial bliss, while the king of hell, enthroned on a tall chair with an open seat, crams other sinners into his mouth and then excretes them into an azure bubble from which they drop into a pit?

The fiendishness and perversity of such phantasms suggest again and again the Black Mass, and may easily have been inspired by tales of it, but there is no factual support for the theory that Bosch belonged to the heretical Adamite sect, or that a certain Jacob van Almangien, whom Bosch must have known, was the sect's grand master and Bosch's mentor in occult symbolism. Jacob van Almangien was a converted Jew who entered the "furiously respectable" Confraternity of Our Lady but left it after ten years when he returned to the Jewish faith. Bosch could easily have gained his acquaintance with Jewish folklore from this man, but that is the end of it.

Jewish folklore is only one of a dozen identifiable ingredients in the Bosch nougat ("nougat" is not as odd in this context as one might think, for a painting by Bosch can be as densely packed, and its color can be as fresh, and as sweet), but the ingredients in Bosch's time were not as esoteric as they now seem. Alchemy, astrology, sorcery, tarot cards, and reports of heretical ceremonies are among them, and as sources of symbolism they intermingle like the beasts, plants, minerals, and human beings of Bosch's world. The egg, for instance, which occurs again and again, re-formed and transformed, may shift in and out and back and forth between references, as a sexual symbol, as a symbol of life, as a pagan symbol of fertility, as a Christian symbol of resurrection—all familiar. In alchemy the egg begins as a symbol of the alchemist's crucible and not only ramifies in every alchemical direction but by its own alchemy of suggestion is related to the gourds, the bubbles, the bladders, the hollow trees, that occur and occur again. In this Gordian knot of symbolism, some meanings are known, some have been decoded recently, and many must remain forever lost.

But since he was working with traditional symbols, Bosch cannot be thought of as the wild, visionary mystic—or at least the extreme eccentric—that he would have had to be if his paintings were pure inventions. The fantasy was inherent in the material, just as it is in a photograph of a two-headed calf even if the photographer is the most commonplace of men. But Bosch could not have been quite that. His assembling of hundreds of individually fantastic elements is more than an agglutination. He was at least a superb stage designer when he synthesized the theatrical spectacle of *The Garden of Delights,* and at least a great melodramatist of the weird when he concocted his hell. And beyond all that, how can we account for his constant and contradictory preoccupation with moralizing on the one hand and sensuality on the other? He is always speaking of the presence of the devil—evil is ubiquitous—and of the punishment of sin, but at the same time he delights in the forms that sin—and punishment—can take. At this point conjecture as to what kind of man Bosch was becomes unsafe.

We know only that he maintained a respected position in a small, conservative town all his life and hence must not have displayed erratic behavior that the conflict between sensual obsessions and a strictly moral point of view may produce to send individuals to the psychiatric couch today. Perhaps the obvious joy that Bosch took in representing the aberrant sweetnesses of the flesh served as a kind of safety valve for impulses of which he was unaware. But here we are already entering the quicksands of presumption.

As an artist, Bosch can hardly be tied to any tradition that might normally have produced him (although he has been firmly joined, after four hundred years, to the surrealist movement in its explicitly naturalistic representation of the unnatural). Attempted demonstrations that his fantasies are anticipated in Gothic and Romanesque hellscapes are forced and tenuous at best. And he found no true followers, despite a popularity attested by the quantities of copies of his paintings made during his lifetime and for a while after his death. After two generations he found the nearest thing to a follower in Pieter Bruegel, but Bruegel's drolleries are those of a humanist, not a fantasist, of a sociologist, not a moralizer. Efforts to endow Bosch with any of the humanistic learning of his century have been fruitless.

His interest in the fantastic is apparent from the beginning, but his early work is relatively sober. (It must be admitted that in relation to *The Garden of Delights* almost anything else is sober.) His work never seems closely tied to his time or place, and the impression of its isolation has been exaggerated by its virtual transplantation to Spanish soil. During the century after his death, Bosch became the favorite painter of Philip II, who collected Bosch so avidly that this Flemish painter is best seen in Madrid. In truth he cannot be seen at his full stature anywhere else. His combination of sensuality, puritanism, and macabre fantasy would have been much more comprehensible in a painter of the Inquisition than in his own country where it grew like a plant from an exotic seed that should not have been viable in a cold climate. Bosch belongs to no climate except the one he created, and how it happened that he created it, we shall probably never know.

There is always something sad about the tag-ender of a great school. That thankless role fell to Quentin Massys, an expert and intelligent Netherlandish painter who arrived a little late, and to another Netherlander, the much less impressive Jan Gossart, known as Mabuse.

Quentin Massys (*c.* 1466-1530), whose name also appears as Matsys and Metsys, inherited a Gothic spiritual tradition that could no longer sustain itself within a booming commercial society and a booming Renaissance intellectualism, but he achieved the remarkable feat of bridging the gap without seeming to straddle it awkwardly. Probably a student of Dirc Bouts, he was a cultivated humanist, a friend of Erasmus and More. With consistent intelligence (a valuable asset to a painter, but not one that guarantees greatness) and with great respect (always dangerous), he continued the tradition of the earlier Netherlandish masters in religious subjects, but was most at home in secular ones. *The Money Changer and His Wife,* in the Louvre, a combination of character study, genre piece, and staggeringly detailed still life, is probably his best painting, although one must also admire his Madonnas for the skill and discretion with which he adapted the medieval formula to sixteenth-century taste. Two sons, Cornelis and Jan Massys, followed him as artists of the Antwerp school, of which he can be called the founder.

Jan Gossart (Gossaert), called Mabuse, was born between 1470 and 1478 and died in 1533. He went to Italy as a retainer of the Duke of Burgundy and thus came into contact with the full Italian Renaissance. As a mature artist working within the Netherlandish tradition, Mabuse had been more archaistic than imaginative, and after his contact with the Italians he did not improve greatly. He is always called important for his introduction of Italianate mannerisms into the art of the Low Countries, but he grafted them onto his own style rather awkwardly, not making the best either of his native (if badly weakened) Gothic heritage or of the inventive vigor of the South. Hybrid styles are frequently tremendously attractive. But in Mabuse's case—no.

The phenomenon of Netherlandish painting had no parallel (and hardly anything that could be called an echo) elsewhere in northern Europe during the fifteenth century. But if no unified schools of great importance flourished in France or Germany, some artists of individual stature did. The great Frenchman was Jean Fouquet.

Fouquet lived for about sixty years, was an extremely busy artist, and was so highly esteemed that he not only became painter to the King of France but accompanied a delegation from the French court to Rome, where he received the rare honor of permission to do a portrait of the Pope. He made such an impression in Italy that Vasari was still hearing echoes of his illustrious reputation a hundred years later. Judging from his existing paintings, he deserved the position he held, and he can stand not only as the greatest French painter of his century but among the great in any country during that fantastic hundred years, even though his extant paintings—beyond numbers of miniatures, in which his genius was somewhat cramped—can be ticked off on the fingers of one hand, leaving the other five free for a list of shaky attributions.

If his paintings have largely disappeared, Fouquet himself vanished entirely during the seventeenth and eighteenth centuries. With his miniatures lying in libraries and his few paintings scattered, he fell into such obscurity that when he was re-identified in 1830 as the painter of a set of miniatures in a volume in the Bibliothèque Nationale in Paris, there were no biographical facts to link with his name and his life had to be reconstructed to the extent that we now know it.

Fouquet lived and worked in Tours. By the evidence of a papal brief of the year 1449 he was born there about 1420 in what might be described as a state of maximum illegitimacy, his father having been a priest and his mother an unmarried woman. The brief legitimized Jean Fouqet (*sic*), cleric, of Tours. The "cleric" indicates not priesthood but a form of laymembership shared, incidentally, by François Villon, the dissolute genius who was Fouquet's contemporary. The date of Fouquet's death is unknown, but it was probably shortly before the end of 1481, since a record of his parish church, again in Tours, mentions his widow and heirs in November of that year. He must have achieved an early success, since he was sent on the mission to Rome in 1446, when he would have been about twenty-six.

Fouquet's miniatures are superb exceptions within the generally decaying tradition of manuscript illustration of his time, but his panel paintings reveal the full scope of his powers. There are three portraits of middle-aged men—one of Charles VII of France, another of Chancellor Guillaume Juvénal des Ursins, and one of Etienne Chevalier, a middle-class court official, accompanied by a young man in the guise of Chevalier's patron saint, Stephen (the first two portraits are in the Louvre, the third is in Berlin).

These portraits, as portraits, are hardly surpassed in the painting of any country or time—a broad statement, but it is true that each of these men exists with a completeness that goes beyond the technically impeccable delineation of features into the inexplicable area where an artist transmutes those features (which could belong to anybody) into a revelation of individual character.

The double portrait of Etienne Chevalier and the young man posing as St. Stephen, which is generally considered to be Fouquet's masterpiece, was originally half of a diptych, or possibly the wing of a triptych, in combination with the famous *Virgin and Child* that usually comes first to mind when Fouquet is mentioned. Allegedly, the Virgin is no virgin at all, but Agnès Sorel, Charles VII's mistress. The picture must be the most audacious Virgin and Child ever painted. It shows a pretty woman, her bodice unlaced to bare one perfectly hemispherical breast, who has all the allure and the high style (if also the affectation of a bit more piety) that would be expected of a royal courtesan. The doll-like features sufficiently suggest those of Agnès Sorel's funeral effigy at Loches to justify an identification. And since Etienne Chevalier, together with the financier Jacques Coeur, was the executor of Agnès Sorel's will, it also seems reasonable that when Chevalier commissioned an altar for his birthplace, Melun, he should have done so in her memory. The Sorel–Virgin, which is now in Antwerp, and the Chevalier–St. Stephen were sold separately when French treasures were carelessly exported after the Revolution.

This Virgin and Child are so startling that it is no wonder they have become the earmark of Fouquet's manner, but there is something just a little outrageous about them. The poetic conception of the surrounding cherub Angels of Day—painted a solid, brilliant scarlet with golden highlights—who support a jeweled throne along with Angels of Night—painted in a contrasting solid deep, bright blue—barely lifts the picture from audacity to religious fantasy, but leaves it, in any case, one of the most extraordinary paintings in the history of French art, and a painting of sophistication that one feels to be peculiarly French.

Beyond these pictures, we have a single life-size altarpiece in all probability from Fouquet's hand, a *Pietà* in the parish church at Nouans—damaged, cut down in size, and partially repainted, but still a majestic shadow. From this meager list we can infer that Fouquet revivified panel painting in France during the years after the disaster of Agincourt, combining in perfect equilibrium the high finish and the delight in objective realism of detail that he saw in the work of his Netherlandish contemporaries with the breadth and intellectualism of the Italians that he saw at first hand. And he added to the mixture a French elegance that, all told, gives his art a flavor not quite like any other, a flavor perhaps the more concentrated because we must savor it in such small quantity.

The next ten painters form a kind of appendix to this chapter. They were delightful artists, all of them. The first four belong to a French Netherlandish tradition; the last six are German, with inevitable Netherlandish connections. Though they may be considered minor, they cannot be skipped in anything like a comprehensive survey of Northern painting in the fifteenth century.

Melchior Broederlam (active 1381-1409), of Ypres, was an early Northern master of the International Style and, by far, the most important of the proto-Eyckian artists whose work still exists in sufficient quantity to make a judgment of rank possible. He was an artist of great originality who seemed to be striving toward an Eyckian spatial expression with rounded volumes revealed in harmonious light. But he lacked the technical means perfected by the Van Eycks that allowed them to transform the Gothic mass of realistic particulars into a logical whole.

Broederlam was held in great esteem by his patron, Philip the Bold, and performed the various services beyond painting expected of a medieval master at court, such as the design of architectural ornament, of banners and other paraphernalia of celebrations, and the gilding and coloring of sculptures. He is an enchanting painter whose fancifulness is more apparent to us today than his acute eye and his struggles to expand the expressive resources of painting.

Jean Malouel, or Maelweel (active by 1396; died in 1415), was one of the earliest panel painters in Europe, and represented, with Henri Bellechose, a strongly Italianate school, more conservative than the manuscript illuminators of the time. He was an uncle and early benefactor of the most important of the illuminators, the Limbourg brothers. Although a Fleming, he worked in France, first in Paris for Queen Isabeau of Bavaria and then, beginning in 1398, for the dukes of Burgundy. For Philip the Bold and John the Fearless he executed portraits and also religious paintings that combine mystical symbolism with a courtly French delicacy and stylishness. Upon his death he was succeeded as court painter by Henri Bellechose, also a Fleming. Between 1400 and 1444, the years of his recorded activity, Bellechose continued the tradition Malouel had established, but he suffered badly from the rise of Jan van Eyck.

Nicolas Froment, active from 1450 to 1490, was a leading—or even the leading—painter of the loosely connected group working in Provence and centered at the papal court in Avignon. He modified the school's Italianate cast with a strong dash of Flemish realism. His *Triptych of the Burning Bush,* which remains in the Cathedral of Aix-en-Provence, for which he originally painted it, is one of the fascinating paintings in early French art, combining medieval allegory with courtliness, and blending Italian and Flemish elements into a personal style. (This is one opinion. The painting is not universally admired. Some critics find it an ill-assembled group of well-executed exercises.)

The anonymous French painter called the Master of Moulins (active between 1480 and 1500) so strongly influenced by Hugo van der Goes that he can be called Hugo's disciple, worked at the Bourbon court in Moulins. He brought a degree of Renaissance amplitude to the lingering Gothic tradition, and a degree of Hugo's intellectualized mysticism to the elegance of court painting. Usually thought of as second only to Fouquet in his century in France, the Master of Moulins is connectible with, but cannot be identified with, the painters Jean Perréal and Jean Bourdichon.

Conrad Witz (1400/10-c. 1447), who worked in Basel and Geneva, was born and educated in Constance. He is the Master of Flémalle or even the Jan van Eyck of German painting. Witz has a claim to a pinpointed historical position as the first artist we know who painted a "portrait" of an identifiable landscape, instead of following the usual practice of synthesizing one. His *Christ Walking on the Water*, signed and dated 1444, now in the museum in Geneva, places the event upon an accurately rendered stretch of the lake and its shores. (Witz also used the marketplace of Basel and the Basel Cathedral as settings for Bible subjects.)

Pictorially, however, it is more important that Witz observed Jan van Eyck's treatment of refractions in water, and perfected it. But he never absorbed the Eyckian ideal of living space: he tends to clutter his pictures in the manner of the Master of Flémalle. As an incidental detail, this painter whose style was marked by a dignified simplicity belonged to that confraternity of artists who, as brawlers in the street, gave as much trouble to the police as they gave satisfaction to their patrons.

Lucas Moser (active 1431-1440) was the first exponent of fifteenth-century Northern modernism—that is, of the new art flourishing in the Netherlands—on German soil. Very little is known about him, but that little is sufficiently striking. His only unquestionably identifiable work is the *St. Magdalen Altarpiece* for the church at Tiefenbronn, and it is as famous for an inscription he added to it as for its advanced character. "Wail, art, wail and lament," he wrote. "No one cares about you any more, alas!" (*"Schri. Kunst. schri und klag dich ser/ Din begert jecz nemen mer./ So. o. we."*). The dirge sounds like the plaints today of conservative painters who have been left behind by the rush of modernism. But with Moser—his altarpiece is our evidence—it could have been only the objection of a progressive artist whose vanguardism is not appreciated. His realism, solidly Flemish in character, must have been learned abroad—directly or indirectly from the Master of Flémalle. But this, like everything about Lucas Moser except his altarpiece and its inscription, is speculation by deduction.

Hans Multscher (*c.* 1400-1467) settled in Ulm in 1427 and ran a productive shop there for forty years. Best known as a painter by the eight remaining panels of his Niederwurzbach altarpiece of 1437, he was primarily a sculptor, and painted like one. In his case this meant that the grace and delicacy of the International Style gave way to a less polished and more vigorous expression with a powerful, almost crude, German accent. His realism makes him, with Lucas Moser, probably the most "modern" German painter of his day.

Stephan Lochner (1410/15-1451), an altogether charming artist, is the leading master of the school of Cologne, but he probably received his early training in the Netherlands, either under the Master of Flémalle or in a closely associated workshop. The influence of Jan van Eyck is discernible in Lochner's understanding of color and light, but for all his modernism—in Germany, Lockner was an advanced painter—he remains in spirit a representative of the International Style. His narratives of holy events are lively, personal, and sensitive rather than powerful or (like those of his contemporary Rogier van der Weyden) emotionalized, although some enthusiasts have found his hell scenes prophetic of Bosch's.

Lochner is frequently mentioned in the archives of Cologne, where he married, settled down, and was a member of the city council. He died early, between the ages of thirty-five and forty, probably of the plague.

Michael Pacher (*c.* 1435-1498) was a painter and sculptor (in wood) who was born and lived all his life in the southern Tyrol. Pacher, as a Tyrolese, inherited and hybridized in his work both the German and Italian traditions—which in his time were separated by the whole distance between the late Middle Ages and the Renaissance. Pacher's manner—so arresting that one wonders why he is not more widely admired—remained primarily Northern. He certainly traveled in Italy (although perhaps not as far as Venice), but such Italianisms as he adopted served only to enhance the intensity of a rather violently convoluted style sometimes called "late-Gothic baroque." From the Italians Pacher learned the use of deep perspective with low horizons against which figures in the foreground assume monumental scale. But where his models, which included first of all Mantegna's frescoes in Padua, treated space as a static volume, Pacher conceived of it as an arena of action.

Pacher's major work, an altarpiece for the high altar of the Franziskanerkirche in Salzburg, begun in 1484, has survived only in fragments, but his earlier *St. Wolfgang Altarpiece*, in the village church of St. Wolfgang, Salzkammergut, Austria, is stylistic proof of his contact with the Mantegna frescoes and would alone establish him as the most important bridge between North and South before Dürer. Dürer may have seen Pacher's work when he crossed the Alps en route to Italy, and was possibly influenced by it in later woodcuts.

Martin Schongauer (*c.* 1430-1491), trained as a goldsmith under his father, became an engraver (115 examples are extant) and painter, and the first German artist to attain an international reputation. Although he worked in Colmar, he probably spent some time in the Netherlands, since his work often reflects an acquaintance with Rogier van der Weyden's that could hardly have come at second hand. Rogier's linear intensity, his crisp drawing, and the frequently two-dimensional emphasis of his pattern, all were sympathetic to an engraving style.

Schongauer is unexcelled as an engraver by any artist in

history, even including Dürer. Dürer, when he was twenty, made a trip to Colmar to see Schongauer, but arrived to discover that his idol had died. Through Dürer, Schongauer was a powerful influence on the German Renaissance; he has also been claimed as an ancestor by twentieth-century fantasists, notably the surrealists, on the strength of such engravings as *The Temptation of St. Anthony,* with its combination of eerie supernaturalism and precise definition.

It is possible to call Schongauer the greatest of all engravers technically without fear of starting a really serious quarrel. No other engraver combined to the same degree that special crystalline rhythm of line producible only by the engraver's burin with tonal gradations so subtle—from silvery gray to brilliant black—or with textural effects of such phenomenal variety.

3

THE EARLY
FLORENTINE
RENAISSANCE

At this juncture it might be well to offer a reminder that in following fifteenth-century painting thus far, we have been tracing one branch of a forking that occurred about 1400. While the fathers of Netherlandish painting—the Master of Flémalle, Jan van Eyck, and Rogier van der Weyden—were bringing medieval painting to its apogee in the North, a brilliant Florentine triad—the sculptor Donatello, the architect Brunelleschi, and the painter Masaccio—were setting off what we have already called the grass fire of the Renaissance in Italy. By chronological reckoning we are dropping back a century to 1400. But chronology deceives. By ideational reckoning, the Italians represent the transition between the Age of Faith and modern times, and it is a temptation to think of them as having worked a hundred years later than the Flemish masters who were, in fact, their contemporaries.

Surely no city can ever have been more wonderfully,

confidently, and enthusiastically alive than Florence between 1400 and 1450. It was both an old city and a boom town, proud of its past, proud of its new strength, proud of its citizenry, ambitious and hardheaded in practical matters but fascinated by intellectual exploration. As the city that had successfully defended its independence and thus scotched the plans of the Duke of Milan to conquer all Italy, Florence was not only a powerful city-state but a symbol of independence. And the most extraordinary aspect of Florentine pride was that the city was prouder of its intellect than of its muscle. The strength of Florence lay not only in its geographical position and the caliber of its citizens but in the achievements of its writers and artists. Giotto and Dante, dead for more than sixty years, played as prominent a part as living diplomats and warriors in the Florentine victory over Milan. The people of Florence were making money, and they liked to spend it on buildings, paintings, and sculpture—not reverently and not as collectors as we know them, but with enthusiasm as citizens eager to make the city the visual embodiment of its greatness, and to make their own parts of it —their palaces, or their churches where they might donate a chapel—the visual embodiments of their own self-won eminence.

Conscious that Italy's classical inheritance had sunk under the Goths, the Florentines called their revived city "The New Athens," and went the Athenians one better by admitting sculptors and painters to the company of philosophers and poets and, eventually, princes, as ancient Athens had never done. In a curious mixture of Christian and pagan ideals, interest in life on earth from day to day competed with the joyous promise of eternal life in heaven. Men became more interested in themselves as themselves than as vassals in a celestial feudal system. Thus adopting the Greek ideal of man as the measure of all things, the Renaissance artist revived the sculptural and architectural forms of antiquity. (Classical painting was unknown; its most important existing records were still buried within the ashes of Pompeii and Herculaneum.)

Painting became the most expressive art of the Renaissance, but the most influential single artist of the century was not a painter but a sculptor, Donatello, who in a lifetime of eighty years—he was born about 1386 and died in 1466—set painters in directions ranging from the serenest classicism to the most tormented realism. As a scientist-artist he explored in low-relief sculpture the painter's problem of illusionistic perspective; and in the new fascination with the human body he studied its anatomy as a realist while posing it in stances derived from the classical ideal.

The scientific cast of early Florentine art is even more apparent in painting, however, than in Donatello's sculpture, since painting, as a process of diagramming form and space, is more harmoniously adaptable to theoretical demonstration than sculpture and architecture, which are factual applications. The Florentine passion was for realism—which might, as we will see in the case of Ghirlandaio, mean little more than an interest in the trivia of daily life, but might also mean the exploration of material forms as vessels worthy of noble spirits. Such exploration was the essence of Giotto's revolution, which had been assimilated only in fragments until the appearance of Masaccio.

Tommaso di Ser Giovanni di Mone, called Masaccio, was born very nearly with his century—on December 21, 1401. Before he died, at the age of twenty-seven, he had created the seminal paintings of the Italian Renaissance. The little we know about him as a person we owe to his nickname. Not quite translatable, "Masaccio" has been approximated as

"Simple Tom," "Slovenly Tom," or "Hulking Tom." It was a name given him in affection. The stories that explain it were still current a hundred and fifty years after his death, enabling Vasari to leave us this one description: "He was most careless of externals. He had fixed his mind on art and could by no means be induced to care for worldly things, such as his own personal interests, and still less for the affairs of others. He gave no thought to his clothing and did not collect debts until he was actually in want."

Vasari adds that a better or kinder man could not be imagined. Falling into the hazard of visualizing Masaccio through his paintings, we see a shock of dark hair, perhaps a swarthy complexion, and a large, heavily muscled but flexible body flowing with vigorous appetites that were satisfied upon demand in the natural course of living from day to day in the excitement of satisfying something more important—the appetite to create that welled up in Florence from new springs and from old springs replenished.

Our own reverence for the old masters adulterates the color of the time: somewhere in the back of our minds there persists the aberrant idea that the Renaissance artists were painting old-master paintings from the beginning, and that the proud new buildings were conceived as the historical monuments they have become. We can tell ourselves that the new style was revolutionary, but we cannot feel its newness. And Masaccio, of all the great Florentines, is the most disappointing to most people—seems the least fresh and original —for reasons we will get around to shortly.

His birthplace was the town of San Giovanni Valdarno, but he was in Florence by the time he was sixteen. At twenty or twenty-one he was working in the Arte dei Medici de' Speziali: the record of his payment of two lire to the steward, on October 26, 1422, is still in existence. When he was twenty-four he painted one of the supreme masterpieces of the Renaissance, the fresco of *The Holy Trinity with the Virgin and St. John* in Santa Maria Novella. During the next years he was at work at different times in the Brancacci Chapel of Santa Maria del Carmine, and in 1427, when he was twenty-six, he painted a comparable masterpiece, *The Tribute Money,* in that chapel. His death the next year is not recorded, but is referred to by a writer of his own century, Antonio Manetti, as having occurred in Rome when he was "about twenty-seven."

Various painters have been proposed as Masaccio's first teachers, but none could have taught him much beyond technical processes. He had so short a time to learn that it is easiest to think of him as having been born knowing everything. Among his contemporaries, he must have learned by example from Donatello, and he certainly learned by association and collaboration with his friend Brunelleschi. But his true master was Giotto.

After a hundred years, during which artists had busied themselves with approximations of Giotto's three-dimensional realism, Masaccio brought it to technical fulfillment. He corrected proportions, eliminated awkwardnesses, drew bodies that could stand or move naturally in a space that deepened Giotto's shallow stage toward infinity. But this technical fulfillment would have meant nothing if Masaccio had not also recognized the expressive purpose of Giotto's realism. He was the first painter since Giotto to understand that realism, with all its appurtenant problems of accurate perspective, true anatomy, and the like, can be the gate to the ideal—that if a painter can represent the visual world accurately, he can then paint man ideally. For ideally, a man is worthy of a world that has an eternal order and purpose beneath the distracting ephemera that confuse him and obscure the human values on which anything better than an animal world must subsist.

Masaccio may not have put this essentially classical premise to himself in any such way, although he was certainly a thoughtful man and was probably an educated one. But its implicit acceptance made him the first humanist painter of the Florentine Renaissance. His given subject matter was the Christian story and the Christian mystery, but he neither told nor felt them in terms of medieval religious passion. Rather, he declared the dignity of man in the world by his balanced, grave, and monumental figures disposed logically within convincing space. In the way that Giotto had been Masaccio's teacher, Masaccio's Brancacci Chapel became the schoolroom for the generation of painters that followed him, and *The Tribute Money* has its natural descendants in Leonardo da Vinci's *Last Supper* and Raphael's *School of Athens*.

And yet the first sight of the chapel is always a disappointment. The visitor half sees (for the light is wretched) Masaccio's portions of the frescoes juxtaposed and intermingled with others by Masolino, who worked in the chapel at the same time, and by Filippino Lippi, who completed the series of paintings fifty-seven years later. The colors are disappointingly turgid—as well they might be, since the frescoes were damaged by a fire in 1771 and cannot be satisfactorily cleaned. When a small portion that had been covered by a projection of an altar was recently revealed after the projection was removed, the original (or approximately original) colors turned out to be clear and luminous.

In *The Holy Trinity* of Santa Maria Novella there is less for the visitor to overcome, but even here he must cope with a damaged surface. He reads his guidebook and is reminded that the perspective scheme was probably worked out with Brunelleschi, who without much question also designed the painted architectural setting. He is then likely to become involved in an effort to admire the perspective (which as a geometrical problem could of course be solved by any beginner today) without understanding that its function is not mere illusionistic trickery but the creation of logically ordered space. He waits in vain for the visceral impact that contemporary attitudes toward art have led him to expect. Masaccio is a scholar's painter, whether the scholar is an art historian or a humanist philosopher—or the happy combination of both that occurs now and then.

We are fortunate that Masaccio exists at all except as history in words. The frescoes in the vault and the upper tier of the wall of the Brancacci Chapel were destroyed in redecorations in 1748, but these were Masolino's. Earlier, toward the end of the seventeenth century, the whole chapel had been saved from destruction when a plan to, as we would say, update the chapel was blocked. The frescoes were saved by members of the Academy and other citizens who turned for help to Vittoria della Rovere, the widow of Ferdinand II and the mother of Grand Duke Cosimo III. If she had not stepped in, Masaccio's only existing painting of great consequence would be *The Holy Trinity.* Its salvage, too, we owe to something of a fluke.

Brought to light in the 1860's during restorations, *The Holy Trinity* had been covered by a large painting by, of all people, Vasari. The great good fortune is that it had been merely covered and hence only partially defaced instead of destroyed in the first place. Without these paintings, Masaccio's art could be reconstructed only from verbal accounts and from the small body of minor works that still occupy scholars in a constant process of attribution, re-attribution, and de-attribution. All these are "early works," a sad phrase when we remember that the works that can be called "late" are late only because Masaccio's life was so short.

Masaccio's companion painter in the Brancacci Chapel is, perforce, immortal by association while suffering from comparison. Masolino da Panicale (Tommaso di Cristoforo di

Fini) was born in 1383 or 1384 and died in 1447. Although Masolino was seventeen years older than Masaccio, he seems to have been Masaccio's pupil rather than, as Vasari thought, his teacher. He was a facile painter, decorative in effect and gently lyrical in mood, a superior representative of the International Style, until his association with Masaccio, when his work took on greater breadth and simplicity. Masolino is perhaps a more satisfactory painter in his Gothic manner; but it must be admitted that his portions of the Brancacci frescoes would be more impressive if they were not alongside those of Masaccio.

In Italian Renaissance painting, the Christian story was frequently little more than a peg from which a painter could hang a bit of secular realism; or, more admirably, it would supply a series of incidents adaptable to illustration through an intellectualized study of form and space. But during the first half of the fifteenth century, when realists and scientific formalists were flourishing so mightily in Florence, there flourished also the last and sweetest and purest voice that medieval faith produced in Italy.

By birth the painter called Fra Angelico was Masaccio's immediate contemporary, having been born about 1400, a year before Masaccio. He was ordained a monk of the Dominican order about twenty-five years later, while Masaccio was beginning work on the Brancacci Chapel. He painted little until 1428, by which time Masaccio was dead at the age of twenty-seven; but during his remaining twenty-seven years, he painted a great deal. He died in 1455 at the age of about fifty-five—in Rome, as a monk must want to do.

Fra Angelico has many names: Fra Giovanni da Fiesole, Fra Giovanni da Firenze, Guido di Pietro in secular life, "Angelico" became attached to him as an official nickname after his death and could not be more appropriate (since never before or since has an art been more angel-like in its happiness and purity), unless the even later nickname "Beato" surpasses it in its combined suggestions of saintliness and a state of blessedness in life. Fra Angelico's life, by every evidence, ran its course without a question, without a doubt, in uninterrupted service to God in the exercise of a God-given talent.

Fra Angelico's angels sing the praises of the Lord and the Virgin as if there were no Satan. His Virgins receive the Annunciation from the angel Gabriel with the dignity of women and the pretty innocence of young girls. (Fra Angelico was always reconciling opposites with absolutely no difficulty.) His saints accept their martyrdoms with joy but without hysteria, and in his strongest works—Crucifixions, Descents, and Entombments—he abstracts from a story of anguish and grief all the faith in redemptive grace (if not quite all the majesty and little of the passion) that is at the heart of Gothic lyricism.

Fra Angelico managed, as if without trying, to simplify the sometimes rather fussy pageantry of late-medieval painting without thinning it—he weeded it and gave it room to grow—and to unite heavenly sweetness with earthly truth as if any question as to their identity were ridiculous. Compare him with a musician, since his angels are so fond of playing their lutes, trumpets, and tambourines at the celestial court: Masaccio had revealed the power of full orchestration with improved instruments; Fra Angelico recognized the significance of the revolution, but was content to modify the old arrangements, instead of discarding them.

He is often called a reactionary painter, a medieval tag-ender, an anachronism left over from the Age of Faith. He was all of that, if we must insist that the virtues of a new age invalidate those of the age that preceded it. While the

Renaissance was busy revalidating the humanist spirit of classical antiquity, Fra Angelico drew on a more immediate heritage in maintaining—not as a theoretical conviction but simply in, for him, the natural course of things—the continuing validity of faith. His only failures (and the term is a comparative one) were his late frescoes in Rome. In these he apparently felt an obligation to live up to the grandeur of that city and pay homage to the papacy on an inflated scale that he had never needed in expressing the glory of the Lord.

Fra Angelico's painting is divisible into three periods with exceptional neatness: the Fiesole period, the Florentine, and the Roman. As Fra Angelico da Fiesole he was still close to the medieval tradition of detailed illumination. He came into full flower as Fra Angelico da Firenze after 1436, when Cosimo de' Medici gave the Fiesole Dominicans the ruined Monastery of San Marco in Florence and the chapter moved there. During the years of the building's restoration by Michelozzo, in a Renaissance style as pure and as serene as Fra Angelico's painting, Fra Angelico, who certainly knew the architect and was now in much closer contact with Florentine painters, absorbed such Renaissance innovations as could best serve him.

In 1445 he was called to Rome and spent most of the rest of his life there. But the Monastery of San Marco, now a museum, with his frescoes still in place and with others of his paintings transferred there, is the summary of Fra Angelico's art and as fine a monument as any painter can boast.

Because of his gentleness, Fra Angelico is often underestimated as an artist even by his admirers, who tend to settle for his sweetness without recognizing his strength. As a working painter, rather than as a monk for whom the depiction of holy scenes was a form of worship, Fra Angelico reconciled revolution and tradition by reconciling Masaccio's realism —the projection of figures in light and space on a monumental scale—with the essentially miniature technique of late medievalists such as his probable teacher, Lorenzo Monaco.

Lorenzo Monaco, who was born Piero di Giovanni about 1371, died about 1425. Originally Sienese, he went to Florence and entered the Camaldolite order, working in its famous school of miniaturists and manuscript illuminators in the Monastery of Santa Maria degli Angeli. Beginning as an illuminator in the old tradition of flat form and gold background, he became a convert to the International Style. With Gentile da Fabriano he is historically important for his introduction of this late medievalism into Florence.

The first generation of Florentine Renaissance painters included two great painter-monks, Fra Angelico and Fra Filippo Lippi. The remarkable piety of Fra Angelico's life and the remarkable laxity of Fra Filippo's provide an edifying demonstration of the flexibility and range of mores in that extraordinary city.

Fra Filippo Lippi was born probably in 1406, the son of a butcher. He was orphaned as a child, was put under the protection of the Carmelite monks in the Monastery of Santa Maria del Carmine in Florence, took the vows of the order at the age of fifteen, and at the age of fifty eloped with a young nun and raised a family. Of course a great deal happened during the thirty-five-year interval between fifteen and fifty—including his rise as a painter of religious subjects in a spirit appropriate to monkish piety—but there is always the necessity, in considering Fra Filippo Lippi, to recognize at the beginning the seeming disparity between his life and his art. Now that the salient facts have been stated, perhaps they can be threaded together in chronological order and then reconciled, although to Fra Filippo's contemporaries the disparity needed no reconciliation. It was perfectly acceptable in the normal course of things, and any effort toward defending Fra Filippo's life in order to defend his art would have seemed only quixotic.

By the time he was twenty, Fra Filippo was already established as a dependable artist. At thirty, he had executed important altarpieces and was working independently; he had probably left the monastery late in 1432 (his name disappears from its records after January, 1433). He would have been twenty-six when he set out on his own, still a Carmelite monk, but probably with a fairly normal experience of the world outside the walls. He was continuously in demand in various cities to paint altarpieces and murals in churches and monasteries, but he must also have been always short of funds. Vasari reported, a hundred years later, that this was because he always relished the pleasures of love and spent his money on them, but Vasari was in all likelihood only making an interesting supposition consistent with certain known facts.

Fra Filippo's income went, at least in part, to meet other demands. "God has left me with six nieces to marry off who are sickly and useless and for whom I am the only, if meager, support," he wrote to Piero, the son of Cosimo de' Medici the Elder, in a letter of 1439 making a vigorous plea for funds. He was thirty-three, an age when six sickly and useless nieces would be a terrible burden to any man. In 1450, when he was forty-four, he was reduced to a more desperate expedient than a begging letter: he forged a receipt for a sum of money that was to have been paid to an artist named Giovanni di Francesco, was apprehended, accused, and convicted after confession under torture.

Two years later, however, he was appointed chaplain to the nuns of San Niccolo de' Frieri in Florence. There are no details of his activities there, but he was not there long. He became rector of the Church of San Quirico at Legnaia, near Florence, but was "relieved of his duties" in 1455. (All this time he was painting as usual.) And now we find him appointed chaplain to the nuns of Santa Margherita at Prato. This was in 1456, and he had reached the dangerous age of fifty, but we can hardly suppose that his elopement with Lucrezia Buti, the pretty young nun, was brought about by an eruption of pent-up emotions after so long a time and so checkered a career. A more reasonable explanation would make a parallel to the late marriage of a philandering bachelor who had avoided the matrimonial trap until middle age.

In recounting this story, with the liveliest relish, Vasari for once failed to make the most of a sensational detail. Lucrezia was a full-fledged member of the sisterhood rather than the ward or novice that Vasari called her. He was right about the conditions of the elopement, which was staged in a manner that would have done credit to a picaresque novelist. Once a year, on the occasion of the exhibition of the Sacred Girdle, the nuns were allowed to leave the convent. Lucrezia did not come back, and in the next year she bore Fra Filippo a son, who became the painter Filippino Lippi.

In 1459, Lucrezia, the mother of a two-year-old fruit of illicit love, was received back into her order, renewing her vows in full ceremony along with her sister Spinetta, also a nun, who had followed Lucrezia's example and had bolted the convent soon after her, and three other nuns whose defections had turned these individual flights into something of an exodus.

But the situation did not remain patched up for long. By 1461, Lucrezia was back with Fra Filippo. Spinetta, too, was a member of the household, as we learn from the "Ufficiali di Notte e Monasteri" of Florence, which in that year accused Fra Filippo and a notary of Prato of immoral behavior.

The victory of love was officially acknowledged by Pope Pius II, who, in response to the intervention of the Medici, released both Lucrezia and Filippo from their tattered vows. The couple were recognized as man and wife, and Lucrezia bore another child before Filippo died in 1469 at the age of sixty-three. He had been hard at work on murals in Spoleto, and he was buried there at the request of the city council, which argued that Florence was filled with the tombs of eminent men, while Spoleto had very few.

The obvious explanation today why a city should plead for the honor of enshrining the remains of a man who was a painter, but who was also a convicted forger and an adulterous monk, would be that personal foibles may be forgiven an artist and, indeed, are expected of him in unusual measure. This obvious explanation is altogether wrong. Fifteenth-century Italy simply saw no connection between a man's creative achievement and his personal life. The romantic notion that art and morals are identical twins has been disproved again and again; when they harmonize, as they do so conveniently in the case of Fra Angelico, they do so largely by coincidence.

Fra Filippo the artist never lost the respect or the patronage of his contemporaries either in or out of the Church, but his history so embarrassed the nineteenth century that futile efforts were made to regard its facts as libelous fiction. Even Browning poeticized the painter's story in a rationalization where physical love and reverent religious painting are rather pathetically emulsified. If the case of Fra Filippo Lippi can be used today to prove anything, it is that the exercise of a healthy extroverted sexuality is a natural accompaniment to the fulfillment of other capacities that need have no direct connection with it.

The above history, then, may be forgotten in any discussion of Fra Filippo's painting. A primary fact about him as an artist is that he was the only one of the Florentine painters of his generation who must surely have had a direct connection with Masaccio. He may, indeed, have been Masaccio's pupil. The great man was painting the murals in the Brancacci Chapel of Fra Filippo's own Santa Maria del Carmine when Filippo was still there at the age of about twenty. *The Tribute Money* schooled Filippo's generation in formal spatial composition by example. Filippo was particularly well placed to learn by observation of work in progress and even in conversation with genius.

Fra Filippo's art hybridizes a Gothic tenderness, expectable in the art of a man conditioned, in spite of everything, by the life of the cloister, with Masaccio's innovations. It would be too much to say that Fra Filippo made the best of both ideals. His harmonization reduces the intensity of Gothic spirituality and the grandeur of Renaissance formality to a level that barely escapes, but does escape, the commonplace realism and the sentimentalism that his detractors like to find in him. But at the same time, great effort is required to build him up to the level of innovator where his most fervent admirers like to place him.

He may express lyrical tenderness coloristically in a way somewhat ahead of his time, and his interest in the expression of motion by linear pattern is exceptional. His dancing Salome in the Cathedral at Prato, which was taken directly from a well-known sarcophagus, is an early example of a painter's following antique sculpture as a model for maenads and other figures in wild movement. He transposed into painting the fluttering draperies and flowing locks that sculptors had adopted decades earlier, and Botticelli, who brought this linear excitement to its climax in painting, may have found an example in Fra Filippo.

It is even possible to say that the gentle reveries of Fra Filippo's Madonnas fertilized a seed that became rooted and flourished in Leonardo's sibylline females. But on the whole, Fra Filippo Lippi was less an originator than a receptive vessel in a place where new ideas were burgeoning with such fecundity that their assimilation was enough to make a very fine artist of a man who in a less fertile environment might have languished into mere eclecticism.

Filippino ("Little Filippo") Lippi, the son, was twelve years old when his father died in 1469. He studied under Botticelli, whose style was allied to his father's, and early became a busy and admired painter in Florence. He also made excursions to execute commissions in Rome. Between 1481 and 1483 he completed the Brancacci Chapel frescoes that had been waiting since Masaccio's death more than fifty years earlier—and which his father, as a youth, had seen Masaccio working on. That he was entrusted with this work indicates the respect that the Florentines had for Filippino Lippi. The frescoes were revered almost as holy objects, quite aside from their religious content.

Filippino is an appealing artist, more than talented, who never quite fulfilled himself. He was intelligently and sensitively receptive to such diversified influences as Botticelli's linearism, Masaccio's classical breadth, Roman dramatics, and Flemish realism—as well as the Gothic intensity of Hugo van der Goes. Without sinking to an imitative level he absorbed all of these influences. The unifying characteristic of his art is a tender, and rather anxious, spirituality that often seems repressed. He died at the age of about forty-seven in 1504.

Uccello—perspective. The words have become almost synonymous in art history, and can hardly be set down without releasing, by conditioned reaction, the anecdote told by Paolo Uccello's wife after his death. Uccello used to stay up all night in his studio trying to work out vanishing points, and when called to bed would reply only, "Oh, what a lovely thing perspective is!" and keep on working. Or so, seventy-five years later, Vasari said that Uccello's wife said.

What Uccello figured out during his nightlong sessions with his true love and mistress can now be mastered over a weekend by any bright schoolboy with the help of an elementary perspective manual, a T-square, and a draftsman's triangle. Perspective for Uccello was no more than a problem in stereometric projection, although it was a problem he worked out alone. He was delightfully innocent of the aesthetic and philosophical extensions that brainier Renaissance artists found in the subject. But Uccello's ebullient innocence is his charm, and his famous sentence can be echoed with "—and what a delightful painter Uccello is!"

Uccello was born about 1397, the son of a barber. He entered the workshop of the sculptor Lorenzo Ghiberti* at the age of fourteen, stayed there seven years, and then was properly admitted to the guild of Florentine artists. But he worked within the Gothic tradition until the 1430's—that is, until his own middle thirties—when he joined the more progressive ranks of artists who were investigating the world on its own terms. The great Donatello (who took perspective in his stride) was Uccello's friend, and chided him for the narrowness of an obsession that made him "neglect what we know for what we don't know." According to Vasari, Uccello would shut himself away like a hermit for weeks and months at a time, trying to formulate exact methods where most

---

* Lorenzo Ghiberti (1378-1455) won the competition for the doors to the Baptistery in Florence in 1402—a competition that, like Brunelleschi's building of the dome of the Cathedral, was a symptom of Florence's great surge of pride in her new position as the century opened. Although he made use of nominally classical motifs, Ghiberti remained essentially a Gothic sculptor. His shop, where he was occupied with the first doors from 1403 to 1424, was a training ground for numerous artists who served as his assistants. Donatello, Masolino, and Uccello were among his apprentices. The first doors were so successful that Ghiberti immediately received a commission for a second pair, which occupied him from 1425 to 1452. In these he showed that he, in turn, had learned from his students' discoveries, particularly in perspective.

artists, content with empirical practice, were satisfied if they could get their perspective to look right, without bothering about the rules.

The odd, and most engaging, thing about Uccello's perspective is that although he worked out the rules and applied them strictly, they backfired in his hands to give his paintings a most curious unreality. The function of perspective, of course, is to give an illusion (or expression) of third dimension, but Uccello paradoxically thought, and painted, in terms of only two. His scenes remain absolutely flat; the angles made by lines in perspective become semiabstract distortions of the objects represented, and although human figures grow smaller in the distance, in obedience to the rules, they seem only dwarfed—miniature men going about their business in the immediate company of normal-sized men who go about theirs in the foreground.

Also, Uccello's arrangements of figures and objects is of an extraordinary artificiality induced by the inflexibility of his adherence to perspective rules that he only partially understood. In his *Rout of San Romano* in the National Gallery in London, one of three famous scenes celebrating the Florentine victory at San Romano, all the lances dropped by the contestants in the fray have fallen not higgledy-piggledy upon the ground but exactly parallel or at right angles to one another and to the spectator, in order that they may recede, like railroad tracks, to a common vanishing point. And a fallen knight, seen feet-on, has obligingly lined himself up with them. The warriors and horses still entangled in battle are conceived as the most superbly decorative objects imaginable, but Uccello's unawareness of the spatial volumes that perspective supposedly serves is proved by the fact that neither men nor horses are given a third dimension to occupy. In three dimensions their existence would be as impossible physically as their pattern is delightful optically in two.

Total loss and severe mutilation have robbed us of most of Uccello's work, but records indicate that he must have been kept busy until his last years, when, other records make plain, he was reduced to poverty. According to Vasari, Uccello was always poor, the implication being that he was more interested in his research than in making money. He died in 1475 at the age of about seventy-eight.

Leonardo da Vinci's *Last Supper* is seldom questioned as the most impressive version of that subject ever painted, but Andrea del Castagno's, which was painted some fifty years earlier, about 1445-50, is to some extent the prototype of Leonardo's. And in the affections of some people, Castagno's is not only the greatest of all Last Suppers but one of the half dozen or so finest paintings of the early Italian Renaissance.

"Some people" need not mean many: Castagno does not have a very large fan club. But the club members bear this strange, stern, and violent artist a loyalty as unyielding and as unqualified as the very forms that he painted—forms as hard as rock, even when they represent flesh or drapery, and, like some rare stones, stained with bizarre mineral tints in unexpected combinations.

In Castagno's *Last Supper* the disciples are lined up at a long table that stretches the width of a small enclosure, a closet-like room so uncompromisingly defined by rigid geometrical perspective that the space becomes less a room than a large, shallow box lined with slabs of simulated marble. Six of these slabs, ranged just above the disciples' heads, cover the long wall against which the figures are pressed, and although each slab is individualized as a special type of marble by its veining and spotting, the one above the head of Judas is more than a simulation; it is an expressive burst of swirling color in a pattern that has reminded some writers of a bolt of avenging lightning. It has reminded at least one surgeon of the patterns and colors found in freshly cut sections of certain types of malignant tumors. And, suggesting malignance in another sense, it could be taken as an expression of the betrayer's state of mind. Excised from the picture and offered as an independent work of art, it could stand as an exceptionally successful example of modern abstract art in the tradition of Kandinsky, who believed that line, pattern, and color, without any narrative reference, can carry the total burden of emotional content.

Of all the disciples, Judas alone is seated on the near side of the table, so that he is the only one of the thirteen figures who is fully seen. And although Castagno was following a medieval convention that thus separated Judas as unworthy of the company of the other disciples, the effect here is to make him the central figure of the composition. With his black hair and beard and the pungent, morbid colors of his robes, he all but overpowers the gentler figures that face him. The figure of Christ is relatively inconspicuous; the psychological play is between Judas and John the Beloved, whose head is bowed in grief within a few inches of two overlapping hands—one belonging to Christ, raised as if in tender blessing, and the sinister hand of Judas holding the piece of bread he has just received.

The disciples exist in a state of suspension, each isolated from his fellows as if paralyzed within an individual spell. Where one regards another, or gestures toward his neighbor, the glance or the gesture appears frozen as if blocked by an invisible wall that bars communication. The closeness of the room is almost claustrophobic, and although every form is absolutely motionless—every fold of drapery, every hand, every face, every hair on every head—there is no feeling of quietness or peacefulness, or of either fear or resignation before the impending tragedy of the Crucifixion. Absolutely still, the scene is impregnated with a sense of latent violence that would corrode and shatter any forms less self-contained than these in their own hard strength. If they are like stone, they are also like iron, and the tortured extremity of their hardness is in itself a kind of violence.

Castagno's first recorded commission, when he was about twenty years old, was to paint effigies, on the walls of the Palazzo del Podestà, of a group of men hanged as traitors to Florence. Such commissions were not uncommon; criminals were often represented in this way in public places as a form of warning. But Castagno's murals (later destroyed) seem to have been extraordinarily impressive: they earned him immediately the nickname Andrein degli Impiccati—"Andrea of the Hanged Men." We do not know enough about him to reconstruct a clear personality, but the one that seems to show through his work was powerful enough so that Vasari, whose taste ran always toward sweet harmonies, could believe that on a medallion in a painting now lost Castagno "placed his own portrait with a face like that of Judas Iscariot, whom he did resemble both in face and in character," and could then go on to say that Castagno murdered, by beating, his friend and collaborator Domenico Veneziano, from envy of Domenico's skill.

In fact, Domenico outlived his supposed murderer by at least four years, as was discovered in 1862 by research in Florentine archives, and there is no reason to believe that Andrea del Castagno was the envious, quarrelsome, rancorous, and brutal man Vasari describes. The presumption that a man who painted with such power, and whose work so frequently carries an undertone of threat, must have been a villain, is indefensible. Actually, the artists known without question to have been villains in their private lives have as artists usually been dedicated to mawkish grace.

Castagno was born in 1421 or 1423 in the mountain village of that name. He was the son of a farmer. Whether or
not there is a connection here, his art was marked by a primitive vigor that ran counter to the increasing trend among his
contemporaries toward gentle sentiment, a trend that eventually produced the conventional Florentine conception of
holy figures as an arbitrarily graceful and refined company.
The disciples in *The Last Supper* have the lined and weathered faces of the common men the disciples were. But even
so perceptive a historian as Bernard Berenson could speak
of Castagno as a mere vulgar realist, guilty of substituting
muscular force, rodomontade, brutality, and "the insolence
that often accompanies an excess of vitality" for a deeper
strength and subtler talent that were denied him. To many
people with an inelastic taste for the suave, Castagno's art
seems taciturn and perverse, or even coarse with the coarse-
ness of a mountain peasant who never—intellectually—lost
his rough edges.

The rough edges apparently did not bother patrons, if
rough edges can be admitted in an art of such precision. Castagno was an extremely busy artist. Italian archives yield
filed contracts for work and receipts for payments in a heart-
breaking record of works completed but later destroyed or
lost. Vasari saw many of them, and admired them too, whatever else he thought of the artist. The refectory of the Bene-
dictine Monastery of Santa Apollonia in Florence, where
Castagno painted his *Last Supper* along with scenes from the
Passion, is now a small Castagno museum housing works that
have been moved there. (It is probably, considering its importance, the least visited museum in the city.) Beyond these,
only a few Castagnos are spotted around the museums of the
world.

Castagno was not only prolific; he was also an artist of
tremendous influence. Mantegna, the greatest Renaissance

artist of northern Italy, bears Castagno's mark. And in what was perhaps Castagno's last painting, the beautiful *David* in the National Gallery in Washington, he created a figure that in its flowing energy and taut grace anticipated a new direction in Italian art that was to blossom in the Pollaiuolos and reach its climax, and fade, in Botticelli.

Castagno, somehow, is easiest to think of as a man rugged in his middle age. But he was only thirty-four or thirty-six years old when he died in Florence on August 19, 1457, eleven days after his wife, who, like him, was carried off by the plague. He died in debt, but Vasari gives him credit for having lived in the style of a gentleman, as an artist should— between murders.

In the few years of his life Castagno had been an innovator in many ways. When he used perspective to create the illusion that he was staging *The Last Supper* in an extension of the room for which it was painted, he set a model that became standard and was not greatly changed until Leonardo deepened the space and exploited it as a psychological element of the event taking place within it. In his straightforward realism Castagno gave impetus to a new profane but powerful impulse in Renaissance art. He was greatly influenced by Donatello and would himself have made a wonderful sculptor: in painting certain figures as if they were statues in niches, and in simulating carved frames and moldings in paint, he was at the beginning of a *trompe-l'oeil* tradition to which Masaccio's use of architecture in *The Holy Trinity* also belongs. He experimented with effects of light and shade that were developed by the next generations of painters, and in doing so he made fantastic shifts of color between illuminated and shadowed areas of a single object.

Critics who do not respond to Castagno are capable of writing in the same sentence that he had a "passionate intensity," yet "no sense of inner life." This is not necessarily a contradiction, but it is one in the case of Castagno. It is true that he never relays to us any quality of spiritual reverie, but there is more than one kind of inner life, and in Castagno it took the form of an immense repressed tragic energy that was finally to be released by Michelangelo.

Castagno's supposed victim, Domenico Veneziano (or Domenico di Bartolomeo da Venezia), is one of the most important painters of the early Florentine Renaissance, although not quite important enough to be ranked second only to Masaccio, as one group of supporters now contends he should be. So little is known of his life that he is a hopeless subject for the biographer; by way of compensation, just enough is known about his origins, his activity, and his influence as an artist to make him an inexhaustible subject for scholarly research. His name indicates that he was born in Venice (probably about 1410), and he is known to have died in 1461. Letters and other documents indicate that he came early to Florence, that he was highly regarded there, and that he was a good, vigorous, practical manager of his affairs in competition with other painters. Vasari makes him out a moonstruck fellow fond of serenading, but this must be a fabrication on Vasari's part, a good bit of dramatic counterpoint to his equally fabricated tale of Castagno as the ruffian who murdered Domenico.

The quality of Domenico's work, however, does suggest a gentle spirit. In the paintings that survive (there are very few) he is a lyric poet among Florentine scientists, a painter exploring the quality of light where other Florentines were obsessed with drawing. His dreamy, luminous quality seems to not have been recognized by his colleagues, but they must have admired him as a master of spatial organization. The serenity of his existing masterpiece, *Madonna and Child with Saints* in the Uffizi, is powerful evidence that Piero della Francesca, who as a young man worked with Domenico, may owe him a double debt as a colorist and as a master of geometrical space.

Piero della Francesca (Piero di Benedetto de' Franceschi) was born in the small town of Borgo San Sepolcro, probably about 1416. By this birth date he would have been seventy-six years old when he died in 1492, one of the most illustrious names of Italy. His long life was singularly undramatic; nothing much happened to Piero della Francesca in terms of storybook biography. But he painted a series of frescoes in the choir of the Church of San Francesco in Arezzo that many people would be willing to choose as the greatest single monument of the early Renaissance, and that a few, in the recent enthusiasm for Piero's art, would not hesitate to call the greatest cycle paintings in the world. And he wrote a treatise on pictorial perspective that has become the classic statement of that science as a form of philosophical mathematics.

Piero worked in Florence, in Rome, in Ferrara, in Rimini, and at the ducal court in Urbino (where he was both mathematician and painter to the duke, Federigo da Montefeltro), as well as in Arezzo and Borgo San Sepolcro, nowhere providing a biographer with any narrative anecdotes. No explanation offers itself as to just why he left the great centers, Florence and Rome, to work in provincial ones. He returned from time to time to the town of his birth, held civic offices there, died there, and is still its most eminent citizen. His *Resurrection*, in the tiny municipal museum, must surely be the least visited of all paintings in the world in proportion to its majestic position in the history of art. Aldous Huxley once called it, quite flatly, the greatest painting in the world.

Such judgments on the art of Piero della Francesca belong to our century as part of the rediscovery—in some ways, almost the first discovery—of the nature of Piero's genius. His noble gravity, his restraint and discipline, were not to the taste of Italian artists during the century after his death, and during the next two centuries, when Italy became a school for Northern artists, Arezzo and Borgo San Sepolcro were seldom visited. Even if Piero's works in Florence and Rome had survived, they would probably have been treated merely with the respect attached to his reputation as an artist historically important in the development of perspective but otherwise not very interesting. During the nineteenth century, popular taste was for the prettier and more sentimental schools of Italian art, although toward the end of that century historians began to suspect that Piero had qualities outside the conventional canon.

But it took the revolution of modern art to reveal his full stature. Our understanding of Piero has come to a large extent through our understanding of an artist who bears little resemblance to him on the surface—Cézanne. Some of Cézanne's statements about his own art could almost as well have been made by Piero about his—for instance, Cézanne's "I do not want to reproduce nature; I want to re-create it," and his insistence that all the forms of nature should be reduced to geometrical equivalents unified by perspective.

Perspective for an artist like the naïve and delightfully enthusiastic Paolo Uccello was a system of lines adaptable to the representation of static objects on a flat surface. For more intellectual theorists like Brunelleschi and another architect, Alberti (Piero's great friend), perspective was a system of realistic representation adaptable primarily to the picturization of architectural volumes. For Piero it was this and more. Perspective as a mere mathematical or representational system was of little interest to him except as a means toward more important ends. He enlarged the concepts of architectural perspective to include all natural forms, the human figure among them, as part of the supreme architecture of nature, the architecture of universal order that exists beneath the surface confusion of the world. This order could be revealed through the "re-creation" of objects integrated as volumes in perfectly ordered space.

Perspective for Piero was also a means for the study and definition of ideal proportions, of human figures and of the relationship of these figures to one another and to their environment. In his work the open spaces between objects are not mere emptiness but have shape and scale—the "negative volumes" of modern sculpture. Finally, Piero applied perspective to the human body in movement. The figures in the *Cycle of the True Cross* in Arezzo are as firm and solid as monuments, but they are imbued with the quality of progression across their painted stages, as if engaged in a ritual procession.

The quality that endears Piero to contemporary artists and critics is his essential abstractness. To understand his use of perspective we must always remember that he was not at all interested in illusionistic tricks. He made no effort to deceive the eye into believing that space exists where it does not; his sense of the wall in his Arezzo frescoes is every bit as strong as his expression (not illusion) of space and volume, contradictory as this may sound.

In creating his universe, a universe of dignified remoteness, of ideal clarity, Piero developed a physical type in which the head, with the features slightly flattened, is a perfect ovoid balanced upon a cylindrical neck. Bodies, when nude, are similarly geometrized, and when clothed take on a columnar simplicity. Piero's is a universe that would be almost harsh in its unrelenting grandeur if it were not tempered by his blond color schemes and his silvery light. He seldom used a pure color; his pinks and blues share one another's tints; his reds are modified toward shades of plum or terra cotta; he uses the most dangerous color, lavender, as a form of gray.

Piero painted the Arezzo frescoes between 1452 and 1466. After 1478 (about his sixty-second year) he stopped painting and devoted himself to the formulation of his theories. He had begun his great work "De Prospectiva Pingendi" in 1470, and he completed it in 1490, two years before his death. The manuscript, in the library of the Duke of Urbino, was known in copies and through plagiarisms, but was not published for another four hundred years—in 1899.

Piero's influence was wide. His uncompromisingly defined forms contributed to the artifices of the rather dry style of Ferrara and the hard-bitten manner of Signorelli. His peaceful, lambent space was reflected in the often oversweet art of Umbria. Possibly his majestic volumes were an example for Raphael, whose *School of Athens* in the Vatican replaced destroyed frescoes by Piero. But no artist recognized (or at least none tried to emulate) Piero's formal synthesis.

Umbrian by birth and Florentine by early experience, Piero like Signorelli is called an "Umbro-Florentine," but he is virtually a one-man school. The breadth of his art is such that of all Renaissance artists he most closely approached the Greek ideal, without ever reflecting Greek forms, and at the other end of the chronological scale he anticipated, without rejecting nature, the current ideal of abstraction. It is in a way appropriate that we know so little about him as a person. He remains an intellect—cool, detached, analytical, exquisitely distilled.

Great periods of art carry along with them the kind of painter who trails the masters not quite as a parasite but as a talented and charming adapter of their surface attractions. Benozzo Gozzoli was a superior example of the breed in the early Florentine Renaissance.

Born in 1420 or 1421, he was a member of the second generation in the revolution that began with Masaccio, but there is little in the spirit of his art to show it. He remained all his life devoted to the decorative elegance and sprightly detail of the late-Gothic style, which he modernized superficially by graftings of whatever served him best in the way of perspective, foreshortening, and realistic drawing.

Gozzoli's place in the history-of-art books, where he was once conspicuous, has shrunk drastically in recent years, but his conservatism did not hamper his career in Florence. He was as busy as the most adventurous of his colleagues whose innovations were so exciting to his patrons. He is thought of now, first of all, in connection with his frescoes of *The Journey of the Magi* in the Medici Palace, which are as popular a tourist shrine as ever. Aside from their decorative appeal, they have strong associative interest as a souvenir of the Medici, among whose portraits is a youthful one of Lorenzo, the great patron of the second half of the century.

Covering the walls of the small, high-ceilinged chapel, the Magi and their retainers progress through an invented countryside toward an altar where an *Adoration* by Fra Filippo Lippi supplied a proper spiritual focus for a procession that Gozzoli made resplendently mundane. The Kings of the East are portraits of three princes alive at the time, shown in their finest trappings—the Emperor of Byzantium and the Patriarch of Constantinople, who in 1439 had made a state visit to Ferrara, and the young Lorenzo. Gozzoli included his own portrait among their followers, and in the background regales us with huntsmen and animals and birds in a landscape where exotic plants rise in geometric perfection from engagingly theatrical patterns of hills and fields. The plants are direct descendants of Fra Angelico's (Gozzoli as a young man worked for a while with that gentle painter), and the hills and fields are more suavely organized echoes of Paolo Uccello's.

In his small paintings, miraculous events become gossipy narratives saved only by their air of innocence. Gozzoli's liveliness and his skill in decorative organization must never be discounted. They failed him only once. When he was an old man—he died in 1497 at the age of seventy-six or seventy-seven—the High Renaissance was just around the corner, and he seems to have felt that he should do some catching up with things. Executing an Old Testament cycle in the Campo Santo in Pisa, he made an effort to apply the most advanced theories of perspective and to employ solidly designed classical architecture in his backgrounds. The results were not so fortunate as to make the deterioration of the frescoes, first from exposure and then from serious damage in World War II, quite as regrettable as it might have been. Gozzoli was most charming when he lagged furthest behind.

As a conclusion to this chapter, although hardly a dramatic one, Alesso Baldovinetti may serve, since he may be regarded either as a junior Florentine of the early Renaissance or a senior one of the second half of the century. His dates—about 1425 to 1499—tie him chronologically to the latter group, but his allegiance to Domenico Veneziano in the freshness and tranquility of his poetic style, make him a spiritual brother to the earlier group. He certainly worked with Domenico, and perhaps had some earlier contact with Fra Angelico. Exceptionally among painters of the time, he came of a patrician family, which may in part explain his conservatism. He was a designer of mosaics and stained glass as well as a painter.

4

THE LATER
FIFTEENTH CENTURY
IN FLORENCE
AND UMBRIA

Masaccio, who initiated the Florentine Renaissance, was born at the beginning of his century, in 1401, and Piero della Francesca, whose majestic art represents the culmination of the Renaissance in its early phase, lived almost to the century's end, until 1492. But Piero's supreme achievement, the frescoes in San Francesco in Arezzo, were painted about 1455, and thus afford a neat marker for a division of the century into halves for historical purposes.

The Florentine painters of the second half of the century lost much of the monumental assurance, the gravity, the sedate balance, and the celestial calm of Masaccio and Piero. Some (like Domenico Ghirlandaio) sacrificed these virtues to a placid and rather dull, mundane realism; others grew away from them in a new expressive direction. The new generations were a more nervous breed, more intense, restless, more personal, and frequently more sophisticated in their terms of expression. As scientists they had nothing new to discover about perspective, but they explored anatomy passionately. The brothers Antonio and Piero Pollaiuolo, and Luca Signorelli, were probably handier at the dissection of cadavers than the physicians of their time. As classicists, painters like Botticelli, and in his very curious way, Piero di Cosimo, shifted the artist's point of view from the revivification of monumental antiquity to the illustration of Greek and Roman legends or myths, and to the interpretation of philosophical doctrines derived from the ancients.

A shift in the artist's concept of drawing accompanied— we might say, was demanded by—his shifted interests. Drawing remained the Florentine obsession, but now instead of thinking in terms of simplified volumes, painters thought in terms of line. They intensified their dramatic expression (and the personalism of their various styles) by the use of line to convey emotion or sentiment as well as action. Each of the men already mentioned—the Pollaiuolo brothers, Signorelli, Botticelli, and Piero di Cosimo—developed a linear style as individual as any signature. In the case of Botticelli, line both as an expressive-descriptive device and as an independent abstract visual delight became so important that the contours of his figures frequently retain only a residual connection with the third dimension of the forms they bound.

Outside Florence, the Renaissance was flowering with local variations (in Padua, in Ferrara, in Venice, as we will see). Of all the local schools, the one that interbred most significantly with Florentine art was the Umbrian, with Pietro Perugino as the epitome of its virtues and shortcomings. Nominally, Umbria also contributed to the second half of the fifteenth century the genius of Luca Signorelli (just as, nominally, it had contributed the genius of Piero della Francesca to the first half), but Signorelli concluded the century—to the year—with a supremely Florentine vision of the end of the world.

These various painters are the subject of this chapter; the Italians further north, busily at work all this while, will be the subject of the next.

Born in Florence in 1449 as his great century approached the halfway mark, and buried in Florence in 1494 with the end of the century in sight, Domenico Ghirlandaio (Domenico di Tommaso Bigordi) supplied both a conclusion and a warning, without meaning to do either. He was indubitably a master of all the resources of picturemaking that the century had developed for the painter. That is, he knew the rules of perspective, he could draw realistically, he was adept—truly adept—at the organization of figures in space. From the point of view of technique simply as the application of pigment, whether in fresco or on a panel, he was equaled by many of his contemporaries but excelled by none. Yet his pictures demonstrate inadvertently that none of the techniques of realism mean anything unless realism serves an imaginative or intellectual purpose. Ghirlandaio was a skilled and honest workman whose prosaic talent was backed up by the discoveries and the popularized ideas of great innovators in one phenomenal city in one phenomenal century, but any efforts to make him something more are hopeless.

He was an excellent man, whose biography can be skipped, since it would merely add up to a list of works that kept him too busy to do anything much but paint before he died at the age of forty-five. He was such an excellent painter (in distinction, here, to artist), was such a hard worker, was so dependable, performing his assignments not only conscientiously but with enthusiasm, that he had the respect of large numbers of good, solid patrons—who, except for the Pope, were pretty definitely the lower bracket of the top clientele. Ghirlandaio was not a favorite of the most cultivated patrons;

they probably found him rather obvious and dull, as—increasingly—we find him today.

In a few portraits Ghirlandaio rebukes this judgment. These are so splendidly drawn and painted that a presence is evoked through the sheer power of costume and physiognomy expertly described and patterned within the limiting rectangle of the frame. And in a single double portrait, the Louvre's *Old Man and His Grandson,* the old man ugly, with a deformed nose, and the little grandson fresh and beautiful, the play of tenderness between the two is so poignant, yet stated with so much tact and reserve, that one wonders why Ghirlandaio did nothing else that approaches the expressiveness of this picture. One decides that it must have been at least half accidental.

Vasari wrote of Ghirlandaio that "he drew all by eye alone." The reference was to his ability to draw the antiquities of Rome in absolutely accurate proportion without measuring them. But "by the eye alone" could as well refer to Ghirlandaio's faith in the validity of sheer factual objectivity. His use of classical incidentals—bits of Roman architecture incorporated in his *Adoration of the Shepherds,* in the Sassetti Chapel in Santa Trinità, for instance—demonstrates the popular awareness in Florence of antiquity as a cultural requisite, but is without expressive or humanistic reference.

Ghirlandaio had the good fortune to conclude his career with the finest of his several series of matter-of-fact illustrations of religious narratives staged in contemporary Florentine costumes and interiors, a sequence of the lives of the Virgin and St. John the Baptist in Santa Maria Novella. They are famous for the portraits of prominent Florentines, dressed in their best, who stand about posing as attendants in various episodes. The complicated assemblages of dignitaries, sainted participants, Renaissance palace architecture, furniture, and incidental paraphernalia are expertly arranged.

They are valuable records of modes of Florentine dress and decoration, and, to give them full due, are entirely pleasurable as demonstrations of Ghirlandaio's mastery of a realistic surface. Offering a recess from the strains of wrestling with the deeper truths of the spirit, they can be a source of comfortable enjoyment. This relaxation of intellectual challenge in an artist who seems to be in the tradition of Masaccio accounts for Ghirlandaio's popularity during his time (it is a mistake to imagine that all Florentines really understood the nature of their Renaissance) and also for the eminent position he held with art lovers during the nineteenth century. The twentieth, with its emphasis on abstract values, has made his historical record and predigested storytelling less attractive.

Vasari says that Ghirlandaio once yearned to paint the entire circumference of Florence's city walls with storytelling pictures. And he could have done so if given time. With his brothers Davide (1452-1525) and Benedetto (1458-1497), both painters, he ran a well-organized shop with numerous apprentices (including one boy named Michelangelo), who assisted in turning out the steady stream of commissions. The elder brother, Davide, was Domenico's general manager; he took care of the details of contracts and also painted when he had time. After Domenico's death, Davide worked largely in mosaic, but had no great career as an artist. The younger brother, Benedetto, was first a manuscript illuminator, then, when his eyes weakened, a painter. He worked for a time in France, probably at the court of Charles VII, but it seems impossible to build up much of a body of work for him.

Domenico Ghirlandaio also had a son, Ridolfo (1483-1562), who became a painter. He was only eleven years old when his father died, and hence was not his pupil. A minor artist of his generation in Florence, Ridolfo left some graceful portraits. He was sufficiently without a style of his own to produce paintings once attributed to Leonardo da Vinci and Raphael—a distinction of sorts.

The names Antonio and Piero Pollaiuolo evoke attractive images of two vigorous, intelligent, hardworking, successful, brusquely outgoing, and agreeably decisive fellows. That these brothers were hardworking we know from the number of contracts, still on file, that they fulfilled. That they were successful we know from the eminence of their patrons. That they were intelligent is an obvious deduction from such of their work as has survived. But the feeling that they were brusquely outgoing and agreeably decisive is nothing more than a response to the character of their art.

By the same response, one tends to visualize Antonio and Piero as rather ornamentally fierce of countenance and very ornamentally muscled. As the Florentine artists most preoccupied with anatomical study, they created, in sculpture and painting, some of the most unyieldingly muscular male nudes in the history of art, and in order that each muscle should be flexed for maximum inspection and description, they engaged their subjects in the most strenuous possible activities—preferably hand-to-hand combat. As scientist-artists the brothers anticipated the anatomical studies of Leonardo da Vinci, although they remained objective explorers, unconcerned with philosophical extensions. And their high-styled athleticism endeared them to a later generation, the mannerists, for whom their almost strident masculinity was a point of departure for an often effeminate celebration of masculine force.

The brothers' family name was actually Benci. Their adopted one was derived from the family's business: their father was a poulterer. Antonio was born in 1431 or 1432 and died in his late sixties, in 1498. Piero, who was probably born in 1443, was about twelve years younger, but he died before his brother, probably in 1496, at the age of fifty-three.

Antonio and Piero seem to have collaborated on a number of paintings, but without leaving any record indicating which brother was responsible for which parts. In spite of this ambiguity, Antonio's own work leaves no question but that he was the dominant talent. He was trained first as a goldsmith, and the precise, demanding, sharply defined, essentially miniature technique of goldsmithery continued to be reflected in his painting and sculpture, even when these were at large scale.

The records show that during the 1460's and the 1470's Antonio executed all manner of fine gold- and silverwork—reliquaries, altar frontals, crucifixes, other religious objects, jewelry, and tournament armor and helmets. Virtually all of these have disappeared, victims of that familiar disaster by which objects of precious metal are melted down in order to realize from the metal a fraction of their worth as objects of art. Antonio was aware (or so Vasari tells us) that the kinds of objects he was creating were vulnerable to destruction by war and ignorance and, concerned for his immortality, took up painting, learning the techniques within a matter of weeks from his younger brother. Whether or not Vasari's story is true, the fact remains that Antonio began painting rather late in life and that Piero, who (as tax records show) had an independent studio as a painter in 1480, would have been the natural source for any technical instruction Antonio needed.

Antonio's major surviving sculpture is the bronze tomb of Sixtus IV in the Vatican Grottoes. The old man's effigy, magnificently robed, lies surrounded by exquisitely modeled allegorical figures of the Virtues, and everywhere the ornament has that special combination of force with delicacy that, in Antonio Pollaiuolo, is the apotheosis of Florentine technique. But in the old man's face, collapsed with age and illness, Antonio's realism is merciless—as unsparingly objective a study of an old man in death as any that Antonio might have sketched from the anonymous corpses he dissected.

But even when his subject is a dead man, Antonio's art is charged with a ferocious sense of life, which he counters by an extreme discipline of forms. He did one engraving, a frieze of battling nude men, in which this combination of violence with rigid control attains a perfect balance. The subject seems to have been chosen as a good one for a study of nude figures in attitudes that reveal each muscle of the body as part of a machine; in two instances the same attitude is shown from front and rear. The figures are all but flayed for maximum definition; they also demonstrate his ignorance of one characteristic of the body as a set of muscles, which is that for every muscle that tenses in any serial action, another muscle relaxes. But no matter. If the men who struggle in *Battle of the Nudes* seem made of metal rather than flesh, that quality is appropriate in an engraving done with a jeweler's precision by the hand of a sculptor. Except for the best examples by Mantegna, fifteenth-century Italian engraving produced nothing to compare with it.

Antonio Pollaiuolo represented a force that changed the character of Florentine style in the second half of the fifteenth century, a force that was most widely disseminated through an artist a few years younger than he. Andrea del Verrocchio (*c.* 1435-1488) was like him a goldsmith and painter as well as a sculptor. Unfortunately for him he succeeded the great Donatello as the leading sculptor of Italy and thus falls under the shadow of an incomparable predecessor. His contribution of nervous energy, spirited grace, and extreme elegance of ornamental detail (this last in the tradition of goldsmithery) to the art of sculpture seems less a contribution than a settling for second best in the light of Donatello's exceptional achievement. And as a painter (nervously energetic, gracefully spirited, and extremely elegant in a decorative way), Verrocchio must suffer from comparison in the opposite direction chronologically, having been the teacher of Leonardo da Vinci. But his workshop and his example were determining factors in the shift of style. Both Verrocchio and Pollaiuolo were strong influences on the artist who brought the style to an extremely personal consummation—Sandro Botticelli.

Botticelli, literally translated, means "little barrel." With its connotations of rotund jollity the name could hardly be less suitable for the artist of tender melancholy to whom it has become attached. His real name was Alessandro di Mariano Filipepi, and he was born in Florence in 1444 or 1445. The contradiction between his name and his art (and his personality, from all we know or can deduce) is at least an appropriate introduction to an artist who presents one contradiction after another. Botticelli is a maddeningly elusive artist. He should not be, but he is.

Painting by painting, Botticelli's art is explicable as a combination of references to the classical past, to the Christian story, and to people who were his contemporaries. Except for two years when he was in Rome executing three frescoes on the walls of the Sistine Chapel, Botticelli's life can be visualized against Florentine backdrops that still exist or can be reconstructed with certainty. He moves as an active participant within a historical context that is all you could ask for dramatically—the rise and fall of the Medici, his patrons; the quicker rise and the terrible fall in flames of Savonarola, his hero. He is on stage from beginning to end, and his part is a rich one—the tanner's son who becomes a favorite painter, and probably the colleague, of a circle of intellectuals, princes, and dilettantes, but abandons worldy advantage for a moral and mystical ideal that becomes a lost cause, and at last dies sick, alone, and in poverty.

Yet when it is all over and we leave the theater, we realize the central character has not delivered a single line of dialogue. He has been completely present and absolutely removed, just as he is in the Uffizi's *Adoration of the Magi*, where he has painted himself standing to one side, unattached to the action, wrapped from chin to ankle in a heavy cloak, his head turned away from the Virgin and Child and the ranks of their worshipers to look us straight in the eye, but with neither a question nor an answer.

It is an arresting face, virile, sensual, composed, and alert, a harmony of contradictions. The full lips, with the upper one curled and the lower projecting just a bit, could be petulant if they were not so firmly modeled. The nose is large and strong, full-nostriled and with a prominent arch to the bridge, too much nose for a small face but a good nose for a man with that great chin and jaw. The chin is softened by the hint of a matinee idol's cleft, and the heavy eyelids just fail to droop. With the curling lip they could give an impression of haughtiness, and they must partly account for the feeling that we are curtained off from the person behind the eyes who looks out at us with such absolute steadiness, divided between something more than curiosity and something less than arrogance, perhaps skepticism. But at this point the would-be physiognomist becomes confused. Isn't there a hint of perversity in so much contradiction and concealment? Yet how can there be, in a face and head so strongly formed? And can we finally consider it an ascetic face—having begun by finding it virile and sensual—or is the asceticism inherent in the manner of drawing rather than in what is drawn? Or are we reading asceticism and hints of perversity into the face because of what we know of Botticelli's life?

What it comes down to is that we do not know much about the part of Botticelli's life that counted most, the inner life reflected in his paintings as one long, restless dream tormented by nostalgia for a lovely past that never existed and forebodings of a future that did materialize in anguish. Venuses and Madonnas people the dream equally and are not very different from one another, twin symbols of that curious pagan-Christian dichotomy of the Renaissance, fused by Botticelli into an art so personal that it cannot be understood within the generalities of the two traditions it seems to expound.

It is standard information that Botticelli's paired masterpieces, *The Birth of Venus* and *Primavera* (now in the Uffizi), were inspired by the convolutions of Neoplatonic philosophy popular in the circle of artists, poets, and intellectuals who were patronized by the Medici; that Botticelli's Venus, shown born from the sea in accord with the Greek myth, is historically important as the first large nude figure of the pagan goddess modeled after antique sculpture to appear in the Renaissance; that Neoplatonism held to a doctrine of physical perfection as the emblem of a noble spirit, and that a Venus could be interchangeable with the Virgin Mary in the philosophical rationalizations of Botticelli's prestigious friend Marsilio Ficino, who worked out an impossibly complicated system of universal divine beauty. The humanistic iconography of the paintings has been interpreted and counter-interpreted and re-interpreted in detail with conscientious scholarship, sometimes on rather uncertain grounds as allegorical reference to Medici family history. Botticelli has been seen as a Renaissance link both to the mystical passion of Gothic art and to the ascetic morality of the Reformation, and with equally good reason. As subjects for analysis, his paintings seem to be inexhaustible; as subjects for conjecture they are stimulating and flexible; and from any interpretative point of view they are fascinating material.

But their magic is in their evocation of dream. Their exceptional iconographical knottings and interlacings were probably worked out by members of the Florentine Neoplatonic circle and dictated to Botticelli for picturization as they would have been to any other artist. But only Botticelli could have given them the mood of hope and fear, promise and regret, reminiscence and tender melancholy, that is his distinctive expression. And no matter how specifically he may have observed a Neoplatonic pattern, philosophical reasoning gives way in his work to the personal mysticism of the dreamer.

Botticelli's dreams have nothing conventionally visionary in their presentation. A dream while it is happening does not seem a vision, but a reality. Botticelli's absolute definition, the wonderful lines that bound his forms with a life of their own, have nothing to do with the vagueness and fuzziness of the usual dream representations. Yet nothing is quite real within this unyieldingly explicit definition. While the other artists of the century were preoccupied with all the devices by which the real world could be represented accurately, Botticelli ignored them. Perspective? Botticelli has multiple perspectives within a single picture, which means that by the logical, geometric systems worked out by the perspectivists he has none at all. Anatomy? In spite of his early connection with the brothers Pollaiuolo, who were the most passionate anatomists of all, and although his figures seem to be constructed upon normal skeletons with normal musculature as a reference point, his gods and saints and even the individuals in his portraits seem to belong to a special race—more spare, more taut, more angular here and more sinuous there, than the rest of us. His beings do not inhabit a physical world; they are the inhabitants of a mood and a recollection.

The hazard of preciousness, of affectation, is inherent in any style as nearly eccentric as Botticelli's, but it is more than countered by the virility and control of the linear patterns, which, when imitated, so often grow flaccid and effeminate. It took Botticelli's imitators among the Pre-Raphaelite painters of the nineteenth century—men like Dante Gabriel Rossetti and Burne-Jones—to show just how saccharine his style and his sentiment could become at second hand; yet the critics who were associated with these painters—Ruskin, Pater, Swinburne—were the ones who were perceptive enough to rediscover Botticelli, after two centuries of obscurity, as a major artist rather than a sentimental eccentric.

The Adoration of the Magi, with Botticelli's self-portrait, was painted about 1478, when he would have been about thirty-four, and is a group portrait of his patrons, the Medici, and some members of their circle. *The Birth of Venus* and *Primavera* are from about the same year. Botticelli's Roman trip came three years later (he was there in 1481 and 1482, working in the Sistine Chapel). He returned to Florence and spent an extremely productive decade, but with the turn into the last decade of the century Florence's troubles and Botticelli's agony began.

Lorenzo de' Medici died in 1492; his successors fled the city after what amounted to civil war between the ruling families; French invaders set up the inspired but fanatical monk Savonarola as head of the Republic in 1494; six years later after a tragicomic performance by the Florentines, swinging on a pendulum between public prudery and private licentiousness, Savonarola was convicted of heresy and executed, or murdered by hanging and burning, a martyrdom that might one day have led to his canonization if he had not lacked so completely the requisite virtue of charity.

Botticelli was an avowed follower of Savonarola, not by the temporary hysteria of conversion through the monk's evangelism, but by the total dedication of a spirit in which an ascetic compulsion had always chastened sensuous impulse. Botticelli's Venus may be the loveliest ever created, but she is also the least fleshly, more virginal than voluptuous. Now his style became more austere, yet more nervous, more spare, and more intense. In the *Calumny of Apelles* (Uffizi), he translated his Venus into the figure of Truth standing naked, calling on heaven to witness the infamy of a court where an innocent victim (the banished Medici? the martyred Savonarola?) is dragged before a false judge and accused by the furies—Envy, Fraud, Deception, Suspicion, and Ignorance. The allegory has a direct classical source, Lucian's description of a painting by Apelles, but in Botticelli's hands it is like a scene from a hell where the heroic moral obligation of Christianity has been denied.

Two years after Savonarola's execution, Botticelli painted a Nativity, now in London's National Gallery—a curious, rather dislocated composition filled with angels and adorers whose attitudes of exaltation and joyous greeting are hardly distinguishable from those of despair and battle. He inscribed it with his name and with the year 1500, "during the fulfillment of the Eleventh Chapter of St. John, in the second woe of the Apocalypse, in the loosing of the devil for three years and a half." And although he added that the devil would be chained, according to the Twelfth Chapter, this was a prophecy that was not fulfilled on schedule. The painting could hardly have failed to be recognized as an indictment of the forces that had murdered Savonarola. These forces were still in power, and hence Botticelli's declaration of allegiance to the victim may have had something to do with his being charged with sodomy in 1502. Such a charge was rather freely thrown around when personal or political efforts were being made to discredit a bothersome citizen. The charge against Botticelli was dismissed.

From 1500 until his death in 1510, at about sixty-five, Botticelli painted very little. He had never been a widely popular artist; his style, always a little archaic in flavor, now seemed altogether outdated to a generation that knew the softened harmonies of Leonardo da Vinci and the rising thunder of Michelangelo. There were no more commissions. The Medici sent him funds that kept him alive, but if he painted at all during the last years, he painted for himself. But that, in a way, is what he had always done in the long soliloquy that has left us wondering what kind of man he was.

If Vasari had not established him once and for all as a prize eccentric, obsessed by bestiality to the point of madness, Piero di Cosimo might have come down in history on the evidence of his paintings as an intellectual with a bizarre sense of humor. The paintings can support both views: they are full of the wildest kind of fantasy where men and beasts intermingle, but they also expound an interpretation of pagan mythology that was approved by the ancients themselves, by St. Augustine, and by some solid thinkers among Piero di Cosimo's contemporaries.

The probability is that Piero di Cosimo was a benign eccentric and a semi-intellectual—neither a madman nor a scholar—but Vasari's account must come first, no matter how much of it may be exaggeration or pure invention, for it is almost all we know about Piero except for birth and death dates and the times and places and patrons of his pictures.

Piero, whose real name was Piero di Lorenzo—the Cosimo is adopted from his teacher, Cosimo Roselli—was born about 1462 and died in 1521. He must have been a lonely and unhappy old man toward the end of his life, and Vasari reports that he was afflicted with a palsy that reduced him to furious rages (understandable enough) when he tried to use his brushes. His symptomatic eccentricities as a younger man are listed here, with some modifying parenthetical comments not Vasari's.

He had a taste for shutting himself up for days, refusing to see anyone at all (perhaps nothing more than a symptom of a strong need for privacy and concentration, which makes some people take the telephone off the hook or barricade themselves behind a secretary).

He let his garden run wild (any busy man's temptation) because "nature should be allowed to take care of herself"— an idea consistent with Piero's interest in the primitive world and its forests, which were the concern of his major paintings.

He was fascinated by strange birds and beasts (we all enjoy the zoo) and liked to keep them around him to draw and study (as did Leonardo da Vinci, among other artists not regarded as eccentric).

Noise bothered him, for example the crying of children and the coughing of men (universally irritating, both), as well as the jingling of bells (which just might be compared to automobile horns today) and the chanting of friars (which is all very well in its place, just as opera on the radio may be, but not when it is going on next door and you are trying to work).

He liked to see rain streaming from the roof and hear it splashing to the ground (most people enjoy standing at a window to watch a good downpour). He did not like lightning and thunder (as many people do not), and when the thunder was loud he would "wrap himself up in his mantle and, having closed the windows and locked the door of his room, he would crouch in a corner until the storm had passed."

He was varied and original in conversation and "sometimes said such extraordinary things that he made his listeners rock with laughter." (A man like that is good to have around.) He hated doctors (as did Molière, whose wisdom is famous) and loved long lonely walks (as did Thoreau, among many others).

"He cared nothing for his own comfort," Vasari says, which is true of many artists and of many people so absorbed by a single activity that they have no time to arrange comforts, "and reduced himself to eating boiled eggs, which, in order to save fuel, he cooked when he was heating his glue, and not six or eight at a time but some fifty, and, keeping them in a basket, he would eat them by and by," which sounds odd until it is recognized as a wonderfully practical measure.

Finally, in his old age, "flies enraged him," but who likes them? "Even shadows annoyed him." He refused to have assistants "standing around," and "his foolishness robbed him of all possible aid." Vasari was only ten years old when Piero died, but this would still put him within close range of something more than pure hearsay. Most historians are willing to believe that Piero was what we now call "deeply disturbed."

Vasari's account of Piero has some corollary historical interest in being an archetypal account of the artist-as-freak, a persistent idea today born only a few years earlier than Vasari himself. When the late Renaissance recognized the artist as an exceptional being endowed with a Divine Fire that made him a fit companion for princes—a superman, like Leonardo da Vinci, Raphael, or Michelangelo—it also conceived of the Divine Fire as something that might miscarry and make the artist a fit candidate for the insane asylum. Vasari's fascination with this idea accounts for his exaggerations. For these exaggerations, Piero di Cosimo supplied some excellent material.

Piero seems always to have had a talent for the bizarre, and one of his most famous creations was a float designed for the carnival of Florence in 1511, which was so well remembered that Vasari could describe it as enthusiastically as if he had seen it in that year (which was the year of his birth). Actually, he could have gotten a pretty good description of the float by referring to Petrarch, who had supplied Piero's model nearly two hundred years earlier in his "Trionfi." Black, enormous, sepulchral, the float was drawn by oxen and bore a macabre burden of sarcophagi beneath a towering figure of King Death and his universal scythe. A cortege of horsemen in black tights painted with white bones like skeletons accompanied it, and from time to time, when the float stopped, other skeletons would rise from the sarcophagi and all would chant a dirge warning the revelers in the street that they, too, would one day be dead.

Piero may have been the ideal artist for the assignment, but there are numerous reasons for refuting any idea that this theatrical morbidity was simply an expression of his curious nature. For one thing, the subject was surely assigned to him. For another, the Petrarchan model might have been followed just as closely by any other artist, with no reputation for being slightly mad. Also, the float is believed to have had political overtones, making it more than a pure fantasy by a man isolated from life. And the Florentines loved it. When Vasari described it forty years later, the doggerel verses that had been chanted by the skeletons were still being sung, and in a light spirit. The whole thing was more entertaining than sinister.

Although death itself has never been very popular, the Florentines at that time, loving life as much as any people have ever loved it, were able to contemplate death with wry levity or, on a poetic level, as a poignant reminder that life is sweet but that men are mortal. About 1500, Piero created as tenderly lyrical an expression of this attitude as has ever been painted, *The Death of Procris,* now in the National Gallery in London.

In the rather complicated classical myth, Procris is killed by her husband, who hurled her own spear at her (a spear endowed by the goddess Artemis with unerring accuracy) when he mistook her for an animal moving in the underbrush. The tale is recounted in Ovid's "Metamorphoses," where Piero doubtless knew it. But he did not try to echo the classical past in ideal forms as another artist would have done. Instead, he painted realistically a beautiful girl lying dead in a meadow, mourned by a faun and by her own dog, while in a serene landscape behind them life goes on as birds fly, animals hunt, and ships ply the waters of a lake.

The dog in *The Death of Procris* is famous as the first of its kind, romantically endowed with the human sensitivities that we still like to attribute to our favorite animals. And in his most famous series of paintings, Piero created a world where half-human animals and half-animal human beings engage in riotous communal living, including indiscriminate lovemaking with one another, that seemed for a long time to justify his reputation for half-bestial obsessions. But the paintings are now known to have been conceived not as half-hallucinatory inventions but in accordance with a school of classical thought that can be traced back to Hellenistic times and was revived, along with everything else classical, by the insatiable fifteenth century.

Piero's classicism is utterly opposed to the Neoplatonic reveries that Botticelli was painting at the same time, and utterly unrelated to the kind of classicism exemplified by Mantegna with his re-creation of what he thought ancient Rome looked like. Piero re-creates an imagined primeval world that man is engaged in conquering by his own powers. In spite of all the fantasies involved in Piero's account, man is shown achieving a better than bestial state not by the paternalistic intervention of the gods, but by the means he learned for himself when he discovered the potential of natural resources and the ways to control and use them. The exceptionally gifted individuals who made these discoveries became the pagan gods—which is where mythology takes over from anthropology in this ancient approximation of the theory of evolution. The men who served Plato as classical Darwins included Virgil, Ovid, Lucretius, and Vitruvius —as Erwin Panofsky demonstrated in 1939 with the publication of an iconological study that rediscovered the meanings of a series of paintings that for nearly four centuries had been regarded as pure fantasies.

Piero's exposition of mankind's progress divides it into stages. Shortly after 1490, he did a series of paintings for a rich Florentine merchant, Francesco del Pugliese, showing the transition from primeval days when men and beasts commingled to the days when men learned to order their world under the tutelage of Vulcan.

Hunting Scene and *Return from the Hunt,* twin panels in the Metropolitan Museum, show, in the first picture, a savage world where men and animals and creatures half man and half animal quarrel, kill, and mate, with indiscriminate violence, and in the second, a world still savage but one in which the violence has abated and men are making their first efforts to control their environment. In a third picture, *Landscape with Animals,* in the Ashmolean Museum, Oxford, the monsters produced by the mating of men and animals are still present in the forest, but men are building crude huts from broken trees, and are domesticating the first beasts of burden. Then, in two large paintings, *The Finding of Vulcan* (Hartford, Wadsworth Athenaeum) and *Vulcan as Arch-Craftsman and First Teacher of Human Civilization* (Ottawa, National Gallery of Canada), men emerge from savagery under the instruction of Vulcan, the god of fire, who has taught them to forge tools and hence to develop the practical arts.

Piero continued the story, for another patron, in two paintings illustrating our progress in another direction. Having learned to make life tolerable, men now learned how to make it enjoyable through the discoveries of wine and honey, with Bacchus as referee in the consequent festivities. *The Discovery of Wine* and *The Discovery of Honey* in the Worcester Art Museum are Piero at his most individual. Much of their fantasticality—what with their satyrs, their exotic animals, their revelry, and their general air of a cross between a costume fete and an anthology of zoological curiosities—comes from Piero's literal transcription into pictorial forms of the classical texts he followed. But there is an air of frolic, a high-spiritedness, a drollery, that is all Piero's own. The pastoral idyll of conventional mythology becomes a bit dull by contrast—a party you wish you could leave to go to Piero's.

The gaiety of these paintings has been interpreted as a conscious dodge employed to get around their conflict with the scriptural account of the Creation. Piero was doubly vulnerable, having violated not only the purity of Neoplatonic idealism but the authority of Christian miracle as well. He was not quite in line with modern anthropology either, but he is closer to it than he was to the other two. And during the past several decades, he has begun to look more and more modern as a painter. His sources can be pinned down as classical, but by pictorializing them through his own imaginative vision he created a poetry of the extraordinary that forecast the romantic movement of the nineteenth century and has made him a patron saint of the surrealists in the twentieth.

Piero di Cosimo was an independent spirit and perhaps an eccentric, but he was neither a visionary nor a hysteric. In his way, he must have been a reasonable and consistent man. His remaining unaffected by the frenzies that swept Florence under Savonarola is evidence of it. He was about fifty-nine when he died. According to one story, he was found dead at the foot of a staircase. According to Vasari, he died in bed adamantly refusing the services of a priest.

Piero's first master, Cosimo Roselli (1439-1507), must be given a few words here. A dull painter who ran a busy workshop in Florence, he was one of those many pedestrian artists who somehow make good teachers. In the extraordinarily unimaginative quality of his painting there is nothing to connect him with his pupil's genius for fantastic invention, or with another famous pupil, the rather placid Fra Bartolommeo. According to Vasari, he had at least one eccentricity, a passion for alchemy, and he finally bankrupted himself with alchemical experiments.

The twentieth century has put Pietro Perugino in the unhappy position of being either detested or excessively admired, in both instances on the basis of his worst work. And on the basis of his best, his very real virtues appear unexciting, because they only echo those of a greater predecessor, Piero della Francesca, or foreshadow those of a greater follower, Raphael. This is a terrible spot for an artist to be in.

Perugino's saints and Madonnas, which he turned out assembly-line fashion from stock patterns kept in his workshop, and which were degraded during the nineteenth century as the stock patterns for thousands upon thousands of mawkish holy pictures, assume graceful attitudes and gaze heavenward with a pious sweetness that still appeals to souls who cling to the sentimental standards of nineteenth-century art appreciation at its popular level. But for most people today, "sentimental" has become the most pejorative of adjectives, and Perugino's religiosity seems false enough to verify an unflattering report made by Vasari.

According to Vasari, Perugino was an irreligious man who in rough language denied the immortality of the soul, a moneygrubber intent on cranking out a salable product. A more flattering interpretation of the same facts might recognize that in the fifteenth century the artist was not a man who necessarily painted according to the dictates of his personal beliefs or even as an expression of his own nature, but was a craftsman with a workshop who supplied a demand. In supplying a demand (and delivering an impeccably crafted product), Perugino may have been no more hypocritical than, say, a vegetarian butcher who sells good meat at honest prices.

At his best Perugino is an altogether admirable painter. As a young man he probably knew Piero della Francesca, a fellow Umbrian a full generation older than he, and learned from this master something of the monumental possibilities inherent in perspective as a means of organizing deep space inhabitable by figures in receding planes. Perugino's *Delivery of the Keys* in the Sistine Chapel of the Vatican is a truly dignified, logical, and almost impressive composition in planar architectural space, stable and legible although it may not rise to the level of being "monumental," the adjective that in opposition to "sentimental" is reserved today for art that can be venerated with safety. And when he did not overdo it, the sweetness of Perugino's saints and Madonnas can be appealing enough. It was here (as well as in the placement of figures in space) that he pointed the way for his pupil Raphael (a full generation younger), who capitalized on the formula with greater skill and infinitely more tact.

Perugino remains the star painter and the typifying painter of the Umbrian school, even though he holds the position by default. Both Piero della Francesca and Signorelli were—aesthetically—naturalized Florentines, and Raphael shifted his allegiance twice, first to Florence and then to Rome. Perugino also worked in those two cities, and is on record as a member of the painters' guild in Florence in 1472, one of the main reasons for establishing his birth date as about 1450. He worked in the Vatican, not only in the Sistine Chapel, but as the decorator of the ceiling of the Stanza della Segnatura, above Raphael's walls. He also worked on a project in St. Peter's, now destroyed, in which he might have responded to the Roman spirit with the same effectiveness that is apparent in *The Delivery of the Keys*.

But Perugia was his city (from which his nickname; his real name was Pietro di Cristoforo di Vannucci), and Umbria his heath. In one area Perugino needs no defense. His landscape backgrounds convey all the gentleness, the tender air and soft skies and blue distances, of Umbria. Against these backgrounds his lay figures posing as saints may be forgiven a certain lack of skill in their enactment of dramas too profound for their talents, and we may bypass the too obvious mechanics of compositional schemes worn threadbare by repetition.

His repetitiveness destroyed his career. If Perugino is in an unhappy position today as far as the response to his art is concerned, he ended his life in a position nearly as unhappy among his contemporaries. For twenty years, from the age of about thirty, he was one of the most admired painters in Italy. But the times outgrew him. He was unable to assimilate the weightier dramatic style of the High Renaissance, and by 1500 his reputation was declining. The anticlimax dragged on for more than twenty years, until he died of the plague in 1523 in his early seventies.

Bernardino Pintoricchio, a Perugian, was a decorative muralist who worked in the style of a previous era. Born about 1454, and hence a few years younger than Perugino, he assisted that painter with his frescoes in the Sistine Chapel in 1481 or 1482, and showed signs of his influence for some time thereafter, but for most of the remaining thirty-three years of his life he lagged far behind in the course that painting followed.

Admittedly, an artist's merit need not depend on his modernity, but Pintoricchio (although this may not be the general evaluation) hardly made sufficient capital of the old style to justify his sticking to it. He was an excellent decorator of walls, but so uninventive that one wonders why he was so successful. The reason apparently was that when assigned a subject he could illustrate it well.

It is true that most artists were assigned their subjects, that even Michelangelo was assigned his subject when he painted the Sistine Ceiling. But the popes and other patrons who employed Pintoricchio were wise enough, or lucky enough, to choose him as illustrator for less demanding themes than the creation of the world and the fate of man.

Pintoricchio's nickname, a diminutive for the word "painter," was a reference to his small physical stature rather than to his limitations as an artist. His real name was Bernardino di Betto di Biagio. The little man's biggest single commission, among many, was for extensive decorations in the Borgia apartments in the Vatican. Reverting to the crowded compositions and the liberal use of gold with brilliant color that were more typical of Gothic painting than of the art of his time, he produced a set of decorations sufficiently festive to please Pope Alexander VI. Pope Innocent VIII had also been his patron; later, Pope Pius III became one.

Pintoricchio was always an efficient painter. His sturdiest claim to being something more is a set of murals for the Piccolomini Library in Siena. Here, between 1503 and 1508, he realized some of the spaciousness and clarity promised by his earliest work under the influence of Perugino. He died not long after the completion of this assignment, in 1513, at the age of about fifty-nine.

Born in 1438 at Forlì, in the Romagna, Melozzo da Forlì was in Urbino about 1473-76, working at the court of Federigo da Montefeltro. Possibly he had been a pupil of Piero della Francesca's. If he was not one by direct contact, he was certainly one by example. His art is a blending of Piero's spacious architectural style with more vehemently dramatic elements traceable to Mantegna. He might or might not have seen Mantegna's illusionistic ceiling in the Camera degli Sposi in the Ducal Palace of Mantua, painted just before he came to work in Urbino. At any rate, his figures, like Mantegna's, are drawn in illusionistic perspective and planned from a very low eye level, appearing to occupy space that opens up into infinity. In the course of his subsequent development, in Rome, where he did important frescoes, his increasing mastery of monumental figures in architectural settings brought him to the edge of the High Renaissance, and a fondness for painting accessory figures hovering overhead (angels, for instance) makes him a prophet of the baroque. It is odd that an artist who offers so much stirs us so little. Somehow, in spite of his intelligent invention, Melozzo lacks an igniting spark. He died in 1494.

Although Pedro Berruguete's importance as a painter is overshadowed by that of his son Alonso as a sculptor, he was a most respectable artist who made an intelligent fusion of Flemish, Italian, and his native Spanish traditions in pictures of spectacularly original invention. He was born about 1450 in Castile of Basque ancestry, and it is possible, even probable, that he went to Italy when he was in his early twenties and stayed ten years. If so, he must have been Peter the Spaniard ("Pietro Spagnuolo") who worked for Piero della Francesca's great patron, Federigo da Montefeltro, duke of Urbino.

In any case, Berruguete was back in Spain by 1483. As the namesake and favorite nephew of an influential Dominican monk, he came into favor with the inquisitor general Tomás de Torquemada and received important commissions for altarpieces and decorations at the Dominican Monastery of St. Thomas in Avila. He acquitted himself well on the first of these (he was still at work on others when he died in 1504) and came to the attention of the court. As court painter to Queen Isabella he was given a hereditary title of nobility, shortly before his death. Apparently his family had always been respectable, since he had married the daughter of a wealthy nobleman. Of the six children she bore him, Alonso was the oldest.

Hopelessly dull as a painter, Alonso Berruguete (c. 1489-1561) was a brilliant sculptor. An early stay in Italy (where he knew Michelangelo) brought him into contact with the late, anguished work of Donatello, and he retained much of its humanity while developing theatrically manneristic and tumultuously baroque forms. He is one of the greatest figures (by many critics' judgments, the greatest) in an undervalued chapter in the history of art, Spanish sculpture of the Renaissance.

Francesco Francia, whose real name was Francesco di Marco di Giacomo Raibolini, was born in Bologna about 1450 and perhaps owes his nickname to early training under a French goldsmith. Although technically Bolognese, he is more appropriately classified as an Umbrian, since Perugino and Raphael influenced him more than did any other painters, with the Ferrarese as runners-up in his eclectic stable.

As a goldsmith, Francia was in wide demand and very productive; however, little of his work in this field remains. A number of sculptures have been attributed to him. As a painter he is still all over the place, although he is less sought after now than he was during the nineteenth century, when he was thought of as all but a second Raphael. A second-rate Raphael, in truth, is just about what Francia is at his best, if we forget Raphael's great Roman paintings and compare Francia's only to the less impressive and highly sweetened earlier Raphaels so dear to art lovers a few generations ago.

Whatever his limitations, Francia was consistently an excellent workman. He made good use of the Umbrian formula of rather languid saints, soft-faced Madonnas, and gentle landscape, applying it with unwavering efficiency if not much originality or much evidence of deep feeling. There is, however, one highly emotional if totally implausible legend connected with Francia: he is supposed to have died in a swoon upon seeing a Raphael.

If he really did, death would have had to occur from the cumulative effects of his admiration for that painter, since Francia died in 1517 or 1518 in his middle sixties. Raphael was at the summit of his dazzling career, and Francia's work shows that he had already seen too many Raphaels by that time.

Luca Signorelli, born in Cortona perhaps as early as 1441 and perhaps as late as 1450, is nominally an Umbrian painter. But like Piero della Francesca, the master given him by tradition, he absorbed and developed the scientific disciplines cultivated in Florence. With Piero as the first generation, Signorelli is the second generation of what is virtually a two-man school, the Umbro-Florentine. And the "Umbro" is there largely as a matter of courtesy, even though Signorelli remained a staunch and prominent citizen of Cortona until his death, around the age of eighty, in 1523.

Signorelli's greatest work, an awesome account of the end of the world, remains in nearly perfect condition on the four walls of the San Brizio Chapel in the Cathedral of Orvieto. His finest panel painting, an arcadian allegory called *The Realm of Pan,* was destroyed in World War II, which is as close, so far, as the end of the world has come.

The Realm of Pan (sometime called *The School of Pan*) showed gods and shepherds in an idyllic landscape. No other painting, not even Botticelli's *Birth of Venus,* ever evoked more alluringly the sensuous and intellectual cast of Florentine humanism. Indeed the picture has a specifically humanistic theme: it was a metaphor, perhaps a little flattering to its central character, of the Florentine Arcadia, where the shepherds were the artists, the philosophers, and the cultivated *amateurs* who gathered around Lorenzo the Magnificent in the Medici villa at Fiesole.

The contrast between Signorelli's epic drama of the end of the world and this vision of Arcadia is less extreme than one might think. The most celebrated of the four wonderful frescoed walls in Orvieto shows the damned being cast into hell, but it is a hell conceived in humanistic terms. The date is most convenient: Signorelli painted the frescoes in 1499 and 1500, as if to make a final statement, exactly at the end of the century, of the humanistic philosophy that made such a hell conceivable. By double coincidence, Hieronymus Bosch's *Garden of Delights* terminated the century in the North with the summation of the medieval concept of hell as a spiritual nightmare.

There is nothing nightmarish or visionary about Signorelli's scene of damnation, even though angels of judgment stand in the sky as referees above a one-sided battle. Figures fall or are dragged downward into a writhing mass where naked sinners in every attitude of anguish, horror, and despair are belabored by naked demons whose athletic bodies are wildly tinted in changing colors—greens, reds, lavenders. Every muscle in every body, whether a sinner's or a demon's, is bunched or stretched by the force of the struggle.

There is no air of the supernatural. This is no phantasmagoria. Not only are the sinners real men and real women; the angels, dressed in armor, are men in the role of knights, and the devils are men in the role of appointed executioners. The scene is a formal entity where the chaotic contest has been defined with absolute clarity, not only in the uncompromising description of each straining muscle in each straining figure, but in the relationship of each figure to the mass of what seem to be hundreds of figures. A lesser master might have given us only a squirming horde, but in their dense confusion they have been as carefully organized, if for different effect, as the serene and open congregations so majestically disposed in quiet space by Masaccio and Piero della Francesca.

Signorelli's hell is a real and reasonable hell where the agonies suffered are reasonable punishment for offenses committed in full knowledge by men who have the capacity to control their actions. The sinners, victims of their own wrongdoing, remain men and women like ourselves; they are not transformed into monsters in a mystical struggle between good and evil. If a scene of damnation can be reassuring, Signorelli's is indeed so. It insists upon the humanistic premise that man is strong enough to shape his own destiny. Even the Greeks had not been as sure of themselves as that; they always left a loophole for inexorable fate as the final invincible weapon of the gods.

To say that Signorelli theorized in any such fashion and then set about to create a pictorial expression of the theories would be foolhardy. We are on safer grounds when we assume that Savonarola's prophecies of doom and his castigation of the loose living that would bring it about—prophecies for which the French invasions of Italy were a concrete corroborative symptom—contributed to the powerful conviction that Signorelli's fresco still carries. Whatever the origins of this "humanistic hell," the concept was characteristic, in its moral implications, of the culture that produced it. And Signorelli's style was the perfect one, aesthetically, for its pictorial expression.

This style, entirely Signorelli's own whatever its sources, combines Piero's aloof, semiabstract formalism from the first half of the century with the keyed-up realism of the second half. As a young man, Signorelli probably assisted Piero on the great Arezzo frescoes, absorbing Piero's conception of space as a three-dimensional volume to be occupied by solid forms reduced to their geometrical equivalents. At the same time, Signorelli's almost obsessive interest in the anatomical structure of the body shows the influence of Antonio Pollaiuolo, and his interest in movement links him with Verrocchio.

Signorelli worked in Florence in the 1470's and gained a reputation sufficient to win him a call from Pope Sixtus IV in 1482. For Sixtus he completed a fresco begun by Perugino in the Sistine Chapel, and did two of his own. Later, along with Pintoricchio, Sodoma, and Perugino, he began work on frescoes for the Stanza della Segnatura in the Vatican, but these beginnings were destroyed when the job was handed over to Raphael.

The Chapel of San Brizio in Orvieto remains Signorelli's monument, and if it is something like a fifteenth-century summation, it was also a fountainhead, for it was so admired by Michelangelo that its influence flowed through the Sistine Ceiling and the *Last Judgment* into the next century. The decoration of the chapel had been started, in its vault, by Fra Angelico—a painter who never really believed in hell—and after Signorelli took it over, the commission was extended to include the walls. The paintings are fiercely masculine in their force, so much so that a traditional idea of Signorelli as a personality endows him with a violent nature. But even when Signorelli is dealing with violence, he chastens it with an austerity that none can miss except a casual observer who reacts only to the subject matter and to the strained musculature of the nudes.

As an anatomist, Signorelli, like Pollaiuolo, never realized that all the muscles of the body do not function at one time. For this reason his anatomical drawings of nudes have an aggressiveness that is, actually, incidental to their first nature as scientific delineations of a fascinating construction, the human body. The factual record on Signorelli as a personality does not support any association of violence, but on the contrary reflects a stable, dignified, and kindly man.

Signorelli is the only artist of his generation included in Vasari's "Lives" that Vasari could remember from close personal contact, and the story is as appealing as any that Vasari recounts. When Vasari was only eight years old—this would have been in 1519, with Signorelli in his seventies—the artist was staying with the child's uncle, Lazzaro Vasari, in Arezzo, where he had gone to supervise the installation of a painting. "The good old man was most courteous and agreeable," Vasari reports, and once, when the boy broke into a nosebleed, old Signorelli treated it for him "with infinite tenderness . . . a recollection that I will cherish as long as I live." Signorelli called Vasari "little kinsman" (and there was perhaps a blood tie), admitting him to the company of artists because the child was always drawing, and told him to "study well." After Vasari grew up, he held that excessive study had reduced Signorelli's style to "dryness and crudeness," a fault he also found in Botticelli and others of that generation, for his own sympathies lay with the grace and fluidity of the Raphaelesque tradition.

Vasari also reports that Signorelli "lived like a gentleman, not an artist," and the records of Cortona show that in his home city he was elected to the office of prior twelve times between 1479 and 1522, was its chief magistrate in 1488, and served as Cortona's ambassador to Florence. He was twice married and several times a father. After 1500, with the completion of the frescoes in Orvieto, Signorelli developed very little as a painter, but supervised the production of his prosperous workshop in Cortona for the remaining twenty-three years of his life.

5

THE
FIFTEENTH CENTURY
IN NORTHERN ITALY
AND VENICE

Although painting in northern Italy had no Masaccio, it found an odd kind of father in Francesco Squarcione, who was born in 1397 at about the same time as that great Florentine and died in 1468. He is a somewhat controversial figure, with a few defenders among scholars devoted to his native Padua, and many detractors elsewhere. But none deny the importance of his workshop as a propagative center for certain elements that characterize the early schools not only of Padua but also of Ferrara and even Venice.

Until 1429, Squarcione appears in documents as a tailor, and only thereafter as a painter. The difference is not quite as extreme as it sounds: craftsmen were frequently active in other fields than the one in which they were registered, and Squarcione as a painter seems to have run his workshop much as if it had been a tailor's. There are only two paintings generally accepted as his own, but there are large numbers (as many as 137 by one conscientious estimate) that were turned out under his direction by his numerous apprentices.

Squarcione's apprentice-assistants included adopted sons, but not because he was subject to paternal yearnings. Childless craftsmen often adopted a talented apprentice as a practical measure for maintaining the father-to-son arrangement by which shops were kept going from generation to generation. If affection sometimes entered into the adoption, sound business was the prime consideration. Squarcione adopted not one but several sons, and at least two of them, Andrea Mantegna and Marco Zoppo, finally had to go to court as mature artists in order to get free of him and retain for themselves the profits from their independent commissions. Squarcione fought these actions bitterly and was also resentful when Mantegna married into a family of eminent artists—the Bellinis.

Altogether, Squarcione spent a great deal of time in the courts, although not always in so unpleasant a role. His name appears many times as an arbitrator in disputes, as a judge of the quality of works of art, and on committees for the making of contracts and the supervision of their execution. He must have been a respected citizen.

Squarcione's workshop, too, was respected as a secondary center of the humanistic discussions carried on at the University of Padua. He was one of the first artists to concentrate on the collection and study (and perhaps the profitable sale) of fragments of classical sculpture and architecture, which he went to Rome and, conceivably, even to Greece to acquire. He insisted that his students copy these fragments with archaeological exactitude as part of their training. The combination of these motifs with ornamental swags and garlands of leaves, fruits and vegetables—also suggested by the antique but handled with almost metallic dryness and precision—became the basis of a decorative formula that links the several schools of the area. In the hand of minor artists the formula does grow wearisome, but in the hands of Mantegna it is brilliantly decorative and increases an expressive power to which Squarcione may thus be credited with having contributed a hitherto recessive gene.

Squarcione also did his best to keep *au courant* with Florentine innovations, and his pupils were required to copy Florentine paintings that he kept in his shop. Perhaps, too, the Florentines who came to execute commissions in Padua —notably the great Donatello—visited the shop, adding prestige to Squarcione's historical position as middleman. Undeniably, that is where his importance lies.

Andrea Mantegna was born in 1431 and died in 1506, which means that his life spanned seventy-five years of one of the most adventurous periods in art. In many ways he is the summary of his era, which ended when the early Renaissance merged into its period of fulfillment in Leonardo, Raphael, and Michelangelo. When Mantegna was an old man, his reputation suffered somewhat; he was considered old-fashioned by the young painters in Florence and Rome. But he was spared the agony that comes to some aging artists, the fear of being left behind, the feeling that at any cost they must keep up with the times. This Mantegna was never required to do as the great artist of a provincial capital. To the end he was a painter of fierce individuality uncontaminated by compromise with fashion.

As a child prodigy in Padua, Mantegna was exposed to the new thought of the early Renaissance and to the forms it had taken in Florentine art: realism, inspired by the enthusiasm for the physical world and supported technically by the scientific investigation of anatomy and perspective; the rediscovery of the classical past through its broken sculpture and ruined architecture; the contradictory and continued revelation of the Christian mystery. Though the new science and the new paganism came to Mantegna largely at second hand, no artist surpassed him in the fusion of the disparate elements into a unified expression. With his magnificent hard-bitten style he is one of the greatest artists of a century that produced more great artists than any before or since.

Mantegna: the first associations are hardness, intensity, brilliance. Already we have begun to describe a jewel—a ruby or an emerald—or a polished stone, perhaps agate. And Mantegna's art is as ornamental, as elegant, as these in spite of its fierceness. It is a monumentally static art—gigantic, yet with a jewel's exotic and irreducible character of something transformed from baser materials into a final rare and precious substance.

Mantegna was born the son of a carpenter in Isola di Carturo, but as a small child he was adopted by the painter Squarcione, and by all accounts he became, in effect, the master teacher of Squarcione's workshop. He learned little from Squarcione directly, but the workshop was a clearinghouse for new ideas brought to provincial Padua by painters and sculptors from Florence, already a Renaissance city. The University of Padua was still essentially medieval, but its humanists, who apparently respected Squarcione as an antiquarian, were eager to absorb the new learning. The workshop became a meeting place where artists and scholars discussed classical fragments and classical literature with the intensity once reserved for holy relics and the Bible, and when Florentine artists visited Padua to execute commissions, they came to the workshop as emissaries of the new culture.

By the time he was eighteen, Mantegna was receiving substantial commissions. At twenty-three he married Nicolosia, the daughter of Jacopo Bellini, then the leading Venetian painter. At twenty-five, a highly paid artist of established reputation, he finally managed to dissolve his contract with Squarcione. At this point he could have gone wherever he pleased, and the expected thing would have been to go to Florence, or at least to Venice. But in the crucial decision of his life, Mantegna entered the service of Lodovico Gonzaga of Mantua, and for the rest of his life—nearly half a century —he remained attached to this out-of-the-way ducal court.

Mantegna could and did travel to the great centers when he wished, but he was content to become a distinguished spectator of the later innovations of his century. Developing with a consistency, a strength, and an individuality unmodified by the philosophical questioning that affected artists in Florence and Rome, he remained an artist of the early Renaissance in the fullest expression of its youthful vigor, and brought that vigor to mature power in a lifework that advanced steadily and confidently in a single direction.

The court of the Gonzagas, provincial in comparison with the splendid and aggressive courts in Venice, Florence, and Rome, was still the perfect court for Mantegna. The Gonzagas, of all possible patrons, seem to have shared most closely his own characteristics. Their tradition was stern, reserved. Yet as Renaissance humanists they were fascinated by a romantic vision of the classical past and were avid for learning, not as a path to social grace, but because they felt a kinship between their own vigor and the vigor of an ancient Roman world that they envisioned in heroic terms, a military pageant at a celestial level.

The Gonzagas had a fine sense of the theatrical on a grand scale, and so did Mantegna. Like Mantegna, they made up in masculine energy what they lacked in feminine sensitivity, in strength what they lacked in a taste for contemplation, in alertness what they lacked in subtlety. In his portraits Mantegna shows them—and himself—filled with unquestioning assurance, with a sense of power free of arrogance, calm in the face of our inspection, aware of the presence of the observer without admitting him to their confidence. They are hard, strong, and vital—adjectives perfectly descriptive of Mantegna's art—and each holds himself apart as a man responsible first to himself.

Mantegna, an individualist too, one of the great individualists in the history of art, is so isolated that he is often misjudged. The most devoted lovers of Florentine art complain that he lacks the breadth and freedom, the human warmth, that the Tuscans offer. They cannot see that Mantegna's stoniness, his rejection of movement and fluidity and of softened, sweetened, and gentled forms, was a rejection necessary to the almost fanatic discipline that accounts for the intensity of the emotion he expresses. They find him cold. Yet in Mantegna, emotion is not so much held in check as it is distilled to an essence so pure that it is too strong for most palates.

Mantegna is the most abstract, and hence the most modern, of all early Italian Renaissance painters. At the same time, he is the mightiest Roman of them all. From fragments, from forgeries, from literary references, probably from collections of drawings that artists passed around among themselves as sorts of pattern books, and from the wonderfully evocative but decayed and half-buried architectural stage-set of the ruins of ancient Rome itself, Mantegna synthesized his own ancient world, a world of wonderful completeness and austere purity.

The buildings he invented in the backgrounds of his paintings—buildings never planned to be built but that it would have been possible to build—are some of the most impressive architectural designs of their time on the classical model. But the landscapes surrounding them are fantasies, with their curiously formed cliffs, as sharp-edged as razors, their barren rocks, where a broken tree, festooned with clumps of weird foliage studded with small, brilliant fruits like enameled metal, may rise through the biting rim of a crack. Within this world his Christian martyr saints endure their agonies like sentient sculptures.

Element after element in Mantegna's style can be traced back to Squarcione's workshop, and he shared the majority of his decorative motifs with other north Italian painters. But where his cousin artists often produced little more than meaningless complications of drapery, repetitiously patterned swags or garlands of foliage, ribbons, and fruit, and tinny figures posed in attitudes of affected passion or nicety, Mantegna took this improbable material, this catalogue of mannered tricks, and transmuted it into a vocabulary of unsurpassed expressive power. His emotional understatement heightens the impact of the total picture; the spiritual intensity of the protagonist infuses every object within the painted scene. Not the smallest pebble seems auxiliary; nothing is accidental; nothing can be thought of as temporary or reducible. Every object is charged with the full concentration of the total scene, and all is transfixed forever within a miracle.

As a man, Mantegna was anything but a mystic. He was practical and hardworking in the service of the court, turning out schemes for fetes, pageants, and decorative projects, as well as paintings. He was respected as a friend by the Gonzagas, but apparently never became quite the courtier on terms of equality that the Renaissance craftsman-artist was becoming in Florence and Rome. A severe and even acerbic personality, he could grow testy over small disagreements, and frequently ran into trouble with his neighbors. He was not a man to be trod upon with safety, not a man to expect concessions and not a man to make them. But he was remarkably patient with one charming but rather difficult young patroness—Isabella d'Este.

Poor Isabella! She was a woman of considerable beauty and intellectual cultivation, but her misadventures with her "studio" in the Gonzaga palace have left her forever tainted with a bit of the flavor of a pretentious little bluestocking. At the age of sixteen she married Francesco Gonzaga, and as the new great lady of a small court she took over its cultural direction a little prematurely. Her studio, in competition with a similar project of her brother, Alfonso d'Este of Ferrara, grew into a combination of salon, retreat, art gallery, and flattering backdrop, intended as an apotheosis of the humanistic spirit. Isabella planned that the walls should be lined with a set of appropriate paintings by leading artists, and set about with youthful highhandedness to dictate to them.

The great Giovanni Bellini of Venice drily let her know that he regarded himself as more experienced and more competent than she, but Mantegna, as the Gonzagas' court artist, was more indulgent. Meeting her at least halfway, he completed two paintings—*Minerva Expelling the Vices from the Grove of Virtue* (in which, we may assume, Isabella thought of herself as allegorized in the figure of the goddess of wisdom) and *Parnassus*, both now in the Louvre. Nobody, it appears, will ever know exactly who made what concessions to whom, or what Mantegna had in mind in the so-called *Parnassus*. There have even been suggestions that Mantegna, now in his sixties, might have been very gently pulling his young patroness's leg—an unlikely possibility in view of the general severity of his temperament.

Such a personality was imperfectly adapted to the requirements of ornamenting a salon in an appropriately feminine character, but Mantegna sufficiently modified his manner to create a pair of pictures where sensuous opulence, ornamental elegance, and his own unrelenting formal disciplines are combined into a somewhat uneasy emulsion. It is plain that the dancing nymphs, the graceful god-youths, and the naked Venus of *Parnassus* were not his true vision of antiquity. His antiquity was the Rome of military conquest, a fiercely masculine world where the forces of violence are often shown triumphant in war, but where the uncomprehending brutality of the centurions, magnificent in their brutality if you wish, is defeated in the end by the faith that sustains their victims, the Christian martyrs, in their magnificent agony.

Carlo Crivelli was born sometime between 1430 and 1435, in Venice, and died sometime between 1495 and 1500. Virtually nothing is known about him during the sixty or more years of his life, beyond two isolated documented events: in 1457, when he was in his twenties, he was convicted of rape and imprisoned, and in 1490, when he was in his fifties, he was knighted. After his release from prison he left Venice, and his wanderings from city to city in northern Italy can be followed by means of the paintings he left behind. During these years he developed a style individual sometimes to the point of eccentricity in the expression of religiosity so extreme as to skirt morbidity on the one hand while barely missing mere affectation on the other.

Everything else about Crivelli's life and personality is either question or questionable deduction. He was possibly the son of a painter, Jacopo Crivelli. Another Crivelli, Vittorio, who imitated his style but could never be mistaken for more than an imitator, was perhaps his brother. Carlo might have been trained in the workshop of any one of several early Venetian painters, but he is most easily tied to Squarcione's workshop in Padua, and to the young Mantegna, who worked there. Squarcione's desiccated style with its garlands and antique fragments seems the likeliest point of departure for Crivelli's wiry one.

Since he would have been only twenty-two or at most twenty-seven when he was convicted in 1457, Crivelli was either just out of his apprenticeship or just beginning to get established on his own. He was condemned to six months in prison for abducting the wife of an absent seaman and keeping her sequestered for months in his house, where he "knew her flesh in contempt of God and the sanctity of matrimony."

The questions begin. Just how does one go about such an abduction, and how is the victim kept undiscovered for so long in a city as busy and as compactly built as Venice? A twentieth-century author of thrillers might have answers here. Then there is the psychological puzzle: what curious passion could have demanded satisfaction under such difficulties in a city famous for the variety and accessibility of its fleshly pleasures?

Upon his release from prison, Crivelli fled Venice. Because of the disgrace? Possibly, although other artists in Renaissance Italy suffered legal convictions without hindrance to their careers, and flourished professionally during lifetimes of personal notoriety. Because he feared the vengeance of the wronged husband? It would seem reasonable. Because of a feeling of anguish over the nature of his crime? Any answer here would depend on pure imagination.

After King Ferdinand of Naples knighted him thirty-three years later, Crivelli always added his title to his signature. Professional pride? Why not? Personal vanity? Conceivably. Or the aging man's reiteration during the few remaining years of his life that his early sin had been atoned for by a long history of good behavior and reverent paintings? Any speculations here would drop us into the center of the romantic quicksand.

Whatever kind of man he was, Crivelli as an artist during these decades of self-exile was both busy and isolated—busy with commissions but isolated from developments in the centers where his exact contemporaries, Mantegna in Padua and Giovanni Bellini in Venice, trained in the same workshop tradition as he, were bringing the Renaissance to fulfillment with their explorations. Crivelli might not have been interested in making explorations in any case, of course. What we can see, without speculation, is that working in such towns as Fermo, Macerata, Fabriano, Ascoli, and other places in the Marches, Crivelli turned inward as an artist. He not only devoted himself exclusively to religious subjects, but painted them without humanistic modifications. At the height of the Renaissance he remained a Gothic lyricist.

Crivelli's style is so sharp and thin from detail to detail that the effect is brittle, even spidery, in spite of rich golden backgrounds and the sumptuous colors that he laid across his dry, unyielding forms, forms defined with lines that seem to have been drawn with the edge of a razor and that for all their roundness have no solidity, as if they had been pressed from tin and enameled. The description does not sound flattering. And yet these Madonnas and saints with tendons like wires stretched across thin bones, surrounded by festoons of speckled fruits and vegetables and curled leaves, are all part of a systematic stylization that in Crivelli's favorite subject, the Lamentation, can raise a state of emotional tension to the point of hysteria and freeze it there.

In his very late work, Crivelli's manner sometimes cancels out emotion and he seems nothing more than a supremely decorative painter. But even when he offers nothing but his manner, he offers it so completely that one is tempted to accept the surface and let everything else go. Crivelli is the most brilliant exemplar of the Squarcionesque formula, which gave a special character to north Italian art outside Venice and Padua, the centers of its most impressive developments. And if he can be regarded as *retardataire* in his retention of Gothicisms, he can also be thought of as a prophet of the mannerist artists who in the next century revived them. Altogether, he is one of those painters whose art immediately supplies its own exception to any generality that it seems to prove.

Mantegna, in Padua, proved that the stylistic tricks of his master, Squarcione, could furnish seeds for noble and dramatic expression. From the same source, Carlo Crivelli developed a style combining an ornate manner with extreme emotional tension. Another painter of just their age, Cosimo Tura, demonstrated how excellently the same tricks could be refined and elaborated into a style of theatrical affectation.

Tura was the first great painter of the Ferrarese school, and was at work in that city in 1451, sometime after the age of twenty. (His birth date is determinable only as "before 1431.") He developed his style from Mantegna's example, if not from direct contact with Squarcione's prolific workshop. Also, somewhere beneath the swaddling layers of ornament, a skeleton of Piero della Francesca's monumental figures can be imagined, if no longer felt. Tura's style became the pattern for a school as distinctive, and as elaborately artificial, as any in Italy during his century. It was in a way a reactionary style: although neohumanist themes were pictured, they were pictured with Gothic complications of extreme sophistication.

In his superbly self-conscious exhibitionism, Tura designed serpentine locks of hair as rigid and as gleaming as polished brass, and brazen thrones where decorative details were spun out to hairlike delicacy. His draperies, exaggerating the clinging folds painted by Mantegna, ceased to have more than a nominal relationship to the natural fall of cloth. The joints of his figures were bent with the angular inflexibility of manikins, and their flesh, modeled with exaggeratedly high reflected lights, was like painted tin. Although his paintings are filled with jewels, these are like clearest tinted crystal rather than true gems. In spite of his high style and the great attraction of his manner, Tura bears to Mantegna something of the same glass-as-against-jewel relationship. He is an immediately effective artist, and then before long a rather wearisome one.

The Este family of Ferrara were not the most agreeable of patrons, and Tura suffered from their parsimony. But he does not appear to have been very adventurous, either as a painter or as a man. His style changed very little during his lifetime, and he remained in Ferrara in spite of the frustrations and discouragements he suffered at the provincial court. The greatest of these came with the rise of a slightly younger painter, Francesco Cossa. Although Tura outlived his rival, who died in 1478, he gave up his position as court painter in 1486, when he was nearing sixty. After that he dragged on for another nine years, dying in 1495.

Tura's efforts to graft some of Cossa's themes onto his work, in the hope, perhaps, of their bringing with them some of Cossa's freshness, were not successful. Tura was an estimable painter and a brilliant designer, but his range was limited, and it is impossible to feel that anything much lies beneath the surfaces he painted. His personages, if struck, would ring in their hollowness and probably chip.

Francesco Cossa is usually given second place to Cosimo Tura as the finest of the Ferrarese masters, but he has his own club of enthusiastic advocates who would like to see him recognized in the top spot. Only a few years younger than Tura, Cossa possibly worked or studied with him; his style has much of the same metallic, mannered character. But where the fascination of Tura is in the consistent extremity of this manner, the delight of Cossa is that, though the manner is present with its special hard, dry Ferrarese flavor, it is tempered by a zest for life, a love of the look of animals, a lively response to the activities of the daily world, a great talent for the staging of pageantry, and, in his late work, a humanistic content that is only incidental in Tura.

These rather disparate merits are combined in the surviving work (Cossa has suffered greatly from loss and destruction) by which he is usually judged: his frescoes in the main hall of the Palazzo Schifanoia in Ferrara. Working with the astrologer of the Este court (one Pellegrino Prisciani) and probably following a general plan laid out by Tura, as court artist, Cossa painted a series of symbolical spectacles of the twelve months of the year, along the old medieval formula. Five of these have been destroyed. The remaining seven are beautifully staged pageants of the tasks and pleasures of men under the supervision of the heavens, with a cast of gods and goddesses, knights and laborers, huntsmen and farmers, weavers and embroiderers, ladies and gentlemen of the court of Borso d'Este, and scholars and students of the local university.

The best-known portion of the Schifanoia frescoes is the scene showing the triumph of Venus in the month of April, in which the goddess, decked out in court dress, rides in state on a floating throne drawn by swans, with a panoplied knight chained in perpetual adoration at her feet. But Cossa's vivacity and variety are of such range that it would be difficult to choose between the delightful affectations of this precious allegory and the equally delightful scene filled with realistic observations where workmen are going about their business of pruning vines in the month of March.

Cossa was working on these frescoes in 1469, when he was about thirty-three. Fetching as they are, they merely hint at his developing power. In his later altarpieces he modified the rather tricky stylizations inherited from Tura, approaching Piero della Francesca (a strong influence) in the serenity and sobriety of his modeling. We can only guess at the degree of Cossa's final achievement, since his masterpiece, the decorations for the Garganelli Chapel in San Pietro in Bologna, was destroyed in 1605.

Cossa's career was divided between Ferrara, where he was born (c. 1436), and Bologna, where he died, probably of the plague, and probably at the age of forty-two. We know little about him as a man, or about the events of his life. Vasari confused him with one of his pupils, Lorenzo Costa, thus leaving us without even a faulty early record, and scholars are still trying to separate what remains of his work from the confusions of various misattributions. There are many records of payments for commissions, and Cossa also appears in baptismal records as a godfather—an appealing hint as to the kind of man he might have been. He was touchingly eulogized by friends upon his death, but he remains a vaguely defined personality and, to a distressing degree, a lost artist.

After the death of Francesco Cossa in 1478 and Cosimo Tura's retirement from the post of court painter to the Este family in 1486, the leadership of the Ferrarese school passed to Ercole Roberti (Ercole d'Antonio de' Roberti), who was born in 1450 or thereabouts and died in 1496. Formed by Tura and by Cossa, whose pupil he probably was, Roberti succeeded Tura in the post of court painter. Although attributions are confused, it is apparent that he modified the hard-bitten Ferrarese style with an element of pathos adopted from Giovanni Bellini.

The Ferrarese school reached its end with Lorenzo Costa, who was born and had his training in Ferrara but moved in his twenties to Bologna, where he worked with Francesco Francia. His Ferrarese intensity, learned from the examples of Tura, Cossa, and Roberti, struck a compromise with another extreme, Francia's exaggerated Umbrian sweetness. But Lorenzo Costa retained a connection with the Este family. In 1506, he succeeded Mantegna as court painter to Isabella d'Este in Mantua. He was in his forties at this time in his career, having been born about 1460. He died in 1535.

VENICE

A city as special as Venice is bound to give a special color and flavor to its arts, by the simple and delightfully inescapable fact of its surrounding its artists twenty-four hours a day. Of course Florence, and Rome, and Siena, and other Italian cities and other great cities all over world also have their special colors and flavors, but no other city is as consummately individual, as intensely special as Venice. Florence and Rome, London and Paris, are city-personalities created over centuries by generations of men whose thoughts and activities are reflected in the physical forms they imposed upon their habitats, during a process of continuous change. But Venice took on its extraordinary physical character early in the game, and kept it. Its beauty and the limitations of its site combined to make it invulnerable to drastic change, and it became a city where artists were first of all Venetians. The city affects its inhabitants more than the inhabitants affect the city, and artists accepted happily, as a gift rather than as a restriction, the character that Venice imposed upon them.

The light that was part water, the water that was part light, the buildings rising like visions from the sea, and the self-containment of a small place that, like the neck of an hourglass, served as a two-way funnel between the Orient and the West without being fully a part of either—all this created an ambience so pervasive and so alluring that artists could hardly have struggled for expression in other terms even if they had felt a rebellious obligation to do so. The Venetian ambience generated an art more lyrical than intellectual, more sensuous than philosophical, and except in its most profound expressions more mundane than spiritual.

In spite of its specialness, Venetian art was never provincial, nor was it stultified in its self-containment. Venetian styles grew, decayed, and were replaced by others in the natural course of things; they contributed to the development of styles in the rest of Italy, and drew from them. But Venetian art was always consistently Venetian beneath the changes. Sometimes the painters glorified Venice as a visual fact that had all the fantasy of an improbable invention; always, without trying, they celebrated Venice in their psychological reflections of their city, whose personality had become part of everything they thought and felt.

Venice was a city of such splendor that the picturesque spectacle of its decay in the eighteenth century was as rewarding to artists as its golden perfection had been during the Renaissance, and it is still a city whose specialness no amount of neon, or motorized gondolas, or Coney Island tourists, can obliterate.

The paternity of this or that school of painting is always being awarded to this or that artist, and usually the attribution is disputable. In the case of Venetian painting, however, there is no argument. The title of father belongs to Giovanni Bellini, who during a lifetime of some eighty-six years traveled the whole road from the late Middle Ages to the High Renaissance and traveled it from beginning to end as a Venetian through and through.

If there were any question, Giovanni's father Jacopo and his brother Gentile could be called in as allies, and the title given to the Bellini family as a whole. The period from Jacopo's birth to Giovanni's death stretched over the entire fifteenth century and ran sixteen years into the next. Granting Jacopo his master-painter's papers at a normal age, this means that for something like ninety-five years there was at least one Bellini at work. For thirty years, while he was begetting his sons and training them to follow in his craft, Jacopo was establishing the name alone. Then for twenty years the two generations were at work at the same time. For another thirty years after old Jacopo's death the two sons led the field in tandem, and after Gentile died Giovanni carried on for another decade. The family was long-lived: their average age at death was seventy-eight.

During Giovanni's lifetime Giorgione was born, entered Giovanni's studio, painted during the brief span allotted to him, and died. Giovanni's probable other pupil, Titian, had only to pick up where Giovanni and Giorgione left off, and seems to have begun in the most direct possible way, by finishing Giovanni's final masterpiece. It is a wonderful picture, *The Feast of the Gods,* now in the National Gallery in Washington. Filled with golden evening light, it is an arcadian lyric to the miracle of sensuous experience, chastened by the nostalgia of an old man who knew that even a Bellini could not expect to enjoy Venice forever.

Jacopo Bellini, the founding patriarch of this two-generation dynasty, was born in Venice—the son of a plumber or tinsmith—about 1400 and died there, famous, in 1470 or 1471. We have, at least, Vasari's word that he was famous, and existing records of contracts or payments for commissions certainly show that he was in demand. (The records also show a grant of twenty ducats upon the occasion of his daughter Nicolosia's wedding to Andrea Mantegna.) Jacopo's work has largely disappeared; not one of the recorded commissions exists, and there are hardly enough other paintings signed by him or attributable to him to summon up more than a shadow of the painter that he must have been. But he exists vividly in two books of drawings, one of them in the British Museum, and another that found its way into the Louvre after travels that took it as far as Constantinople, where Gentile Bellini had carried it as a gift to the Sultan in 1479.

Jacopo began his career and probably did his best painting in the so-called International Style, at first under the direct influence of Gentile da Fabriano, and later under the influence, direct or indirect, of Pisanello. Only eight years old when Gentile da Fabriano came to Venice in 1408, Jacopo may have gone to Florence with him as his apprentice when Gentile went there six years later. Jacopo certainly knew him in Florence at some time and came into contact with the cosmopolitan circle there. And if Vasari is right, he regarded Gentile as his foster father.

Jacopo's paintings, such of them as we have, are close to Gentile da Fabriano in style. His drawings often reflect Pisanello's inexhaustibly spirited elegance. But other drawings show that he went beyond both these late-Gothic masters (he outlived his contemporary, Pisanello, by at least fifteen years) to cross the border into the Renaissance. He experimented with the perspective theories of Uccello and Alberti, and spent the last years of his life learning from his sons. There may be some question as to Jacopo Bellini's greatness as a painter, but without any question at all he was a great father. He was also a grateful foster son (if we may believe Vasari), for he seems to have named his own first son after Gentile da Fabriano.

Gentile Bellini was born in 1429. When he was seventy-seven years old he decided it was time to make his will, and he did so, on February 18, 1506. He left to his assistants a set of drawings to be divided equally among them; to his brother Giovanni (who was only seventy-six) he left the obligation to complete a picture that he, Gentile, had begun for the Scuola di San Marco, as well as the payment when it should become due, plus a book of their father's drawings. (Giovanni failed to complete the picture, and the book was to go along with everything else to Gentile's second wife. His first had died when he was sixty-five.) He also asked a little something for himself: he wanted to be buried in the Church of Santi Giovanni e Paolo. One year and five days later, on February 23, 1507, he was.

Gentile's last year must have been the only inactive period in that long life. He was thirty-one in 1460 when he signed, with his father and brother, an altarpiece for a chapel in Sant'Antonio in Padua. From then on the records show a succession of contracts that kept him busy from year to year. He also had his full share of honors attending his professional eminence. By the time he was forty the emperor Frederick III had made him a *cavaliere* of Venice and the Palatine Court, and when he was fifty the Venetian Signoria appointed him an emissary to the court of Mohammed II in Constantinople. Bearing the famous book of his father's drawings as a gift to the Sultan, he made the trip in a state galley and spent a year as the Sultan's guest.

The slight flaw in this Eastern adventure was that Gentile had been second choice for the post. The Sultan had asked to meet Giovanni after receiving some paintings by him as presents from the Venetian Republic in an exchange of diplomatic courtesies. There is always the possibility that Giovanni did not want to make the trip and convinced the Signoria that he should be excused, but the probability is that they were unwilling to risk losing their finest painter on such an expedition and sent another excellent one instead.

This comparison between Giovanni and Gentile must always occur when they are considered together. Giovanni was a very great painter, and Gentile merely a first-rate one

—in a century, however, when genius was bred so prolifically that to be among the first-raters was to excel the standard of greatness accepted in other times.

Gentile's limitation was that his capacity to record the spectacle of external reality sufficed him. Not being very imaginative, he seldom commented or interpreted. But the limitation is offset by the character of the external spectacle that surrounded him. His *Procession in the Piazza San Marco* in the Academy in Venice, while nominally dealing with a miraculous history, records in minute factual detail the appearance of that square—as sumptuously celestial a spot as any that the man-made world offers—on full display as the setting for a religious procession of monks accompanying a reliquary. Any response that is stirred in the observer is stirred by association: Gentile has made no effort to elicit it. What interested him, and what continues to interest us, is his rendering of the look of the place, down to the last detail of the mosaics on the façade of the great church that serves as a glittering backdrop.

In the companion painting, *The Miracle of the True Cross* (also in the Academy), he takes us into the Venetian back streets, telling the story of a wonder in almost gossipy terms. According to the legend, a reliquary with a fragment of the True Cross having fallen into a canal while the procession was crossing a bridge, the monk who dived in to retrieve it from the bottom was miraculously buoyed up by the heavy golden weight and carried to shore. The incident is reported in such matter-of-fact terms that it is not irreverent to notice that the happy monk, as he speeds through the water toward safety, seems less the subject of divine intervention than a water sportsman enjoying a spin with a new form of outboard motor. Ranks of dignitaries and their wives (each one a portrait of an eminent Venetian) regard the event in the attitude of prayer, but their faces and their costumes are more interesting than their states of mind or soul, neither of which, in truth, is described at all. As to the populace, it goes about its business unmoved. So attractive in its explicit actuality is this picture of Venice that the miraculous event becomes little more than a bit of byplay in a locale where even the commonplace is extraordinary.

Gentile Bellini was a draftsman of static objects. Even those nominally in motion seem transfixed: the monk being borne to shore in the canal is arrested forever in that spot, and the wavelets in his wake will never move. The fact that Gentile was not interested in the expression of motion is a negative factor that has taken on a positive character in our eyes: the motionlessness seems enchanted in a way that Gentile never calculated. But his art must not be sold short. If Gentile does not rise above his pictorial material, he rises to it, and under the circumstances that is enough.

Giovanni Bellini is traditionally given the birth date of 1430, which would make him a year younger than Gentile. Actually, Giovanni was probably a bit older than his brother, and perhaps only a half brother. He seems to have been an illegitimate child, born either to Jacopo and his wife Anna Riversi before their marriage, or to Jacopo from another liaison and then adopted into the family. He died in 1516, which gives him a generous allotment of eighty-six years at the least. Ten years before Giovanni's death, Albrecht Dürer met him in Venice and described him in a letter as "very old, but still the best painter of them all." Dürer's Italian friends had warned him "not to eat and drink with their painters," an envious and backbiting lot, but, Dürer reports, "Giovanni Bellini has highly praised me before many nobles." Giovanni wanted something of Dürer's and offered to pay well for it. Everywhere, Dürer was assured that Giovanni Bellini was an honest man.

Whatever else he was, Giovanni was hardworking. The

enormous number of paintings optimistically ascribed to him include far too many by his followers—he had a tremendous influence on younger painters after he reached maturity— but, even so, his own output was prodigious.

His greatness lies in the gentle harmony of light, color, and mood that invests everything he painted, whether pagan allegories or Christian Madonnas, and it is difficult to imagine him as anything but a man of reserved, poetic, perhaps slightly melancholy temperament. He was not too proud to go to Dürer, the young German, rather than summon Dürer to come to him, but he was quite aware that he was the grand old man of Venetian painting and he refused to be dictated to by even the most distinguished patrons. Over a period of six years the ambitious little Isabella d'Este* was determined that he should produce for her a painting after her own recipe, but she didn't get her painting until she gave the old man freedom to do exactly what he wanted.

In a rather contradictory way, Giovanni Bellini was an individualist but not, in a strict sense, an innovator. His consistent development of an increasingly personal mood was stimulated by the work of other artists as he discovered them in sequence, and the account of his self-discovery, his progress toward full realization, makes him sound like the last thing he could ever have been—a borrower and an eclectic. He began, of course, as his father's student, follower, and assistant, and he also learned by the example of Antonio Vivarini, a younger rival of his father's. But the turning point came for him when he encountered Andrea Mantegna. Giovanni was about twenty-three when Mantegna married his sister Nicolosia in 1453, and Mantegna was the dominant influence on his art—dominant except for the eternal dominant of Giovanni's own temperament—for twenty years. During this time he Venetianized (the word is not a very good one, but it

* Or Isabella Gonzaga, as you wish.

must do) the harsh Mantegnesque landscape into somewhat more dulcet forms; he gave the almost morbidly arid intensity of Mantegna's fiercely masculine world a leavening of tenderness, and he began to endow his contours with a lambency that slightly softened the uncompromising definition of Mantegna's forms.

Giovanni Bellini developed slowly, and when he was in his early forties he was still held in check by a Mantegnesque severity that, even poeticized to the possible limit, obdurately refused to bend to Giovanni's gentler, more reflective spirit. But the works of this period are superb; their incompleteness of expression is apparent only in comparison with the last works, and even if Giovanni had died at this time he would have come down to us as the first true poet of Venetian painting. There were technical obstacles to overcome before he could achieve the melting color and the glowing light appropriate to the mood he strove to express. The tempera technique that suited Mantegna in its precise definition of detail could not yield the blended transitions from color to color and from light to shadow that were imperative to Giovanni. He made some advances with the technique of glazing in oil over tempera, but he did not fully realize himself until he discovered Piero della Francesca and then Antonello da Messina in the early 1470's.

From Piero's art he learned how serenely a simplified form could occupy logical space, and from Antonello da Messina he learned the perfected technical formula for oil that gave him control over the light which impregnated that space and deepened and enriched all colors. It is possible, even, that Giovanni's understanding of Piero della Francesca came to him more at second hand through Antonello than through acquaintance with Piero's work.

But the important thing is that after Antonello left Venice in 1476, Giovanni, nearing fifty, came into the fulfillment of his powers. Without rhetoric, without sentimentalism, with no preciosities or affectations of style, he created a poetry of light and color that was as calm as it was rapturous, as much a glorification of the physical world as a meditation upon our mystical relationship to it. He imparted this vision to his young pupils Giorgione and Titian, and in turn learned from their response to it. In his lifetime he had taken Venetian painting from its Gothic senescence through its Renaissance youth and had pointed the way toward its climactic triumph in Titian.

The Vivarini and Antonello da Messina, mentioned in connection with the Bellini, and another Venetian, Jacopo de' Barbari, had best be interpolated just here before we go on to consideration of Carpaccio and Giorgione.

Born in Murano about 1420, Antonio Vivarini died in Venice between 1476 and 1484. Like Jacopo Bellini, he was influenced by Gentile da Fabriano, but his style was more ornate and vivacious—in many ways more appealing—than Jacopo's. Antonio was also a rival, though hardly a close one, of Jacopo Bellini as the head of a dynasty of Venetian painters. His much younger brother Bartolommeo Vivarini (*c.* 1432-*c.* 1491) was of an age with the two Bellini sons, and became a follower of Mantegna in an exaggeratedly tight, dry style. Antonio's son Alvise Vivarini (*c.* 1446-1503/5) was one of the generation of younger painters who came under the influence of Giovanni Bellini. He followed the master's mature, luminous manner with considerable skill.

Antonello da Messina (*c.* 1430-1479) spent most of his life in his native Messina. In 1475 he was in Venice, where Giovanni Bellini, according to Vasari's romanticized account, visited his studio in disguise in order to learn the "secret" technique of oil painting. Vasari also gave Antonello a trip to the Netherlands; it now appears that he learned the technique from Petrus Christus when that artist was in Italy. Antonello is known by hardly more than a dozen signed or documented works and about the same number of attributable ones; he is a mysterious figure still in process of clarification by scholarship, and it begins to appear that he must be recognized as a pivotal figure in Venetian painting, equal in importance—historical importance—to Giovanni Bellini, since through Giovanni he revitalized the school.

Apparently a Venetian painter, Jacopo de' Barbari remains obscure to us until 1500, when, at the age of fifty or sixty, he turns up in Germany and the Netherlands, a conspicuous figure in the graphic arts during the last sixteen years of his life. He was born sometime between 1440 and 1450 and died about 1516. A generation older than Dürer, Barbari was a strong influence on the young German and, in turn, borrowed from him. Among other things (Dürer tells us), he showed Dürer some studies of a male and a female figure constructed in the proportions of a geometrical canon that he would not disclose, and thus set Dürer off on a search for the secret of human movement and the body's ideal measurements that lasted for the rest of his life—a single instance of Barbari's introduction of Italian ideas into the German Renaissance.

But if Barbari was considered a fascinating artist in the North, the Italians—Dürer reported from Venice, in a letter of 1506 to his great friend Willibald Pirckheimer—sneered at the expatriate, saying that if he had been good enough to meet the competition at home, he would never have left. The sneer seems not quite justified, for although Barbari was far from a great master he was a talented artist with a sensuous, languid style of considerable appeal, even though it may seem a bit commonplace by the most poetic standards of Venetian art.

Undoubtedly inspired by Dürer, Barbari created a wood-cut map of Venice in twelve joining sheets, each 26 inches high and 18 to 20 inches wide, that is one of the famous ornamental achievements of his generation. His patrons in the North included Emperor Maximilian I; Frederick the Wise, duke of Saxony; and Margaret of Austria, governess of the Netherlands, who granted him a pension in his old age. She so treasured a sketchbook of his that she would not yield it to Dürer, succumbing to neither his pleas nor his gifts.

Just when he should have been in his prime, something happened to Vittore Carpaccio that changed him from a delightful painter into a second-rater who went through his paces with lassitude for the rest of his life. He was born about 1465, was probably a pupil of Gentile Bellini, and until his early forties, painting in his own special variant of Gentile's lively narrative manner, he seemed incapable of dullness. After that, until his death in 1526, he seemed incapable of anything else.

There is a good chance that what is most delightful to us in Carpaccio's art is something he had no idea he was putting there. He was a chronicler of Venetian daily life in the guise of religious paintings, and his special charm is that he reflects that life with a combination of almost primitive naïveté and youthful worldliness that gives piquancy to work that he certainly turned out without theorizing in any such direction. He was a professional who competed for big commissions and gave the customers their money's worth. Both he and the customers would have been astounded to know that his art might one day appeal through the faint stiffness of its drawing and the innocent enthusiasm of its catalogue of the creatures, the flowers, the houses, the households, the courtesans, the dignitaries, and all the rest of life in a city where everything was a pageant and everybody was enamored of his home town.

Carpaccio was a specialist in the cycle paintings commissioned by the *scuole,* or confraternities, of Venice—brotherhoods of professionals whose halls might be decorated with appropriate histories, ordinarily recounting the lives of patron saints. Carpaccio told these stories with a zest that removed everything prosaic from what might otherwise have been mere pedestrian illustration. So far as he was concerned, he was a pictorial realist. But the faintly archaic flavor of his style, inherent in the period that was just ending, and his use of an encyclopedia of everyday things in staging stories of miracle, give his art to our eyes that combination of objective statement and irrational theme so dear to the surrealists. That he had no such ideas in mind does not change the look of his art for the twentieth century.

John Ruskin rediscovered Carpaccio, though not exactly in our terms, in 1876. Carpaccio's own generation outgrew him. Then the later sixteenth century found him a "very diligent master," by Vasari's estimate, the word "diligent" being one he reserved for artists whose ability was limited to the imitation of nature. In the next century another chronicler of the lives of artists, Carlo Ridolfi, admitted that, although a merely diligent painter, Carpaccio could be praised for having "sweetened" his style. The eighteenth century, with Charles Nicolas Cochin as its spokesman, was equally grudging in granting Carpaccio any merit for his "things rendered with ingenuousness and precision of a lowly nature and without taste, but true." Other writers allowed him some merit as a straight reporter, which is certainly not where his merit lies for us, but it was not until the nineteenth century, with its romantic vision, that Carpaccio seemed anything more than a genre painter with an excessively dry style.

The nineteenth century found Carpaccio appealing without quite knowing why. Some of the critical judgments, while sympathetic, sound very curious. At last Ruskin perceived in *The Dream of St. Ursula* (an episode from a cycle begun in 1490 for the Scuola di Santa Orsola and now in the Academy in Venice) the quality of magic that transformed the objects of a Venetian bedroom into the accessories of miracle. He recognized the special quality of naïveté that Carpaccio never intended, but recognized also his skill in the manipulation of light and his great power as a colorist.

It was precisely as a colorist and a painter of light that Carpaccio seemed to his contemporaries to fall short. Giorgione and Giovanni Bellini had opened Venetian color to full diapason in floods of light. Carpaccio's rich but rather flat color, his simply directed light, and his comparatively rigid form—all harmonizing so beautifully with one another —began to seem old-fashioned and awkward when he was in mid-career. Apparently they seemed inadequate to him, also, but he was unable to build upon them. He fumbled for direction. He pulled himself together for another beautiful cycle of 1502-7 in the Scuola di San Giorgio degli Schiavoni and then, a comparatively young man, gave only an occasional glimpse of his past greatness for the last twenty years of his life. A hardworking professional who was unaware of his special quality, Carpaccio denied his virtues without managing to develop others.

Giorgio (or, in Venetian dialect, Zorzi) da Castelfranco, called Giorgione, stands as a revolutionary artist whose brief activity, occupying a perfect moment, coincided with the terminating career of his probable teacher, Giovanni Bellini, through whom Venetian painting attained its Renaissance peak, and the opening career of his colleague Titian, who not so much carried on where Giorgione left off as brought Giorgione's innovations to fulfillment. Giorgione died so young that even the old Bellini, nearly fifty years his senior, outlived him by six years, and shared the "perfect moment" under the influence of Giorgione's achievement.

Giorgione was born about 1477. Thirty-three years later, on October 23, 1510, Isabella d'Este wrote to one Taddeo Albani in Venice, asking that he purchase for her a certain painting by Giorgione, and was answered under date of November 7 that Giorgione had died of the plague a few days before.

The owners of the picture refused to part with it in any case. Giorgiones were not quite as rare then as they are now, but they were rare enough. The thirty-odd years of his life gave Giorgione only about a decade as a mature painter, and today there are hardly half a dozen paintings that are accepted as his without serious question by the various scholars who try to straighten out and enlarge the obscure facts of his life. But on the basis of these few paintings he holds his position as the central figure of the great Venetian triad—Giovanni Bellini, Giorgione, Titian.

Giorgione was not only the first painter of the full Venetian Renaissance; he was also a prototype of the modern artist. Possibly his contemporaries could have told you whether or not his undisputed masterpiece, which we call *The Tempest* (Venice, Academy) for lack of a title, is based on poetry or mythology, but perhaps, too, the subject was as mysterious to them as to us. No one has been able to attach a literary or philosophical source to it, and critics generally admit that it is time to stop trying and let the painting stand as an independent poetic evocation, as Giorgione in all probability intended it to do.

On a verdant bank, a young woman, clad only in a small white cape that covers her shoulders, sits beside a stream nursing a baby. On the other side of the stream a richly clothed young man leans gracefully on a staff and regards her. There are bits of ruined architecture, a rustic bridge, a few buildings not far away, and in the distance a domed structure. Everything is perfectly quiet except the sky, where a bolt of lightning splits the clouds.

Recent X-rays have revealed that in place of the young man Giorgione had originally painted another woman about to enter the water. So drastic a change enforces the conclusion that Giorgione was making but the loosest reference, if any at all, to a story or other specific source in *The Tempest*—which is sometimes called *Soldier and Gypsy*, although the young man is not a soldier and the young woman is not a gypsy. Giorgione, surely, was interested only in the creation of a poetic mood, a mood independent of any reference outside the picture, and it is here that his modernity lies.

He rejected the illustration or interpretation of legend, of events either religious or secular, and even the exposition of established philosophical doctrines. *The Tempest*, in its freedom from external associations, points the way toward the complete abolition of subject matter in contemporary abstract art. The picture exists for itself within itself; painting becomes a way of seeing and feeling, not an auxiliary to thinking and clarifying. All normal relationships are ignored in order that everything—figures, landscape, sky—may be united in a dream relationship born of sensuous experience. The imagination is given full liberty. In *The Tempest*, art has already begun to exist for art's sake. It was to do so by rebellious declaration nearly four hundred years later as the first principle of the modern revolution.

Even in Florence, where painters, instead of being merely respected as superior workmen, could be adulated as creative spirits, painting had not reached this degree of independence. Giorgione's patrons were members of a special circle where painting, like music, was regarded as a purely aesthetic experience. Giorgione seems to have been an adequate performer on musical instruments, and a person of considerable elegance in his way of life in spite of his probably undistinguished origins. He may have been a member of a group where the teaching of Averroës, the twelfth-century Moslem physician and philosopher, was popular somewhat in the way Neoplatonism was popular in Florence and Rome, though its impact on the artist was markedly different.

Averroism was a materialistic and pantheistic philosophy that denied the immortality of the soul. It was thus harmonious with the traditional hedonism of Venice with its cultivation of the senses, which could produce on the one hand the most opulent brothels in Europe, on the other an art like Giorgione's, poeticizing sensuous experience. It is this transmutation of sensuous experience, hinted at by earlier Venetians and now fully realized by Giorgione, that makes him the first painter of the consummated Venetian Renaissance. His paintings are not only visual but also tactile experiences in the way they relay the warmth of luxuriant flesh, the coolness of grass, the feel of fine stuffs, all bathed in glowing light and caressed by air. To say that Giorgione's paintings are also audible would be, of course, grotesque, and yet descriptions of his work typically indulge in musical metaphors and even the sound of trickling water and the rustle of foliage.

Technically, Giorgione's revolution in sensuous expression was tied to his revolutionary conception of the function of color. At the time of Giorgione's death, Raphael was at work on his Vatican frescoes and Michelangelo was at work nearby on the Sistine Ceiling. Both these artists, even in these supreme expressions of the Renaissance, still thought of color as a tint applied to forms that were already defined by drawing. For Giorgione, form and color had become inseparable, as they are for modern painters. It is, naturally, quite possible to isolate one form from another in his paintings, but trying to separate it is like wrenching an organ from a body. Removing a figure from a Raphael or a Michelangelo would leave a neatly defined hole shaped by the contours of the figure; removing one from a Giorgione would mean the violation of the entire canvas, just as pulling up a plant by the roots would mean violation of the earth around them. The concept of pictorial form and pictorial composition as structures in color was developed more fully by Titian. It was to be approached semiscientifically by the impressionists, to become, with Cézanne, an element in the most drastic revolution in painting since Giotto. Giorgione's share in that revolution arrived at a moment, already called perfect, when tradition and revolution could be fused in harmony.

6

THE HIGH
RENAISSANCE

The names are staggering: Leonardo da Vinci, Raphael, Michelangelo, Titian, Dürer. Over a period of twenty years in the early sixteenth century, all these men were working in the full maturity of their powers. Leonardo painted the *Mona Lisa* and Michelangelo the Sistine Ceiling, probably the two best-known works of art in the world. Raphael created most of his works during these decades, including the ones accepted as his finest. Titian brought Venetian painting into full bloom; Dürer introduced the Renaissance in the North. And the accomplishments of Giorgione in Venice and Grünewald in Germany approach or equal theirs.

The term "High Renaissance" designates the period of fulfillment of a trend in Italian art that began with Masaccio. It is difficult, of course, to see how the art of Masaccio, of Piero della Francesca, of Mantegna, or of a dozen others, could be called less than fulfilled, each in itself. But the art of the High Renaissance has an expansiveness, a harmonious assurance, that distinguishes it from the art of any other period. In works of such abundant power that they seem to have been brought forth without a struggle, conception and technique complement one another so perfectly that the one cannot be isolated from the other.

The bounding dates of the High Renaissance vary from 1495/1500 to about 1520/1527. During the interval, Leonardo, the unrivaled scientist and theorist among artists, raised the Florentine ideal to a universal level. Raphael, younger than Leonardo by an entire generation and a provincial Umbrian when he started out, proved himself, before the end of his brief life, the purest example of the High Renaissance artist: his last series of works, in Rome, are consummate expressions of the ideal of calm, humanistic grandeur. And Michelangelo, supreme among them all, created the unapproachable masterpiece, the Sistine Ceiling. In his late work he questioned the assumption that this ideal order existed and could be discovered within the universe in spite of man's imperfections. With his questioning, the High Renaissance ended. It was not so much a period in the history of art as a brief pause at a point of perfect balance.

Leonardo, Raphael, and Michelangelo are the High Renaissance triad. The fourth great star was Titian—somewhat removed from the others and occupying a special position, like his native city, Venice, where he continued to declare the special harmony of the senses that the Venetians understood, identifying it, late in his life, with a harmony of the spirit.

In 1910, Sigmund Freud published "Leonardo da Vinci and a Memory of His Childhood," a psychoanalytic tour de force brilliant in its way but based on twin cornerstones of error and legend. The key error was the mistranslation of the name of a bird, which made a vulture out of a kite. The legend was invented by the writer Dmitri Merejkowski, as the tasty fictional filler between thin slices of honest bread in an appalling biographical sandwich called "The Romance of Leonardo da Vinci." Merejkowski's fantasies might better have served as the material for a psychoanalytic study of the author than as a source for Freud's study of Leonardo, who in the "Romance," so patly titled, is presented as the illegitimate son (that much is true) of a never-never mother with a Mona Lisa smile who gave him up for the child's own good, but was somewhat consoled by his nightly clandestine visits to snuggle up in her bed.

All this, of course, is today apparent to anybody, in terms of ordinary cocktail chatter, as the Oedipus-homosexual pattern with subsequent sublimations in art, but the picture of the relationship is absolutely unsupported by any records or recollections whatsoever. It is true that Leonardo was born (in 1452, in Vinci, a Tuscan village) to a peasant girl identified only as Caterina, and we know also that shortly thereafter she married one Acattabriga, a kiln operator. Leonardo lived with his mother and foster father until the age of five, when he was taken over to be raised in a more gentlemanly fashion by his true father, a prosperous notary, respected in his profession, named Piero da Vinci, whose own marriage had proved childless. But as E. H. Gombrich has pointed out in a discussion of "Leonardo da Vinci and a Memory of His Childhood," "We shall never know whether Leonardo's mother smiled, wept or was glad to be rid of him." Or whether the boy smiled, wept, or was glad to get away.

Leonardo did leave an account of the childhood memory referred to in Freud's title, telling of an occasion when the "vulture" alighted on his crib and thrust its tail into his mouth. The trouble here is that the psychoanalytic symbolisms that go for vultures do not go for kites. In addition, we have no way of knowing whether Leonardo told the story seriously or was only having a bit of fun satirizing superstitious belief in omens. Fortunately for himself, Freud is on record as regarding the study as a half-fictional invention (of which the factual half is error and legend) intended only as a demonstration of method. Unfortunately for Leonardo, the study is more popular as an authoritative portrait of a personality revealed on a posthumous psychoanalytic couch than it is as the half stunt, half exercise, that Freud found it entertaining to write.

Even so, Freud's reconstruction of Leonardo's personality is more convincing than most, if we allow for its concentration on morbidities, in particular Leonardo's homosexuality, which is admitted by most students to one degree or another. But the study is popular in one circle for the same reason that fictionalized biographies of Leonardo are popular in others: it at least gives form to a profoundly complex figure made even more complex by a plethora of sources (including Leonardo's own writings) all so confused, so contradictory, and so irremediably barnacled with surmise and invention, that we will be lucky if the whole thing is ever straightened out. We cannot think of Leonardo without being affected by this distorting and concealing accumulation, just as we cannot look at the *Mona Lisa* as a picture: it has become so familiar as an institution that we can hardly judge it as a work of art.

The presentation of Leonardo as the greatest genius who ever lived grows tiresome, but he is without question the very type of the genius as a person with endowments so extraordinary that they appear miraculous and must be accepted without being explained. No accomplishment seemed outside his range, whether it was dancing, singing, painting, or writing. But if we knew nothing of him except his handful of unfinished or mangled paintings, Leonardo might seem only a great talent rather than a genius. His true genius did not even lie in the staggering diversity of his talents, but in his insatiable curiosity about the physical world combined with an equal preoccupation with the inner world and his fusion of the two as a scientist-philosopher.

There was nothing in the universe that Leonardo was willing to leave unexplained, from the growth of plants to the formation of mountains, from the operation of the digestive system to the operation of the solar system, from the theory of movement of human and animal bodies to the principles of flight. In his investigations he was an empirical scientist ("No human investigation can be called true science without passing through mathematical tests"), and as such he has been called the first modern man.

But Leonardo also believed that the kind of knowledge obtained by observation and experiment in the laboratory is meaningless in itself, that it must be related to a mystically understood, universal order—and this belief united Leonardo with the centuries behind him. He was the apotheosis of the man of the Renaissance, an age that could still conceive of the possibility of universal knowledge, and did not recognize, as we do today, that the individual's knowledge must remain fractional. He lived during the last period in history when the ideal of total knowledge synthesized into complete harmony could be held to, and even during his lifetime the change was beginning. In the Sistine Chapel Michelangelo, twenty-three years younger than Leonardo, declared the tragedy of man's impotence in his battle against his own frailties, while, in the North, Dürer in his *Melencolia I* symbolically represented creative genius in despair, surrounded by all the paraphernalia of learning but defeated by the mysteries that learning cannot clarify.

Leonardo himself was a defeated genius. If he seems to have learned everything, he never managed to put what he had learned into order, or even to make it available to other people. The notebooks that he kept were not known until after his death, and although now they are being studied down to their last scribble, they remain a wonderful inchoate mass of recorded experiments, notes on ideas for development, random jottings, his best drawings, outlined treatises, jokes, maps, poems, whatever you will. The machines he invented on paper—three-speed transmission gears, pile drivers, water turbines, lathes, printing presses, airplanes, the prototype of the tank that won World War I for the Allies, and a hundred others—may have been only his own versions of ideas that were in the air, but they are so sound as engineering and so explicitly drawn that they have been constructed again and again in this century for exhibitions. His diagrams for these mechanical contrivances are beautiful as pure drawings. Nonetheless, there was a hiatus in his prophetic modernism: what we call the machine aesthetic was apparently foreign to him; he wrote that a merely useful thing could not be beautiful. Even so, he planned a double-decker city that the twentieth century has partially created through necessity but has yet to approach with either the logic or the beauty of Leonardo's scheme.

Leonardo investigated thermodynamics, air currents, and geological forces, inventing entire landscapes with moving clouds, rain, sun, lakes, and mountains in accordance with the natural laws that have created the earth's surface, and he peopled this surface with roads and cities according to the laws by which these, too, grow. He entered space with the study of methods for measuring the distance of the earth from the sun, anticipated some unfortunate developments with the invention of mechanical musical instruments, put forward the ideas of the revolving stage and the machine gun. He dissected bodies of men and animals and made the first true medical drawings, including one of a womb opened to disclose a foetus that is as touching to the emotions and as pleasing aesthetically when seen as pure drawing as it is accurately objective as a description. He drew plants that seem to thrust down their roots and lift their stalks in growth on the page. He accompanied some of the most beautiful architectural designs of the Renaissance with engineering drawings showing how to execute them, and planned a conical valve to regulate the flow of water through a pipe. His extensive notes on the art of painting were assembled into a treatise after his death. He made personal notations as unimportant as laundry lists, scrawled meaningless doodles, wrote down stories, identified the pattern of flowing water with the curling locks of a woman's hair and found parallels to both in air currents, investigated geometry, tied it aesthetically to laws of proportion, and in effect got nowhere with the whole business.

The notebooks are Leonardo. If they or his paintings had to be burned, and all memory lost in the burning, there would be no question as to which should be saved. Yet the notebooks present enough puzzles. There is no telling in exactly what order the notes were made, just where which ideas were changed to others, what the correlations between one subject and another would have been if Leonardo could have realized his intention of organizing the welter into a system. What it comes down to is that the universe was too much for Leonardo, just as it is for us. It was with him every moment of the day and night, we can be sure. Observing the world around him was a constant preoccupation with Leonardo, a way of life; he would try to calculate its pattern, piece by piece, as inevitably as he drew his next breath. And we must remember, if we are to have any picture of Leonardo, that while he was doing all this he was also working as the most respected engineer in Italy, often, and increasingly, in preference to painting. He regarded painting as an art supreme over sculpture, music, and poetry, but its practice interested him less than theories.

At an early age he had entered Verrocchio's shop in Florence, and at twenty he was accepted into the guild. Already in Florence he had become famous and sought after, both as a personality and as a painter. In 1482, when he was thirty, he stopped work in the middle of his *Adoration of the Magi* (now in the Uffizi) to work for Francesco Sforza in Milan, where his engineering projects were as important as the music, the pageants, the painting, and the sculpture that also occupied him professionally. He stayed for seventeen years, until Milan fell to the French in 1499, then in 1500 worked as a military engineer in Venice and Mantua.

Back in Florence for another six years, he spent two of them studying fortifications and engineering projects for Cesare Borgia. By this time he had all but abandoned painting. He was fifty-four when he returned to Milan to do an equestrian statue that was never completed; he returned to Florence in 1507-08, was back in Milan in 1508-13, in Rome in 1513-16 for Pope Leo X, doing various jobs including sets of measurements of St. Peter's. Now sixty-four, he went to France (he had made connections with the French court during his previous stay in Milan) and died on May 2, 1519, perhaps in the arms of the king, Francis I, as the legend-makers would have it.

This is only a list of dates and places, but it is something to cling to. Through it all we imagine Leonardo discussing projects with his patrons, but we cannot quite visualize him —as we cannot help visualizing Raphael—in the role of courtier or even as part of a social company—hardly, even, as part of a rarefied intellectual company where ideas were exchanged on a give-and-take basis. Even during his own lifetime Leonardo became a legend: he was his own intellectual circle, constantly pondering and investigating and filling his notebooks. Unromanticized efforts to discover for him a really close attachment have yielded only one, and that one has disturbed Leonardo's biographers by seeming to besmirch the godlike figure he has become.

In 1490, when he was thirty-eight years old, Leonardo took into his house a ten-year-old boy named Gian Giacomo de' Caprotti, and began a relationship that lasted for twenty-six years. Leonardo referred to the boy (then the youth, then the young man) as Salai—a synonym for Satan drawn from Luigi Pulci's "Morgante." Leonardo also called him a thief, a liar, and a glutton, but he bought him rings, necklaces, and princely clothes, took him with him on his travels, provided a dowry for his sister, and set up his father as tenant in his vineyards. Salai stole money from Leonardo, and from strangers, or, failing that, stole drawings to sell, sold the clothes Leonardo bought him, caroused in the streets, was in every way worthless, deceitful, and grasping—and was as beautiful as only the devil could be. When he was thirty-six and Leonardo sixty-four, Salai died from a gunshot wound, under what circumstances we do not know, but speculation on the subject can be colorful. Whether Leonardo's abandonment of Italy for France was connected with Salai's death, or whether the events were merely coincidental, again we can only conjecture.

Salai cannot be written off as a legend, and neither can the denunciations for sodomy suffered by Leonardo in his early twenties. Leonardo scholars who cannot stomach the record point out that the denunciation was anonymous and that the charge was dismissed. Anonymous accusations are bad enough in any case and loathsome in such a charge, but in Florence at that time, accusations of all kinds were accepted from the *tamburo,* a drum-shaped box in the Palazzo Vecchio available to everybody, and were then posted as public announcements that the cases would come to trial if witnesses volunteered to support them.

The denunciation against Leonardo named an artist's

model, Jacopo Saltarelli, as a youth who was "party to many wretched affairs and consents to please those persons who request such wickedness of him." The informer named four men of the "several dozen people about whom I know quite a lot" who had received Saltarelli's favors: a tailor, a goldsmith, "Lionardo di Ser Piero da Vinci, who lives with Andrea de Verrocchio," and finally Lionardo Tornabuoni. "These committed sodomy with said Jacopo. This I testify before you."

Since Leonardo's father was a solid citizen and the Tornabuoni family was one of the most powerful in Florence, it is hardly surprising that no witnesses materialized when the denunciation was posted in the usual way. The accused were absolved on the condition that the complaint be not repeated. But it was repeated, two months after the original one—again with the same result of conditional dismissal. That is all we know of the affair.

Until recently, especially during the nineteenth century, the anonymous denunciation was treated as an abominable slander against a man whose nobility of spirit made him, naturally, immune to a weakness that was hardly mentionable in any connection. Thus Leonardo was left with no sexual history at all; the field was opened for romantic inventions of a hopeless love between him and the model for the *Mona Lisa,* and Salai, angelic-looking child that he was, was thought of as having been adopted by Leonardo in an equally angelic spirit. Or, worse, Leonardo himself was adopted by unregenerate homosexuals as proof that their aberration and its indulgence are the normal accompaniments of sensitivities superior to the unimaginative passions of the heterosexual rank and file. Neither attitude will do. The homosexual aspects of Leonardo's character have to be accepted and examined if we are not to leave one more major gap in what we are able to reconstruct of his personality.

Several considerations, quite aside from current post-Kinsey social tolerances, make the affair of the denunciation less horrendous than it has seemed. We have to remember that the ancient philosophers provided the Renaissance humanists with a tradition of sorts for love between men, and it is also true that escapades with boys were indulged in as a kind of sport by the less intellectual among Renaissance citizens, with the Florentines and Venetians in the lead. The vice was always called unspeakable when it was spoken of officially, but was nevertheless joked about and engaged in as an aspect of high living that, at the worst, was hardly more reprehensible than carousal in a brothel.

So if we want to conjecture about Leonardo, where does he fit? Certainly not as the habitual participant in casual sexual brawls. The picture is totally inconsonant with everything that we know of him. But as a youth renowned for his good looks he must have been a conspicuous sexual target, and as one renowned for his strength he must have been a virile and inquisitive person strongly pushed toward the indulgence of lusts, natural or unnatural, that would explain at least an experiment or two of the kind he was accused of having committed with Jacopo Saltarelli.

When we come to his little Satan, years later, a different kind of rationalization is needed. If we can imagine a helpless passion stirred in the mature Leonardo by the fantastic beauty of a ten-year-old boy, we can hardly imagine this passion enduring for twenty-six years under degrading circumstances. To do so would require throwing away the Leonardo we know from the notebooks.

And the notebooks clarify things beyond any need of denying Leonardo's homosexual impulses, or condoning them or rationalizing them as a corollary to genius. Leonardo drew Salai again and again, and was obviously entranced by the little monster as a beautiful object. Salai's powerful attraction as a male possibly disturbed Leonardo for the same reasons that he would have been disturbed by an equally strong attraction to an equally beautiful and equally stupid and vicious girl. Leonardo regarded any subservience to uncontrolled impulses, sexual or other, as a defeat. He would have been the last man in the world to explain Salai by "I can't help myself," just as he would never have explained away a fit of anger or any other excess in this way.

Leonardo was not an ascetic or a puritan who regarded sensuality as an offense against a moral or religious code, or even against gentlemanly social behavior. He was a philosopher whose goal of deciphering, controlling, and harmonizing nature through knowledge was jeopardized by any surrender of volition. He refused to accept without examining them the subconscious impulses that all human beings share, that rise in us like appetites in other animals. The chances are that Leonardo was shocked by his youthful sexual adventure (and certainly by his attraction to Salai) as much as people are shocked who cannot accept it in him—but in a different way. Those who admire Leonardo as the perfect man cannot accept in him an action that is physically repellent and socially taboo. Leonardo could not accept in himself an action where spontaneous impulse was stronger than analytical will. Where his conventional admirers would have found a conventional love affair endearing, Leonardo himself might have found it, too, a disturbing symptom of weakness.

The stigma attached to declared and open homosexuality as a way of life never attached itself to Leonardo. He was an idol without feet of clay all his life. And since his writings (as private soliloquies rather than public statements) are filled with condemnations of lasciviousness and sensuality, including one elaborate allegory on lust and repentance, we must believe that, whatever lust might have moved Leonardo to bring the boy Salai into his house originally, Salai remained there for those twenty-six years not as a male mistress but as a model, a part servant, a decorative object, and as a personal devil who, once conquered within Leonardo's spirit, became only the shell of a devil. At the risk of romanticizing, we can imagine that Leonardo contemplated Salai in his day-to-day presence as the symbol of a personal victory—or, since the breadth of Leonardo's speculations makes them essentially impersonal, as the symbol of disorder conquered by intellectual discipline.

Salai could not have been much of a companion, except as a stray and not very gracious dog may be turned into one. Then who were Leonardo's friends? It is appalling to discover that as Leonardo moved from city to city, among all the patrons, intellectuals, and artists he knew and worked with, none emerges as his true companion and best friend. Among all these acquaintances, Giovanni Antonio Boltraffio (1467-1516), a Milanese aristocrat who painted more as a hobby than as a profession, came closest to filling the position, but there is not much indication of boon companionship even here. The mature Leonardo seems to have become by temperament a solitary, and the astral position that he has come to occupy is all the more effective because he stands so alone at the center of a universe that he rationalized into a harmony that, absent in life, must be synthesized by art.

The Last Supper, still in place in the former refectory of the Monastery of Santa Maria della Grazie in Milan, is Leonardo's statement of this synthesis in painting, even though we must read it, in its ruinous condition, only as we might listen to an echo. The painting's long history of decay and abuse began in Leonardo's lifetime, when the experimental medium he had employed began to flake off the wall, and reached its climax during World War II when the sandbags piled around it to save it from total destruction by bombing seemed, after removal, to have produced almost as disastrous an effect through dampness and mold. What we see now is the result of the most expert care directed toward removing everything except what is left of Leonardo's original and holding this soft, powdery, dreamlike ghost in place.

The dreaminess must be altogether discounted. No artist, ever, can have organized a painting more analytically than Leonardo organized this one, in a scheme that fused the interrelated lines and volumes of the geometrical framework with the interrelated psychological reactions of the disciples as they receive Christ's words that He is to die and that one of them will betray Him. Although artists before Leonardo had made a character study of each disciple, none had conceived of them responding not only individually but as a group—responding to the total situation, in chain reaction to one another's responses at the moment of shock, disbelief, and puzzlement. The subject of *The Last Supper,* dictated by convention as a suitable decoration for the end wall of a refectory in a monastery, might not have been the subject Leonardo would have chosen independently as a vehicle to express his synthesis of visual and psychological phenomena, but he made it such a synthesis all the same. *The Last Supper* as Leonardo painted it was neither dreamy nor mystical; except by association it was not even a religious painting. It was an elaborately calculated study by an intellectual who was at once a mathematician and a psychologist.

As for the *Mona Lisa,* it suffers not only from overfamiliarity but from its disastrous reputation as a kind of fetish. When the Louvre put it on brief loan to the Metropolitan Museum in 1963, people lined up by the thousands and had to be marched four abreast past it, with a pause of a few seconds to contemplate it from a distance, as if exposure to its radiant powers could be culturally or spiritually beneficial much in the way that touching a holy relic is supposed to be healing. What they caught a glimpse of was a portrait in not very good condition, much discolored and crackled, of a Florentine woman seated in front of an imaginary landscape of mountains, valleys, and deep sky, a woman with a rather odd face that looked much less odd to her contemporaries. Her eyebrowlessness and her abnormally high forehead were the result of plucking and shaving in accord with Florentine fashion, and her robe, today suggesting that of a seeress, was no such thing. If Leonardo invented it, he invented it along the general pattern of the current style in dress.

But the portrait is obviously intended to be something more than a likeness of an individual, and was perhaps intended to have something of the sibylline character generally attributed to it. Whatever Leonardo's intention, the clue is to be found somewhere within the identification of the landscape and the woman. Landscape backgrounds for portraits were popular enough, it is true, but they were usually little more than decorative backdrops, sometimes with topical reference to the sitter. Leonardo's reference is psychological; the figure and the background are two parts of an indivisible concept. As an invented landscape, this one suggests a primeval (but not savage) world where, in spite of a bridge and a road, we are conscious of the timeless but logical forces that create rivers and mountains. Half scientific as an exercise in geological invention, and half mystical in its evocation of measureless time, the landscape is like the woman, whose corporeal being is described but at the same time transmuted as a revelation of intangibles. If the landscape suggests primeval forces, the woman may also be a symbol of eternal generation —of the ultimate mystery of the origin and perpetuation of life.

Much is always made of the aerial perspective in the *Mona Lisa* landscape—the luminary phenomenon by which, as objects recede in the distance, their solidity and their color are diminished by the intervening air. Whether or not the principle had ever been applied with quite Leonardo's skill to a landscape of such depth, it was a hundred years old in painting before he developed it. Leonardo's innovation is of a different character. A figure delineated in the precisely defined manner of Leonardo's contemporaries and placed before a landscape bathed in the sea of air would have been tremendously effective, but only as an arresting contrast. Instead we have a harmonious softening and obscuring of detail, as if the woman, also, in spite of being brought so far forward in the painting, were yet removed from us.

The haze between the woman and the observer, like an invisible curtain (a yellowed curtain in the picture's present condition, but probably cool and silvery in the original color), is created by Leonardo's *sfumato*. This effect, named after the Italian word for "smoke," was so astonishing to Leonardo's contemporaries that it seemed beyond technical explanation, but it has been abused ever since as a mere soft-focus trick that is not difficult to master. Even Leonardo exaggerated the effect rather unpleasantly in his bothersomely androgynous figures of soft-bodied young men (like the *Bacchus* in the Louvre) that inspired an entire school of even squashier imitations.

The expressive purpose of *sfumato* as Leonardo applied it—in the *Mona Lisa*, at least—was to make the tangible not quite tangible, and it has more to do with Mona Lisa's puzzling and disturbing attraction than the famous smile and the curious, removed gaze—neither of which could have been given their enigmatic quality by precise definition. There is no way of knowing whether Leonardo intended this female to be the personification of enigma that she has become. If we try to discover the answer in his writings, refutation is as easy to find as support. He once wrote, for instance, that "the picture is the most praiseworthy which most closely resembles the thing to be imitated," which sounds like a flat rebuttal, and not at all a sound one, of the principles that guided him as a painter. But to understand, or to conjecture, Leonardo's meaning when he wrote those words, words that had different connotations in his time and that must be modified and remodified within the context of everything else he wrote—to understand exactly what he meant, must be hopeless. As usual with this man who sought answers to everything, the answer turns into a question.

We may take one generality, however, as certain. Leonardo's thought was rooted in the premise that proportion exists in everything, "not only in numbers and measurements, but also in sounds, weights, time, spaces, in whatsoever power there may be." In his belief in universal proportion, and his efforts to raise the theory of proportion to the level of science, there is an implicit identification of the beautiful with the normal that might explain why he considered the picture "most praiseworthy which most closely resembles the thing to be imitated"—and brings us back to the contradictions and the questions.

Contradictions and questions are inherent in any exploration, and the exploration that preoccupied Leonardo was of such scope that, paradoxically, the vast range of his own intellect made a successful conclusion impossible. The universal harmony he wanted to codify could be expressed only by a lesser intellect—one that could accept it in principle without feeling the need to analyze it. This lesser intellect appeared in the handsome person of the artist Raphael. Raphael did not explore: he absorbed. And his genius for absorption, combined with a genius for filtering out any disruptive doubts and complications, made him the culminative painter of the High Renaissance, which Leonardo had introduced.

Raphael (Raffaello Santi or Sanzio) was born in 1483 in the lovely town of Urbino, on what must surely have been a lovely spring day as an augury of the luck that was to follow him for the rest of his life. It was not a long life, but its history reads as if the gods of good fortune had pooled their efforts to concentrate all the worldly things a man could desire within the thirty-seven years that it lasted, and then carried him off in 1520 to the frustration of any gods of doubt, struggle, decline, and disappointment whose turn was overdue. Raphael died in magnificent Rome, as he had been born in gentle Umbria, on a Good Friday. Patly consistent with the good timing that marked his career, this sweet coincidence with holiness parallels the sweet but superficial religiosity of his holy pictures.

This introduction to Raphael may sound heretical, considering the veneration in which he has been held for centuries. Few artists have suffered so little from changes in taste, and Raphael is habitually called the apotheosis of Italian Renaissance art at its classical apogee, its moment of complete harmony and equilibrium. And so, no doubt, he is. But there is always a moment of pause between rise and fall that is less interesting than either, and Raphael's perfect composure in this static position accounts for a blandness in his art that, in turn, explains why you will find almost no one today under the age of ninety (Raphael having been the popular idol of the nineteenth century) who would name Raphael as his favorite painter.

Although he was thirty-one years younger than Leonardo da Vinci, whose intellectual confidence in universal order brought the Renaissance to the point of culmination, and eight years younger than Michelangelo, whose emotional anguish shattered that order in its revelation of our universal frailty, Raphael stands between the two and is less original than either. But to be the least original in such superb company is not to hold too weak a position. Raphael even by the least sympathetic evaluation was a supremely talented artist, or even a genius if the capacity for growth through assimilation can be called genius when it reaches so high a degree.

Raphael must have received his first training from his father, Giovanni Santi, a painter of pleasant if inconsequential altarpieces who was fond of versifying in his spare time. Orphaned by the age of twelve, the boy perhaps continued his training under one Timoteo Viti. But his true teacher, certainly by example and almost certainly by direct association, was Perugino, who was and remains the ranking Umbrian painter and whose formula Raphael learned so quickly that it is impossible, in many paintings, to distinguish the work of the apprentice from that of the master.

Perugino was a busy man who frequently applied his picturemaking formula to assembly-line manufacture, and no heresy is involved in recognizing quantities of his work as repetitious and intolerably saccharine. By the time Raphael was sixteen or seventeen he had already shown that he could apply the Peruginesque formula to make the most of its virtues while skirting its hazards. He did so in a tiny picture, a scant seven inches square, now in the National Gallery in London, called *Vision of a Knight*. He was to paint many more important pictures, but never a more delightful one, or one more complete within its own spatial and expressive dimensions.

Vision of a Knight is a wonderful little painting, remarkable less for having been so expertly put together by a mere boy than for its poetic representation of a dilemma of nascent manhood better understood in retrospect than in anticipation. With all the sweetness and grace that is often appealing but more often cloying in Perugino, Raphael shows a young knight of about his own age asleep under a tree that symbolically divides the picture in halves for the youth's choice. On one side the intellectual and moral virtues are represented by a young woman, appealing enough, who holds a book and a staff (learning and rectitude?). On the other side an even more alluring girl proffers the eternal symbol of the primrose as an invitation to a more immediately rewarding path.

Posing a moral question, the picture presents a foregone conclusion that did not quite apply to its author. Raphael turned out to be one of those rare people who have it both ways. Handsome, gentle in manner, tactful, intelligent, and industrious, he became the great courtier among painters, the intimate friend of popes and princes. And in the worldly and elegant circles where Raphael's personal attraction was as remarkable as his professional skill, his record as an artist is hardly more impressive than his record as a lover.

The young knight's first step was to abandon the provinces and move to Florence (at the age of twenty), where for three years he observed the work of the masters, including Leonardo, and quickly assimilated their greater breadth, their fullness and weightiness. His work grew in these directions, but retained the gentle spirit of Umbria that has made the Madonnas of his Florentine period the all-time popular favorites not only within his own work but in the entire field of Virgin and Child representations. If such examples as the Louvre's lovely (an unavoidable word) picture of the Madonna and Child with the infant St. John (so appropriately called *La Belle Jardinière* with its lovely landscape) have attracted the affection of a wide public through their taint of sentimentality, they have also captured the admiration of an aesthetically more demanding public by their impeccable organization of form—an organization that counters the sentimentality with a redeeming monumentality. Sentimentality and monumentality make for a mixed marriage that seldom works out, and Raphael's way of bringing them into harmonious relationship is an impressive demonstration of his expertise as a tactician.

But the center of art in Italy was shifting from Florence to Rome, where the Church was demonstrating its wealth and power in the rebuilding and redecorating of the city. It was natural that the Pope should call Raphael there, and inevitable that Raphael's style should change again, this time to reflect the grand or even grandiose concepts of the new order. The boy who had begun as a painter of tender sentiment was now called upon to create a cycle of huge frescoes in the Vatican that called for the loftiest intellectualism and the most scholarly exposition. The year was 1509, and Raphael was twenty-six years old.

With a respectful eye on Michelangelo, who was at work on the Sistine Ceiling a short distance away in the Vatican complex, Raphael set to work in the Stanza della Segnatura, a room where the Pope's private library was housed. His job was to cover the four immense walls with murals referring to the four domains of learning—theology, philosophy, law, and the arts, these themes to be developed also in the elaborate decorations of the vaulted ceiling.

The problems of this assignment were acutely demanding in every way. In the first place, the frescoes had to be effective decorations scaled to large spaces: that alone was enough of a problem to tax any artist's powers of organization. Raphael had never worked on such scale, but his solutions were technically brilliant. A corresponding increase in solemnity, weightiness, and majestic drama was also required. It was a task that could have strained the combined powers of a Masaccio and a Piero della Francesca, a task that was made even more forbidding by the high standard of comparison supplied by Michelangelo and raised by him day by day. And by this standard, even Raphael's masterpiece in the Stanza della Segnatura, *The School of Athens,* must fail in passion. But the comparison is not quite valid, since a certain dispassionateness is appropriate to Raphael's subject.

The subject, even so, was of dizzying and even absurd complexity, and hardly one that could be thought of as adaptable to pictorial expression. Yet Raphael managed not only to give it such expression but, by doing so in a clearly organized painting, to make sense of its impossible complications while retaining its severe logic. The intellectual coterie that Raphael had to satisfy believed that any of Plato's poetic propositions could be identified with an analytical proposition of Aristotle's, and had demonstrated this proposition of their own in a system of tortured intricacy. We often hear nowadays of the painter who takes the visual world and reduces it to its essence as a painted abstraction—which is not so difficult. Raphael reversed the trick: he took an abstract philosophical exercise and gave it virtually tangible form, which is never easy and in this case should have been impossible.

Within a vast, calm painted stage that is one of the great architectural creations of the Renaissance, Raphael disposed some fifty figures of artists and thinkers that, ever since, have remained the standard embodiments of the creative and rational spirit, those twin ideals of Renaissance humanism. Gigantic statues of Apollo and Minerva, paralleling Plato and Aristotle as the two halves of this fusion, are painted into the niches at either side of the temple's central vault as the patrons of the immortal band.

Raphael included his own portrait among the personages in the distinguished company assembled below. Even if this had not been a common form of signature for an artist, Raphael deserved such a position among the contemporary representatives of the classical tradition. With a generosity to Michelangelo that Michelangelo would never have shown to him, he placed the master of the Sistine Ceiling in the foreground near the center, giving him an importance second only to that of Plato and Aristotle and paying him the additional compliment of representing him in a completely Michelangelesque style, an open statement of indebtedness. While the other artists and philosophers converse with one another or compare drawings, Michelangelo sits alone, removed within himself in a pose traditionally associated with the figure of Melancholy, and remindful also of the great Jeremiah who looks down from the Sistine Ceiling in solitary contemplation of the puny mortals below. Raphael's venerative tribute is all the more impressive when we remember that it was made to a rival who, although his contemporaries awarded him the epithet *"Il Divino,"* was behaving in anything but a divine manner toward his younger colleague just then. In an all too human way, Michelangelo was attributing his many difficulties with Julius II to the machinations of an envious Raphael who whispered into the Pope's ear.

Raphael completed the Stanza della Segnatura in 1511 and moved on to the decoration of another room, the Stanza d'Eliodoro. Completing a cycle there in 1514, he planned yet another for the Stanza dell'Incendio, which was completed in 1517 but carried out mostly by assistants. A fourth cycle, in the Sala di Costantino, was executed by pupils from his plans after his death.

Progressively, these chambers show that Raphael's genius for assimilation had at last reached the point of surfeit. The schemes of the murals remain irreproachable, but the painted actors, growing more and more agitated, fall into theatrical errors in their efforts to emulate the tragic drama that Michelangelo had completed in 1512. By that time, Raphael's Stanza della Segnatura and Michelangelo's Sistine Ceiling had divided Rome into two camps, supporting (or, more generally, attacking, as the most enjoyable form of defense) one artist or the other. When Raphael began his work in the Vatican, Michelangelo had no rivals, and we have already said that the older man felt some resentment against the newcomer. According to a story Vasari tells, this resentment inspired Michelangelo to say, "You travel accompanied by your court like a prince," when he had to stop in the street to make way for Raphael and his entourage, to which Raphael is supposed to have answered, "And you, you go alone like a hangman." If the unpleasant story is true, Raphael might not by that time have painted Michelangelo quite as he did in *The School of Athens*.

In spite of the competition, Raphael must have been too busy to feel much unease. While work on the Vatican apartments continued, he was occupied with cartoons for a set of tapestries on the Acts of the Apostles that are nearly as widely admired as the Stanze (the cartoons are in the Victoria and Albert Museum in London, the tapestries in the Vatican); on other frescoed decorations for the Vatican and the Villa Farnesina; on a series of altar paintings, large and small, including the most famous of them, *The Sistine Madonna* in Dresden; and on portraits, among them those of both the popes he served, Julius II and Leo X (the first is lost, the second is in the Pitti Palace in Florence), and Raphael's good friend, Baldassare Castiglione (in the Louvre).

As another boy from Urbino who had become as successful a diplomat as Raphael had become a painter, and as the author of "The Courtier," a manual on the theory and practice of being a gentleman, Castiglione was Raphael's perfect subject. The portrait—elegant, calm, assured within its own distinction, but warm rather than haughty—is probably Raphael's best, as well as a reflection of his own best self in identity with his friend.

We owe to Castiglione another of the few relieving anecdotes among all the others extolling Raphael's purity so monotonously that they make him seem too good to be true and much too good to be as interesting as his contemporaries found him. Castiglione relates that two cardinals, indulging in a bit of amateur art criticism, told Raphael that in a certain picture he had painted the faces of St. Peter and St. Paul too red. Raphael retorted that he had painted them thus "after long consideration" because surely the saints' faces "must be as red in heaven as you see them here, having blushed at seeing their Church governed by men like you."

For Castiglione, "courtier" could not mean "sycophant," nor did he confuse good manners with hypocrisy or respectable behavior with prudery. Consideration for others was part of a gentleman's code, and Castiglione insisted that this principle must be rigorously applied for the benefit of malleable ladies and their husbands and fathers. In short: don't kiss and tell. Here, as in the rest of his comportment, Raphael could have served either as the model for Castiglione's courtier or as the best student of his book.

When Vasari attributed Raphael's early death to excessive indulgence in amorous exploits, he was making good copy of something that he doubtless thought of as redounding to his subject's credit, but he was exercising his talent for exaggeration and making an implausible diagnosis. It is true that Raphael's love affairs were numerous. They are worth mentioning because they refute the untenable assumption that the nature of his work was simply a reflection of the kind of man he was (by which assumption Raphael would have been virtually sexless) and because these affairs suggest a human being alive in a certain milieu, instead of the straw-stuffed androgynous idol that the nineteenth century managed to make of what must have been a very vigorous man.

With his great Umbrian eyes, like melting chocolate, his grace, his elegance, his wealth, his reputation, and—something that must have been understood by his prospective conquests—his tact in keeping his conquests unpublicized, Raphael could have been a successful womanizer in a society lenient in fact if not in theory to adulteries. But he seems to have been, rather, a man who enjoyed being in love and managed to combine the pleasures of variety with a single-hearted attachment from affair to affair. And all the while he held to a practical attitude toward marriage: marriage was something that could wait until the proper combination of material advantage and personal attraction came along.

The former half of that combination, and presumably the latter, was offered Raphael in the person of the niece of a patron, Cardinal Bibbiena, when he was twenty-one and still negotiating the passage from Umbrian obscurity to Florentine prominence. But the Cardinal's niece died before the marriage could be celebrated, and our next knowledge of Raphael in relation to marriage comes from a letter, some ten years later, indicating that he had become more than reconciled to this early loss. He wrote an uncle, Simone Ciarla, that he was very glad indeed "and forever grateful to God" that he had not accepted a bride that the uncle had wanted to give him "nor any other," since "I would never have got where I am, with three thousand gold ducats put aside in Rome." This refreshingly straightforward letter, like Raphael's others to his family, is noticeably different from his suave communications to members of his upper circle. Raphael wrote his own letters home, but Castiglione and other literary friends helped him when a more courtly style was desirable.

The only firsthand documents, or near documents, showing Raphael as a lover are his own poems. As a poet he was not much better than his father, but he was ardent. The duality, or rather the completeness, of his life shortly after his arrival in Rome is engagingly revealed by the presence of poems to his current love jotted down on some preparatory drawings for the frescoes in the Stanza della Segnatura. It is pleasant to imagine the young man abandoning for a few moments his struggle to realize a majestic religious and philosophical concept in order to dampen the flames of desire with a bit of versification—a sort of mid-morning poetry break.

Vasari presents a similar picture of Raphael in love a few years later, when the frescoes in Agostino Chigi's Villa Farnesina in Rome were under way but not going too well. Raphael, Vasari's story goes, was unable to give his best attention to the work because he was "a very amorous person, fond of women and always ready to serve them," and could not get his mind off his mistress. Agostino, one of those friends of Raphael's who, as Vasari says rather primly, were "more complacent and indulgent towards his pursuit of carnal pleasures than was probably right," arranged that the lady be domiciled with Raphael in the part of the villa where he was painting, "and in this manner the work was brought to conclusion."

Vasari was only three years old in 1514 when Raphael was at work in the Villa Farnesina, and only nine years old when Raphael died, but gossipy anecdotes like this one, picked up or invented after the event, can often be accepted with the necessary grain of salt as being in the spirit of the truth even when they are factually suspect—on the principle that where so much smoke lasts for so long, there must once have been fire.

When Raphael died suddenly after a week of fever, the news traveled through Italy like the news of a major disaster. He was buried with full pomp and all honors in the Pantheon. He had made a great deal of money and had spent unstintingly, maintaining a princely entourage, a house in Rome, a villa with vineyards and lands nearby, and a house in Urbino. Even so, he left a fortune of 16,000 florins.

Raphael dead remained a stronger presence in Italy than most of his generation who outlived him. His paintings in the Vatican became a combined shrine and school for other painters, and his influence for nearly four hundred years would be difficult to overestimate. When the Italian and French academies were founded, they were founded to perpetuate the principles exemplified by Raphael. The nineteenth century belonged to him. Even the impressionists, revolting against the academy, studied him.

"Unless everybody is flattering me, I have satisfied everybody," Raphael once wrote in a letter to Castiglione. He was speaking of some drawings, and he added in the best courtly manner, "but I do not satisfy my own judgment because I am afraid of not satisfying yours." But Raphael probably came as close to satisfying everybody, for as long a time, as any artist has ever come, even though our century, with its taste for extremes, experiments, and explosions, finds less satisfaction than previous ones have found in Raphael's grace and balance.

Michelangelo cannot be encompassed within a brief essay and can hardly be said to have been encompassed even within the lengthiest books written about him, since he is a figure of such magnitude that any consideration of him could be expanded indefinitely. The words "greatest" and "titanic" must of necessity occur monotonously in anything written about him. And he can be understood only in segments: Michelangelo the painter, Michelangelo the sculptor, Michelangelo the architect, the poet—to list the large divisions—and then Michelangelo in the various facets of his personality: the bitter, quarrelsome solitary, the political idealist, the erotic sensualist self-transformed into the philosophical lover —one of his loves a young man, the other an aging woman—

and Michelangelo the man of deep religious fervor, and Michelangelo the head of a family of brothers and nephews and nieces. And yet Michelangelo was not a man of bits and pieces, nor is he (like Leonardo) a man difficult to separate from his legend. He was—is—the titan of titans, awesome in his powers, superhuman, yet nagged and beset by the commonest human tribulations.

He was born in Caprese (now called Caprese Michelangelo) on March 6, 1475, and died in Rome on February 18, 1564, not quite eighty-nine years old. Fifty-two years earlier, when he was only thirty-seven, he had completed the greatest —surely, everything considered, the greatest—cycle of paintings in the world, the frescoes on the Sistine Ceiling, after four years of what amounted to forced labor for the Pope on a commission that he had not wanted to accept in the first place. Then in 1541, at the age of sixty-six, he had added the *Last Judgment* on the chapel's end wall, concluding his story of the world's creation with an excoriating vision of its end.

As an architect he created Rome as we know it, transforming it from a decaying hodgepodge of a medieval city into the Renaissance counterpart of its traditional imperial grandeur. Rome, studded with its ruins of antiquity, with its medieval monuments rising here and there like islands not quite inundated, and even with its modern veneer, still belongs to Michelangelo. The city is dominated by his dome of St. Peter's and its character is determined by his palaces and the spaces he organized to accommodate them and by the other structures and piazzas that were designed under the momentum of the direction he set.

In sculpture, considering his energy, the length of his life, and the fact that sculpture was his chosen art, he left a relative handful of some twenty major completed works, including half a dozen of the world's greatest statues, a scattering of minor works—if anything his hand touched can be called minor—and a group of uncompleted figures, not wholly released from their stone matrix, of such compelling power that they hold a position all their own in the history of sculpture and the history of expression. For the tomb of Pope Julius II, he conceived what was potentially the grandest of all sculptural monuments, those of antiquity included, and after years of maddening frustration, finally saw the project scrapped.

If Michelangelo's total being can hardly be encompassed, his physical being can be visualized without difficulty from trustworthy portraits and descriptions. He was not a large man, but he was toughly made, with an asymmetrical body of no beauty and a face to match, disfigured by a broken nose, flattened and askew—the result of a blow received from a fellow student, Pietro Torrigiano, when he was fourteen years old. In his ugliness he worshiped the beauty of the male body—not the androgynous male celebrated by Leonardo da Vinci and not the lissome youth pictured in so much Renaissance painting as the physical ideal, but the powerful young giant. He was slovenly in dress, as if he could take no interest in ornamenting so unprepossessing a frame, and when he was working he could have been taken for an unusually rough and dirty laborer. Wildly successful from his early twenties on, he was courted by the great figures of the Church, the state, and the nobility, but he was almost pathologically uncivil except to a few friends. Wealthy, he chose to live in lonely squalor.

By birth he was a member of the patrician class (his full given name was Michelangelo di Lodovico di Lionardo di Buonarroti Simoni, conventionally shortened to Michelangelo Buonarroti). His family had been well established in Florence for more than three centuries and had included various officeholders in the city, but for two generations had been in decline. When Michelangelo was born (he was the second of five children) his father was struggling against the loss of position that comes with the loss of money, and he opposed the boy's determination to become a sculptor as a humiliating loss of caste. According to one biographer (Michelangelo's old servant Condivi, who published his book in 1553 under Michelangelo's supervision), the father beat the son in an effort to break his spirit. In the many letters that Michelangelo wrote later on, he always addressed his father with appropriate filial respect, but never with any indication of affection.

The near poverty of Michelangelo's childhood in a household where Spartan economies had reduced the scale of living to that of countryfolk must account for the sympathy he always felt for common people and even a sense of identity with them. His immediate family—pestering him for money, complaining about his way of life, asking him to help ne'er-do-well relatives out of scrapes, giving nothing and demanding everything—offered little proof that good lineage is a trustable measure of human excellence. Michelangelo retained, however, a real pride in his family's historical association with the city he loved best, Florence, and although in his letters home he complained unreasonably and often untruly about his financial difficulties, he tried as head of the family to shore up its faltering position, buying lands to replace those lost, and arranging marriages with families of high standing for his nieces and—as detailed in numerous letters—his nephew Lionardo.

Michelangelo was practical, but not grasping, in such matters. He was always supplying conditions for model contracts, and he insisted that a suitable bride should be of good blood. To Lionardo he once wrote that it was up to him whether he got married or not, and that the choice of bride was his too, but warned him that "for the sake of harmony" no dowry at all would be better than one that was too large.

His letters to his family make fascinating reading: in them he is a giant plagued by gnats, and occasionally he loses his temper and strikes out at them ("Every time I receive a letter from you I go crazy"), but the gnats surrounded him until his death.

If Michelangelo had created nothing but his poetry, he would enjoy a respectable if minor reputation. Today the poems are difficult to read as independent literary efforts: they have become sidelights on the life of a man whose greatness in other fields dwarfs them. In effect they are Michelangelo's spiritual autobiography, from youth to old age. As a youth he released through poetry an anguished eroticism. In his old age, fervently religious, he implored the love and forgiveness of God. The long years between were filled with his struggle to resolve the conflict between sensuality and faith, or between sensuality and its intellectual sublimation, sometimes in art, and sometimes through the concept of Platonic love between men.

During his lifetime Michelangelo was known as a poet, but the poems themselves were known only to his friends. Fifty-nine years after his death (that is, in 1623) they were published by a grandnephew, but it was not until the early nineteenth century, hardly a hundred and fifty years ago, that they were translated into French and German and really discovered (by the romantic sensibilities of the time) as personal confessions, in the sense that the word had taken on with the "Confessions" of Jean Jacques Rousseau, in which autobiography grew from an account of the facts and circumstances of a life into a revelation of innermost thoughts and feelings, no matter, sometimes, how shameful.

As confessions, Michelangelo's poems became an embarrassment to his admirers, requiring (they felt) a rationalization of the ones among them that were love poems to Tommaso Cavalieri, a young nobleman of great beauty. Mi-

chelangelo was fifty-seven years old when the two first met in
1532, and Cavalieri was not the first handsome youth to have
attracted him. He had written affectionate letters to, and
received them from, a Gherardo Perini and one Febo di
Poggio, and his poems to Cecchino Bracci, when this boy died
at the age of fifteen, can be read in such a way as to leave no
doubt about what is often tactfully described as "an inclina-
tion" in Michelangelo's temperament.

There was no secret about all this during Michelangelo's
lifetime, as is evident from a letter of Pietro Aretino's, the
most malicious ever written by one public figure to another.
The Venetian satirist, yellow journalist, and debauchee took
out his spite by implying that Michelangelo had improper
relations with young men, after Michelangelo had ignored a
hint that Aretino would be willing to receive, with pleasure,
the gift of a drawing.

The concept of Platonic love as a spiritual union between men is virtually impossible for a Freudian-slanted age
to understand except as the sublimation of homosexual desire, a half measure second best to physical intercourse. It is
thought of not as something positive but as a personal compromise that does not remove the stigma but simply makes of
the lovers homosexuals who behave themselves through denial. In Michelangelo's time, however, Platonist circles believed that love between men was an attainable and a spiritually noble ideal, not as male camaraderie, not as fatherly or
filial love, but as a unique intellectual and emotional state.
True, there is little evidence that the ideal was frequently
attained, and Aretino's jibes at Michelangelo probably
echoed gossip and raillery prompted by attitudes similar to
today's.

But the best modern scholars are unwilling to tolerate
the word "homosexual" in connection with Michelangelo.
They believe that in the context of circles where the Platonic

ideals (not alone of love) were cultivated virtually to the point of becoming a religious faith, no rationalization is necessary to conclude that Michelangelo's love for Tommaso Cavalieri was Platonic in the full sense. The nature of the love between him and Cavalieri may be partially grasped if we say that although it was a true love that endured for the thirty-two years between their meeting and Michelangelo's death (with the middle-aged Cavalieri at his side), it was so far from being a love affair that the term is totally inapplicable.

If the idea is ungraspable except in terms of sublimations of base instincts, then so be it. But even in that case, Michelangelo's adoration (allowing the word) of Cavalieri's beauty, no matter that it was generated by an aging man's adoration of the young male body, was transmuted as an expression of the Platonic doctrine that all beauty on earth reflects a divine beauty, the "celestial source whence all life springs," in Michelangelo's own words.

Leonardo da Vinci, in his painting, meant to purify the base world by removing it into an emotionless universe, but Michelangelo in both sculpture and painting always heightened sensation where Leonardo avoided it. His art makes Leonardo's seem emasculated. There is an exalted sexuality in Michelangelo's two greatest male figures, the young David whose statue the Florentines call simply *The Giant* and the Adam rising to life in *The Creation of Man* on the Sistine Ceiling, that makes thousands of tourists who would never think of pinning up a photograph of a naked athlete from a muscle magazine return from Italy with photographs of these two figures and frame them up without realizing exactly what they are confessing.

But the *David,* while undeniably a celebration of a handsome naked youth and a vehement projection of male vitality, is a symbol of Florentine political morality, of the virtues ensuring republican liberty. Vigilance, fortitude, and "anger" —pride of independence, and determination to preserve it against assault and corruption—are given allegorical form through a biblical character, the adolescent hero setting out to slay Goliath. And the Adam, whose great-muscled body is indeed instinct with sexual languor, is the materialization of "divine beauty mirrored on earth." In him are united the Christian concept that God created man in His own image and the Platonic ideal by which divine beauty mirrored on earth frees the spirit from material bondage by the paradox of assuming material form.

For Michelangelo, the ugly man, the beauty of Tommaso Cavalieri was some such proof of the celestial ideal materialized in an alter ego. The passionate terms of address in some of the poems may seem to us more extreme than they were, since they reflect exaggerated literary mannerisms of the day. The drawings that Michelangelo sent to Cavalieri were interpretable as allegories from Platonic and other sources, but had, also, specific personal references to their relationship, references that can never be deciphered but that must have been, for the two men, notations or souvenirs of ideas discussed. Cavalieri was as learned as he was handsome. As a visual delight he might have palled; as an intellectual companion he was Michelangelo's constant solace.

Vittoria Colonna, who did not replace but who coexisted with Cavalieri as Michelangelo's other love, should have been, for the purposes of romantic biography, a beautiful woman. She was not. She was rather plain, a childless widow approaching the age of fifty when Michelangelo, past sixty, met her about 1538. (She was born in 1490 and died in 1547.) Vittoria was a pious woman, and Michelangelo's increasing religious fervor as he aged probably established the strongest bond between them. She has been called his mother figure, in the contemporary cliché, and she might have been in spite of being his junior. Michelangelo's mother had died when he was six years old, and by the evidence of the mothers he created as Madonnas he had no experience of maternal love. For all her gentleness, even the Virgin of the *Pietà* in St. Peter's is nobly monumental rather than anguished in the loss of her Son, while the mother who tries to save her child in the scene of the Flood on the Sistine Ceiling is, at the other extreme, hardly more than an animal.

Michelangelo's Eve is remarkably without the sexual allure of his Adam, and he used male models for the preliminary drawings of other female figures. There is not the slightest suggestion of late-blooming sexuality in his friendship with Vittoria Colonna. Like Cavalieri she was an aristocrat belonging to one of the noblest families of Italy. Learned, and a friend of famous and learned men, she had a considerable reputation as a poetess, but she has not worn well as a literary light. Her writing, including her letters, has a bluestocking preciosity that leaves only the conclusion that as a friend and conversationalist she had much more to offer. When she died, at the age of fifty-seven, Michelangelo was seventy-two and their friendship had lasted about ten years. In an elegiac sonnet he wrote: ". . . heaven hath robbed me of the blaze / of that great fire which burned and nourished me, / a coal that smoulders 'neath the ash am I."

As a great fire that has nourished all men, Michelangelo surely has no peer among artists. His art, seen as a unit from his first exercises as a student to his last transcendent works, is a reconciliation, achieved in torment, between matter and spirit, emotional impulse and intellectual morality, the most passionate adoration of the body and the most profound yearning for the salvation of the soul. His final paintings— *The Last Judgment* in the Sistine Chapel and the frescoes in the nearby Pauline Chapel—have seemed to some critics despairing, bitter, and overblown in their violence, an old man's exaggeration of his great manner. In his old age Michelangelo may have despaired of his fellow man: he saw the Florentine Republic decaying, with no David to save it, and he saw vanity and corruption among the powers in Rome. In his mystical Christianity he began to question the Platonic ideal of divine beauty materialized as physical perfection, and he created a race of supertitans as the material symbols of moral force.

His anger, his agony, and his hope could no longer be expressed in the balanced energies and thunderous harmonies of the Sistine Ceiling; they demanded explosive forms, disruptions so violent that they would shatter any but the supertitans, the colossi, who enact his dramas of sin and salvation. It is a drama that, robbed of its moral energy, would be hysterical and absurd. And absurd it became in the followers of Michelangelo (such as Bandinelli and Giulio Romano) who, borrowing only its inflated forms and its melodramatics, reduced its terrible grandeur to bombast.

The restlessness, the eccentric balances, the violent action, the contorted attitudes that heighten Michelangelo's moral drama prophesied and even generated baroque style in the next century. But as an immediate influence, his art birthed little more than shoddy mannerisms. Rubens was to be his pupil by example and so was Delacroix, but during his lifetime Michelangelo not only took no pupils but would not even abide talented assistants around him. He collaborated with no one on any project; instead of cultivating other artists, he made a point of offending them; he is reviled in letter after letter from artists still quivering from the awfulness of his contemptuous wrath. He could not accept greatness in other living artists, not even in Leonardo and Raphael. There is nothing endearing in Michelangelo's human littlenesses, although there is much that is pitiable as a reflection of his suffering. His littlenesses cannot even be called unworthy of a great man; they are simply inconsequential in a man of such greatness that there can be no questioning the epithet his world bestowed on him during his lifetime: *"Il Divino."*

Tiziano Vecelli—Titian—was so robust a man that it took a siege of the plague to carry him off along with nearly a quarter of the rest of the population of Venice in his very old age. The epidemic occurred in 1576, and according to birth dates accepted until recently Titian was just short of one hundred years old. The dates are now advanced to around 1488 or 1490, giving him only about nine decades. Whether he was ninety or a hundred when he died, he was busy right up to the end.

Titian is one of the four men whose art represents that peak of fulfillment called the High Renaissance, but he stands apart from the other three. Whatever their contrasts, Leonardo and Michelangelo and even Raphael were alike in being artist-philosophers whose masterpieces as intellectual abstractions rose above (if that is the right way of putting it) sensuous experience. Titian was the apotheosis of the Venetian spirit, which put its primary faith in the immediate delights that the world offers through the senses.

Titian's gods and goddesses are neither Olympian personifications nor allegorical figures enacting the humanistic concepts of the Renaissance. If they evoke the ancient world at all they evoke it in Venice's own terms: they are real people—of princely status, it is true, but as richly fleshed as the Venetian courtesans. They are embodiments not of principles but of the pleasures of the natural world, pleasures that come to us through seeing, hearing, feeling, tasting, and smelling it at its richest. This was Titian's world, and he drew on its opulent materiality not only to achieve that poeticization of sensuous experience to which it seems most obviously adaptable, but to render religious subjects that cannot be denied as fervent spiritual expressions.

The facts of Titian's professional life are distressing to victims of the romantic syndrome, who demand a parallel between what a man paints and what he does when he is not painting, expecting him to be a living exemplar of the spirit of his work, as if he had stepped out of one of his own paintings, and who nourish a conviction that if an artist is any good he will not be anything but a fumbler in private affairs. In the light of such expectations, Titian should have been a poetical and passionately religious man moving as a stranger among his worldly fellow citizens along the Grand Canal. He was no such thing.

In the history of art Titian is not unique in having been a good businessman, but he is extreme among painters in having regarded his work not as a personal expression to be cherished but as a form of luxury merchandise over which he had a monopoly and for which he naturally intended to be paid well. His correspondence shows that the desk from which he managed his affairs was as important to him as the studio where he did his painting, and he was equally assiduous at both stations. As a result, he was not only a born prince among painters but a self-made prince in a commercial society. The constant stream of guests in and out of his fine house included every famous or titled person who visited Venice, and the feasts with which he entertained them had an impressive reputation. Along with the courtier Raphael, the "divine" but thorny Michelangelo, and the elusive Leonardo, Titian exemplifies the final stage in the Renaissance artist's shift of status from that of superior craftsman, or at best respected retainer, to that of higher being recognized as exceptional on the strength of his gifts. Where artists had once had to ingratiate themselves with patrons, patrons of the highest rank might now cultivate the favor of an artist in competition with other patrons for the privilege of obtaining his services.

Titian's paintings were so coveted that he could dangle semipromises ("I have almost completed a large Last Supper . . .") as bait in his dunning letters. The number of these letters has given Titian a reputation for avariciousness; on the other hand, the dilatoriness of some of his most eminent patrons is surprising. Although the emperor Charles V did Titian the honor of inviting him to Augsburg as his guest, and gave him the titles of count palatine and knight of the Golden Spur, he was so slow in payment for various paintings that Titian's correspondence with him, and then with his son Philip II of Spain—whose record would never pass a credit bureau today—stretched over years. The letters are tactfully phrased but they leave no question as to their demands, and Titian never made a concession to a defaulting creditor, royal or lowborn. He held to the perfectly sound idea that the honor of receiving a commission from a distinguished personage was repaid by the honor of his accepting it, and that this mutual exchange had nothing to do with the other matter of merchandise delivered for a fee.

Titian also carried on a lively business as an informal dealer in art other than his own and in antiquities. He owned city and country properties, including a sawmill, and in holding on to the income from these various sources he employed devices that would sound familiar to rich men harassed by taxes today. Venice had an income tax, but apparently returns were less rigorously audited than they are now. When Titian was required to prepare a declaration in 1566, after fifty years of enjoying the exemption granted to many artists, his falsifications were outrageous. More legitimately, he avoided immediate taxes by including in his contracts not only annuities for himself but pensions for his children, among other provisions that he made for their security.

Titian had two sons, Orazio and Pomponio Vecelli, and a daughter, Lavinia, a beautiful girl if his portrait of her in Dresden can be trusted. Pomponio, the elder son, was a wastrel, but Titian provided for him all the same. Orazio was his father's delight and standby, serving as his emissary in business negotiations, especially as an international bill collector. Titian loved his children and yearned for grandchildren. By 1545, when he was nearing sixty (or seventy, by the old count), it appeared that he would have none, and he adopted as grandson a boy named Marco Vecelli, a distant relative. Erwin Panofsky has identified three figures in Titian's *Allegory of Prudence,* in the National Gallery, London, painted about ten years before the artist's death, as portraits of Titian himself, Orazio, and Marco (now a youth of twenty or so)—the past, the present, and the future, a concealed reference but an affecting one in its revelation of Titian's strong family feeling.

There is, after all, nothing inconsistent in the combination of a practical concern for business matters with a poetic response to the joys of the world, a deep religious faith, and a love of family. It is only according to romantic preconceptions that Titian the man and Titian the artist seem unreconcilable. His indifference to his paintings once they had left his hands seems at first more difficult to understand. The most famous instance occurred when Titian introduced into a *Gloria* (now in the Prado) a portrait of Philip II's Venetian envoy, a man named Vargas. In commissioning the picture for the King, Vargas had suggested that his portrait be included among the band of saints and angels, and Titian with possibly an excess of tact placed the portrait in the most conspicuous foreground position. But when he delivered the picture to the King he accompanied it with a letter saying that it would be perfectly all right with him if the King had the portrait painted out. "Any painter can, with a couple of strokes, convert it into another person." The portrait was indeed painted out, to become a figure of Job, and more than "a couple of strokes" were required.

To the modern painter the idea that his work is not sacrosanct in the condition he left it is intolerable. Titian's attitude, by contrast, was that of a practical professional, who would no more think of telling a client what he should do with a painting than he would tell him what to do with a piece of land that he sold him. That Titian dismissed his paintings as something finished and done with, and did not feel that they were, in effect, only held in trust by the purchaser, was consistent with his constant activity and growth as an artist. Into every new painting he put something more from his inexhaustible, his increasing, well of creativity. He was one of those artists, perhaps in this respect the greatest of all, whose powers increased until the very end of his life and were still increasing when he died.

Titian probably studied with Giovanni Bellini as a fellow student of Giorgione's, and he certainly worked closely with Giorgione, collaborating with him on some projects, until the early death of that poet-painter. Their early work is much alike, so much so that there are confusions of attribution. By Titian's revised birth date he would have been as much as ten years younger than Giorgione, and the quality of dreamy reverie that the two painters shared would have been Giorgione's mood, adopted by the younger Titian in the double role of colleague and disciple.

Titian as the internationally successful painter we have described was something of a late-bloomer. Nearing fifty when he attained his position as reigning lord of Venetian painting, he had risen against severe competition. During the long stretch between young manhood and old age he was the Titian we usually think of first, with his high drama, his opulence, and the portraits where his perception of character proves that he was indeed a man of the world.

During these years he became the first true painter in oil. The Flemings, the so-called inventors of oil painting in the preceding century, and the Italians who followed them, including Giorgione and the young Titian, had only begun to investigate the medium's potential. It was the mature Titian who brought oil into its full development. Its fluidity, its adaptability to application in a filmy veil or in thick, fatty layers, in a smooth surface or a rough one, and in combinations where one form of application was played against others —its variety of texture, full range of color, and the freedom it allowed the brush, transforming it into an instrument of drawing like an enlarged pencil or pen—all these characteristics of oil became with Titian an integral part of expression as the luscious materiality of his paint fused with the sensuousness of his imagery.

In the intensification of emotional drama characteristic of his religious paintings, in his direct appeal to the emotions through the senses, and in his introduction of figures in motion through deep space, Titian anticipated the baroque. And in his last paintings he approximated the technique of the impressionists, although he did not apply it to celebrations of the out-of-doors. It is quite possible that the dimmer eyes and less steady hand of old age, even when they were Titian's, account to some extent for the softer definition of his last paintings, but if that is so, Titian capitalized on a limitation to reach the only logical conclusion to what had been an uninterrupted spiritual as well as technical development. His broken strokes were applied in a final identification of pigment with light and air, as he returned to the poetic mood of his early paintings with deepened perceptions. The world of sensuous reality remains only as a vibrant radiance illuminating images of man's passage from a world whose beauty is at last eclipsed by the glory of salvation.

7

DÜRER AND GRÜNEWALD

By their conventional organization, books on the history of art follow consideration of the High Renaissance with discussion of the remainder of the sixteenth century in Italy —and then drop back to the century's beginning to pick up the story in the North, where Dürer was importing the Renaissance to Germany.

Perhaps that is the best way to tell the story—long custom seems to prove it—but in this book the two great Germans, Dürer and Grünewald, are introduced at this point in part as a reminder that art did not stop stock-still in northern Europe at the end of Chapter 2 but, even more, to stress the extraordinary character of the first years of the sixteenth century with their unparalleled concentration of masterpieces by Leonardo, Raphael, and Michelangelo, Giorgione and Titian, Dürer and Grünewald.

Dürer's inclusion at just this point is a reminder that he

was a contemporary of Michelangelo and Raphael—although he brought the Renaissance to Germany not in their terms but through his discovery and study of the work of an older generation of Italian artists, with Bellini and Mantegna among the ones he most admired.

Albrecht Dürer is usually called the greatest German artist. His position may be rivaled nowadays by his immediate contemporary, Matthias Grünewald, whose wild and fantastic fervor is more to the modern taste than Dürer's methodical exploration of the world and man's place in it. But even if Dürer is acknowledged to be the "greatest German artist," the assessment carries for most minds an implied restriction, since to be the greatest *German* artist is to be great against competitors who are certainly fewer and in general less impressive than the artists who, not only in Dürer's century but before and after it as well, sprouted so magnificently in Italy and France.

A better introduction to Dürer is simply to say that he was a great artist, restricting that carelessly used word "great" to a handful of names from all countries and all times. Yet his Germanness is intrinsic, and a first mention of his name is somehow incomplete without reference to it. It is, however, a Germanness that should be dissociated from Wagnerian and post-Wagnerian excesses. Mania, disorder, and violence, all of which have characterized recent German history and much recent German art, are present in Dürer's art only as devils that haunt the Northern mind and must be routed by intellectual discipline and spiritual purification. Dürer's two major themes are the will of God and the dignity of man— themes that not all thinkers have found compatible but that Dürer, influenced by the sanity and tolerance of Erasmus, could think of as identical.

In spite of his determination to build his art on a rational basis, Dürer remained part intellectual mystic and part mystical scientist. He studied and recorded nature as the visible expression of a hybrid miracle, created by forces beyond man's capacities to explain, yet within man's power to dissect, much as Leonardo da Vinci did in Italy. Leonardo was always more suave, more subtle, even a bit more guarded. He was also a more objective theorist than Dürer, who was tormented by the problem of the interrelationship between a man, his Church, and his God, a problem that Leonardo was able to dismiss in pondering a man's relationship to himself. But in spite of these differences, Dürer can be called a Northern Leonardo (as he often is) with no more implication of second place than there would be in calling Leonardo a Southern Dürer (which is never done).

Both men were as highly regarded by their contemporaries for their learning as for their achievements as artists. Both made studies of anatomy and geometry, relating them to standards of ideal beauty and to the mechanics of creating works of art. Both went outside the field of art into that of engineering. And both men, when they drew a plant or an animal, were botanists or zoologists as well as artists, interested not so much in the pattern of natural forms as in the systems of growth and construction that accounted for those patterns. Both were fascinated by human beings as natural objects, and as natural objects modified by artifice: they recognized dress, coiffure, and manners not as superficies of style, but as expressions of ways of thought.

The parallels between Dürer and Leonardo could be continued and elaborated as multiple evidence of kinship between exploring minds. But the similarities cease when the end results of the explorations—their applications in art— are compared. Leonardo's art becomes enigmatical, rather soft, often a little perverse. In some of his most elaborately studied paintings, he relinquished the world that had fascinated him as a study and yielded to the languor of escape into a more shadowy world of dream and fantasy. Although his notebooks, never meant to be seen, show us the Leonardo of universal intellect and insatiable curiosity, his paintings are more evasive than inquiring in spirit, a private art.

Not so with Dürer. He remains absolutely decisive even when he is most complicated, and his passion is not only to inquire and to know, but to expound for everybody what he has learned for himself. (His various researches were parts of a treatise on the theory of art that occupied him until the time of his death, just as Leonardo's were.) Even when Dürer recognizes the doubts and confusions that beset us, he recognizes them with anguish rather than resignation. Art for Dürer was a vehicle that served a moral obligation imposed on the artist along with the gift of his talent—the obligation to clarify by rational examination.

Dürer was never satisfied by half answers, nor could he permit himself the kind of answer that has been the most powerful one for many painters—the intuitive response that the artist as a special kind of being can share with us, transporting us to a world that we understand somehow through his guidance although his explanation is never explicit. Dürer is always explicit, and he is always thorough—qualities that almost by definition make a dull person and a tiresome artist, except that Dürer was as passionate by nature as he was rational by self-discipline. He was the perfect Protestant—devout, but unable to leave conventional observances unquestioned; he could accept the mystical and miraculous promise of Christianity only when the final salvation was earned by the daily salvation that a man finds in examining his own conscience. Inevitably, Dürer attached himself to the cause of Martin Luther; as an inevitable corollary, he hoped for a Protestant art as grand as the Catholic art of Italy.

This hope was not fulfilled, although Dürer came as close as any artist to pointing out where that fulfillment might lie—if only the spiritual leaders of the Reformation had been able to recognize it. They recognized instead that art contains elements of luxury and sensuousness, and held them synonymous with corruption. In this one respect Dürer might qualify for the category, so popular today, of the artist unappreciated during his lifetime. But otherwise his life was a triumphant one, in spite of doubts and self-goadings and in spite of a marriage wretched enough to have become famous.

He was born in Nuremberg in 1471 and died there in 1528. It was appropriate that he should die there since, in a way, he never left it, despite his fairly extensive travels. These took him throughout Germany, to the Netherlands, and especially to Italy. The journey to Italy, for a German artist at the end of the fifteenth century, was a matter not only of crossing the Alps but of crossing a century in time.

A hundred years earlier, Italian painters and sculptors had redirected the course of art while the North remained largely indifferent to the change; thus, by 1494, when Dürer made his first trip southward, the Alps stood not only between Germany and Italy but between the late-Gothic style in which Dürer had been trained and a fully developed Renaissance art. Leonardo, the Renaissance man par excellence, was already in his forties when Dürer, in his early twenties, first saw Italy. The entire lifetime of Raphael—the prince of artists, who summarized the classical aspirations of the Renaissance in his Vatican frescoes—was encompassed within Dürer's birth and death dates, with generous margins at both ends. Michelangelo, whose tragic doubts destroyed the serenity of Raphael and marked the end of the Renaissance as a period of optimistic affirmation, was born only four years after Dürer—but between these two artists lay the whole period of discovery and change from the waning of the Age of Faith to the rise of the Age of Power.

Renaissance art had reached the Northern workshops by hearsay—as an echo from the humanistic circles where German artists were not ordinarily included—and by the concrete evidence of a few copies of drawings and engravings. Rough and meager as these copies were, they were strange enough to suggest to Dürer a new world on the other side of the Alps. His first trip, which was to Venice, was a revelation beyond anything he had expected. He discovered a new style, whose importance lay not in the novelty of its forms but in its expression of a new attitude toward life, a new conception of the world, that could not be expressed by the forms of Gothic art.

There had been a startling change, too, in the artist's position in the social scheme. In Italy artists for the first time in history had become members of an intellectual aristocracy, the equals and companions of noblemen and popes. As members of a humanistic profession, the artists of the Italian Renaissance held the position of scholars. And as men of talent they were respected as exceptional beings. But in the young Dürer's Germany the artist was still only a craftsman who might be the respected employee, but not the accepted companion, of the men he worked for. Just as the best carpenters got the contracts for building the finest houses, an artist with exceptional creative ability would get the most desirable commissions, but he was not expected to invent new means of expression. He applied in his own way an accepted set of conventions for pictorial description and storytelling. His outlook was untheoretical and rather narrow. For him the world was a conglomeration of objects that could be reassembled as a conglomeration of standardized symbols explaining the subject of the picture.

It was a formula that had been used by Flemish genius

to produce supreme expressions of mystical faith, but for Dürer it was inadequate and cramping, in an age when theoretical investigation and rational analysis were challenging the legitimacy of blind faith. Dürer's goal was to expand the expressive range of German art by bringing to it the objective disciplines of the Renaissance. He succeeded in this goal. His achievement lay not in the Italianization of German art, which might have produced only a sterile hybrid, but in the elevation and intensity that he brought to his own tradition. Nuremberg, first and last, was home.

Albrecht was the third of eighteen children born, in twenty-four years, to the elder Dürer, a goldsmith, and his wife Barbara. In the tradition by which a son became apprentice to his father, young Albrecht was expected to follow the goldsmith's trade. At that time goldsmithing demanded a variety of skills; the good goldsmith was not only an artisan but a designer, and a designer not only of jewelry but of large and elaborate objects that might share the nature of sculpture. Expert draftsmanship was requisite for the presentation of projects as well as for the engraving of designs on metal with the burin. The father had studied in the Netherlands, and Dürer later on was proud of this once-removed connection with great Flemish painters, although he does not say which ones they were.

Dürer's father was a more than competent draftsman in the Flemish tradition, but the boy Dürer, by the age of thirteen, when he drew the earliest of the many self-portraits he produced in the course of his life, was even better. (The drawing is in the Albertina in Vienna.) In 1486, when he was fifteen, the direction of his talent was recognized by his being apprenticed to a painter, Michael Wohlgemuth (1434-1519). Wohlgemuth was remarkable for extremism in his use of the bunched, tortured, and exaggeratedly complicated forms of the late-Gothic manner. He was a sound craftsman, and in his workshop, for more than three years, Dürer was trained in the standard techniques, including—and this was very important—the technique of the woodcut. It was in this medium and in engraving, the rudiments of which he had already learned from his father, that he was to create his finest work and to bring German art, at last, into the international front rank.

After the conclusion of his apprenticeship in 1490, Dürer traveled through the Germanic states until 1493 and then, in 1494, when he was twenty-three, contracted his unhappy marriage. Agnes Frey has found defenders among Dürer scholars, who have agreed with her that she was a neglected wife, but in general the arguments have gone against her. She seems to have been a rather pretty girl, pleasant enough if not too bright, whose own disappointments in the marriage came when she discovered that her husband was not the typical solid, conventional, dependable craftsman she had expected, a man who would run a steady, prosperous shop, but a man with ambitions toward learning and culture. From her point of view, such ambitions were impractical nonsense; from Dürer's, humanistic investigation of man's spiritual nature was the goal of life.

The marriage, apparently a failure from the beginning, was childless, leaving Agnes nothing but jealousy and resentment with which to fill her time. The couple were married in July, 1494; when Dürer left for his first trip to Italy that autumn, Agnes stayed behind. Only once did they take a trip together, to the Netherlands in 1520-21; Dürer's journal of that trip casts a bleak light on their relationship: it seems that the two hardly ever even ate together. Poor Agnes is even better, or worse, known because of a letter written to her after Dürer's death (but not mailed) by his best friend, the immensely learned humanist Willibald Pirckheimer. Pirckheimer accuses her of having killed her husband with her pious nagging and her insistent demand that he make more and more money (on this score he did quite well as it was). Although we lose sight of it when we see Dürer only through his work, the obtrusive obbligato of this wretched union accompanied his entire creative life. The good Willibald sustained and solaced him as friend, companion, and humanistic mentor.

Two extraordinary self-portraits painted during the five years following his first Italian journey—that is, between his twenty-fourth and his twenty-ninth year—are manifestos of the position he wanted to establish for artists in Germany. Both sound vainglorious: in the first he seems to represent himself as a prince, and in the second he assumes the role of Christ. Both obviously demand explanation.

Dürer always had a fondness for self-portraiture. He was quite aware that he was a handsome man, and we may allow him some normal satisfaction on that score. But his self-portraits are also a reflection of his particular form of tortured introversion, which made him examine not only his own nature but the nature of all artists as special beings. He drew himself at the age of twenty (the drawing is in the university library of Erlangen) as a tense, puzzled, and determined youth in the chaotic state of mind frequently characteristic of brilliant young people who are certain that a great destiny awaits them if they can only clear their way to it. In the first of the two post-Italian portraits the pathway has been found. At twenty-seven, established as his own master with a degree of international fame, Dürer must have felt that the destiny he knew was his was really to materialize.

In the "princely" portrait, now in the Prado, which shows him with his thick, golden hair, elegantly curled, falling across his shoulders, he presents himself garbed— "dressed" is too mild a word—in the most sumptuous of stuffs, cut in the highest fashion. The pose is casual on the surface, but the face is alert, even intense, with an air of hauteur, almost of arrogance. As a painting, this portrait is a forceful display of virtuosity; what is not apparent to us is that at the turn of the sixteenth century it was also a declaration. The self-portrait in Dürer's time hardly existed except as an exercise using a convenient model—the artist himself— or to serve some special purpose such as the commemoration of an event. (Upon the occasion of their engagement, Dürer presented Agnes with a self-portrait, now in the Louvre, showing himself holding an eryngium, the symbol of good fortune in love and marriage.)

The Prado portrait, painted for no occasion and for no customer, but obviously as something more than an exercise, was Dürer's declaration to the world that the artist is not a workman but a gentleman. The air of hauteur hints that he is even something more—the truest of aristocrats, who owes his high position to innate qualities that he has cultivated rather than to the accident of inheriting a name and position that were earned by his ancestors and merely passed on to him. To understand the portrait from this point of view, without seeing it as an outrageous manifestation of vanity, we must remember the predominance of allegory or symbol as the painter's language in Dürer's milieu. Although the painting is a self-likeness, Dürer represents not one single artist making a self-satisfied comment on the position he himself was already achieving, but all artists and the position society should recognize as rightfully theirs.

The allegorical premise is even more important in understanding how Dürer, a religious and reverent man who constantly questioned his own worthiness before God, could seem to assume the role of Christ in the second portrait (which is in Munich). There is no halo; yet there is no question that the resemblance to Christ is intentional. Dürer modified his own features to bring them into an approxima-

tion of those traditionally ascribed to Christ, and by centering the figure within the space to emphasize its hieratic effect,
and placing the right hand in a position where in similar pictures of Christ it would be raised in blessing, he left no doubt
at all about his reference.

Such a self-portrait today would be either an absurdity
or a blasphemy. Dürer's is neither. As a quasi-allegory, it is
a statement of Dürer's conviction that the artist is the re-
cipient of a gift from God, a gift that does not make an individual godlike, but at least makes him a vessel through which
the will of God may be expressed. He is, in effect, a kind of
priest. Thus this self-portrait as Christ is conceived in humility: the artist accepts the divine gift and acknowledges the
obligation to be worthy of it insofar as human limitations
permit him to be. To Dürer's contemporaries this conception
may have been unexpected as an assertion of the importance
of the artist, but it was neither laughable nor shocking as an
allegory. After all, good burghers of the time were customar-
ily portrayed among bands of saints as donors of altarpieces,
and were often shown in attendance at such miraculous
events as the Nativity.

By an odd turn, the intensity of Dürer's conviction that
the gift itself was divine led him away from the idea of divine
inspiration. God did not speak through the artist in mystical
terms. Dürer had no patience with "inspiration" and may
well have objected to Grünewald's fervent, even hallucinatory, art as a wild growth that needed pruning. For Dürer,
the artist was a being who must labor humbly through rational processes to use his gift in expounding the will of God
in didactic terms. In Dürer's rational-mystical philosophy,
the artist's first obligation was to understand, rather than to
feel, and to present with absolute clarity the understanding
he reached through study.

Dürer's art is explicable in every slightest detail—the

product of rational control over the creative process, and a philosophical amalgam in which classical humanism and the Christian mystery are unified through symbols that are harmonized with one another, or even shared. His Garden of Eden (in *The Fall of Man,* an engraving of 1504) is a synthesis of the natural world—accurate as zoology and botany, with animals serving as symbols of the four "humors," fluids that were thought to be combined in man's nature and to have been in perfect balance until Adam succumbed to temptation. The figures of Adam and Eve are not only the biblical Adam and Eve but Dürer's efforts to discover the perfect proportions of the human body, as closely connected to the tradition of antiquity as to the Christian story. Where most artists were content to represent Eden simply as an attractive garden with decorative animals and the symbolic serpent, so superficial a production was, in a double sense, inconceivable for Dürer. In a single work he combined natural fact, philosophical truth, and optical delight, synthesizing the natural world in terms of the harmonious relationships of humanism.

Dürer was now internationally renowned, and in 1505, eleven years after the first trip, he returned to Italy not as a tourist but as a master who had brought German art into the Renaissance current, and who had as much to offer his fellow master-artists as he had to learn from them. He studied Venetian colorism and became interested in the mannerist painters who, paradoxically, were returning to somewhat Gothicized forms. But above all he continued, during the second trip and after his return to Nuremberg, to develop the ideas that he intended to work up as a summary of the theory and practice of art in the service of humanistic learning.

The climactic expression of his genius came in 1513— he was now forty-two—and 1514 with three engravings that, although conceived as individual statements, constitute a trilogy expounding the triple aspect of virtue as represented by three ways of life. *A Knight, Death, and the Devil* illustrates the moral virtue of Christian action; *St. Jerome in His Study* is a wonderfully happy celebration of the theological virtue of spiritual contemplation; and *Melencolia I* examines and questions the intellectual virtues of the world that was most Dürer's own, the world of science and art.

The symbolism of *Melencolia I*, in which Genius sits surrounded by a disarray of scientific instruments, winds its roots through all of classical, medieval, and Renaissance thought, but comes ultimately to the conclusion that genius is at once a condition of power and of helplessness, of privilege and of frustration—a conclusion that Dürer had reached when, in spite of the progress of his researches and his success, he admitted, "What absolute beauty is, I know not. Nobody knows it except God."

The disorder surrounding Dürer's symbolical figure of Genius evokes the defeating complexity of knowledge. At the side of Genius, an infant scribbles on his slate, typifying action without thought, while the thoughtful Genius is rendered incapable of action by the weight of a universe that "nobody knows . . . except God." Dürer's statement in *Melencolia I* is too profound to be bitter, and is saved from ultimate pessimism by the recognition of a Power, a God, that exists and knows the secrets that no learning can decipher. Thus the melancholy of genius is sublime. But so extensive are the connotations and the side currents of this personal testament, conceived over four hundred and fifty years ago, that it can also be read as an anticipation of the philosophies of negation and despair on which entire schools of twentieth-century art are based.

But for Dürer negation and despair were beyond admitting. His last major works, two panels painted in 1526 (and now in Munich), in which the Four Apostles are presented in balanced harmony as the fourfold image of the Divine, were to have been the flanking wings of a triptych reaffirming the unity of man, God, and cosmos. Here Dürer's faith never wavered, but human nature had put a severe strain upon his trust in the first member of this trinity. The panels were accompanied by tablets in which Dürer quoted passages from the writings of the four holy messengers, inveighing against heresy and false prophecy. The quotations were preceded by Dürer's own warning against the radicals who departed from the true word of God. The reference was to the Catholic abuses that had first forced Luther away from the Catholic Church, and then to the Protestant excesses that in turn had forced him into the position of a counterrevolutionary. Dürer had agonized and reagonized over the Lutheran question and his relationship to it, but when he died, at the age of fifty-seven, he was still loyal to a cause that he had frequently feared was lost. Some years earlier, suffering from a lingering illness and conscious of his shortening life, he had again, in a drawing that is now in Bremen, used himself as a model for a figure of Christ, this time showing his nude and ravaged body and anguished face as the Man of Sorrows. To the end he identified man with God. He died on April 6, 1528.

The artist we call Grünewald—which was not his name —is a personage about whom little is certain except that his *Isenheim Altarpiece* rivals Michelangelo's Sistine Ceiling as the one work of art that would have to be included, imperatively, in any list, no matter how curtailed, of the most profound expressions of the human spirit in painting.

As a supreme religious expression, the *Isenheim Altarpiece* is complete within itself, so self-contained that it frustrates efforts to classify it. In its mystical intensity it is an expression of Gothic faith, but it could never be called a Gothic painting. In its unprecedented radiance, in its conception in terms of light, color, and motion, it is a century and a half ahead of itself, a baroque consummation. It skips, in one great aesthetic and conceptual broad jump, the formality and rationalism of the Renaissance century during which it was created. Its philosophical basis is so emphatically the reverse of the humanistic values that Dürer, at the same time, was bringing to their culmination in Germany, that it could stand as a deliberately anticlassical declamation—except that it is not anti anything. It is a full and splendid and unquestioning expression of Christian mysticism—in this respect, a generality. But it is infused also with an intensity that in its personalism is charged with the passionate spirit of one man, the artist.

If the altarpiece has been called both medieval and baroque (or neither), it has also been adopted, with good reason, as the prototype of twentieth-century expressionism, which begins with the visible world as its subject, but transmutes appearances by expressive distortions of form and color into revelations of emotional states of mind. The impact of the altarpiece is so powerfully emotive that the conception is easy to think of as a pure inspiration, but the complex iconography and the masterly organization of the many parts into a dramatic whole are obvious proof that something besides inspiration was at work here. The *Isenheim Altarpiece* could have been created only by a man who combined analytical powers with a fervently emotional nature.

Each of the nine paintings is more than 8 feet high. The altarpiece is 10 feet wide when closed, 21 feet wide with opened wings. Its central carved shrine was equipped with three pairs of painted wings, one pair fixed, the other two pairs movable and capable of closing on the central shrine like double doors. As now set up in the museum in Colmar, a small Alsatian city a few miles from Isenheim, the altarpiece has been dismembered and the wings hung separately. This arrangement avoids constant opening and closing, but sacrifices the successive revelations that Grünewald intended.

When all the wings were closed, the altarpiece presented a double panel of the Crucifixion. A Christ whose twisted body is covered with wounds and putrescent eruptions has just died. The figure's gangrenous and anguished flesh is the symbol of mortality, but its gigantic presence, played against a blackened sky shot through with stormy light at the horizon, makes it the abandoned vessel of a supernatural spirit.

When these wings were opened, the dark scene vanished into a blaze of light. The dreadful spectacle of the rotting tortured corpse gave way to a jubilant scene where music-making angels celebrate the Virgin and the newborn child. On the wing-panel at one side the Annunciation prophesied this joy, and on the other the Resurrection resolved the agony of the Crucifixion. Vast aureoles of red, orange, yellow, and electric blue illuminate the miraculous scenes, and the attendant angels are aflame with rapture.

The altarpiece was painted for the church of the monastery of the hospital order of St. Anthony in the small town of Isenheim. The hospital received patients suffering from venereal diseases, and the extraordinary Christ, with morbid flesh and running sores, has been explained in this connection. The hospital also received patients with mental disorders. Grünewald was a genius whose compassion for living men with rotting bodies and hallucinated minds transmuted putrescence and hysteria into glory. The altarpiece is overwhelming even when it is seen as a museum exhibit. Its effect on the patients received by the monastery can hardly be imagined.

If for no other reason, the altarpiece would be expected to have achieved a kind of notoriety in its own day through its tremendous size and spectacular departures from conventional representations of its subject matter, but it was unknown outside Germany, not very well known there, and finally remained forgotten in the out-of-the-way (if not quite inaccessible) spot for which it was commissioned. Late in the eighteenth century, more than two and a half centuries after it was completed, the altarpiece began to accumulate a band of admirers—who thought it was by Dürer. In the nineteenth century, it became the goal of artistic pilgrimages for German painters, but as often as not they found it repellent, and regarded it as a disturbing curiosity rather than as the resplendent spiritual expression that it is. The recognition of the altarpiece as a rival of the Sistine Ceiling is entirely a twentieth-century appreciation, and Grünewald, as he is still called for convenience, is still only a half-defined, if dramatic, figure reconstructed largely by twentieth-century scholarship.

Grünewald's real name, discovered in this century, was Mathis Nithardt-Gothardt. The second of the surnames (and there are various spellings of both) was probably Grünewald's own variation of the first. If he was burdened originally with the name Nithardt, which suggests a spiteful, ill-humored, or wicked person, he may have adopted Gothardt as suggesting godliness. The change may have come about when Grünewald went through a personal religious crisis during the turmoil of the Reformation.

By any name, Grünewald fell so quickly into obscurity that when Maximilian of Bavaria tried to acquire the *Isenheim Altarpiece* for his collection, no one knew who had painted it. This was not much more than a century after Grünewald's death in 1528. His name was virtually lost by 1600, and the one we call him by was half invented from erroneous sources by the seventeenth-century artist and chronicler Joachim von Sandrart. Sandrart became interested in a group of paintings and drawings obviously from the hand of some single great but unidentified artist but could trace absolutely nothing, either through records or by hearsay, about the man; his interest seems not to have been shared by anyone else.

One documentable fact about Grünewald is that he died in 1528—the same year as Dürer, his antithesis: Dürer the humanist, Grünewald the mystic. They might easily have had exactly corresponding life spans, and were certainly born not too many years apart. Grünewald's birth (probably in Würzburg) cannot be dated more precisely than between 1470 and 1480 (against Dürer's 1471). Grünewald would have died, then, at fifty-eight at the latest or forty-eight at the earliest, and when he completed the *Isenheim Altarpiece,* probably in 1515, he would have been between thirty-five and forty-five.

The absence of contemporary references seems incomprehensible in connection with an artist who was well enough known during one period of his life to have been the subject, by every reasonable conjecture, of the usual records and legends and to have been included in memoirs and chronicles. Melanchthon once mentioned Dürer, Cranach, and Grünewald (under his then name) as well-known German artists, but thereafter the name simply does not turn up. It was probably deliberately avoided by his contemporaries, since his career as a painter was cut short when he became *persona non grata* with his former patron, Albrecht of Brandenburg. Albrecht had been sympathetic to Luther's ideas but was so outraged by the Peasant Revolt that he became a violent foe of the Reformation and in 1525 discharged Grünewald along with other sympathizers at court.

Grünewald sought haven in Frankfurt, but moved on when Albrecht demanded the return of the fugitives. He painted little, and made his living as a hydraulic engineer— he was a specialist in the design of fountains and mills—and perhaps did some work as an architect. But the persons who could have written about him as an artist must have avoided him as a dangerous subject, and if Grünewald ever wrote a word about himself or about anything else, it has not survived.

Exactly what Grünewald's religious convictions were must be surmised. His Lutheran sympathies have been questioned, but he must have expressed some to have been expelled from court in Albrecht's local Counter Reformation. The *Isenheim Altarpiece* had been completed some ten years earlier and is, of course, altogether incompatible with any Lutheran restraints and with the Reformation's objection to paintings as idolatrous objects. Other German Protestant painters continued to work for Catholic patrons, but not with the passion that fills Grünewald's masterpiece. His conversion to Protestantism must have come later. Perhaps, also, it was never complete. Perhaps, even, Grünewald was torn between his social sympathies with the peasants and his natural religiosity. After his death, two rosaries were found in his luggage along with a small library of Lutheran tracts—as suggestive, yet as indefinite, a pair of clues as he could have left if he had intended an enigma.

Of all the great masters, Grünewald is the most isolated historically. The power of the *Isenheim Altarpiece* is such that if it had been painted for a church in a large city it might have changed the course of German art. As it is, even Dürer probably never saw it. Erwin Panofsky points out, however, in his study of Dürer, that although there is no demonstrable proof, the great German humanist might have seen certain other paintings by Grünewald at just the "time when the content of his [Dürer's] prints seems to reveal the impact of a strong emotional experience. . . . It is tempting to think that this crisis was precipitated by an encounter with his antipode."

But Grünewald had no followers, and in spite of our century's adulation, his specific influence on artists is slight. The intensity and personalism of his religious vision should have been incompatible with the monumentality of their expression in the *Isenheim Altarpiece,* but there they are, together, and no painter has been foolhardy enough to attempt their impossible emulation.

8

THE SIXTEENTH-CENTURY CRISIS IN ITALY, SPAIN, AND FRANCE

The artists of fifteenth-century Italy were so certain of their goals, their goals were so definable, and their world was so open for exploration, that the sudden consummation of their ideals with the High Renaissance left the artists of the next generation without a direction. It was as if art had been a ship piloted down a river that had grown wider and deeper day by day until it debouched into an ocean that no one had expected to be called upon to cross. Even Michelangelo, having attained the apogee upon which Italian art had been focused ever since Masaccio (ever since Giotto, for that matter), shared in his later work the general sense of disorientation. And Raphael, the artist who, with *The School of Athens,* had achieved the perfect coordination of Renaissance ideals, indicated early in the century that he was incapable of sustaining this perfected position to the end of a brief life.

During the period of crisis between the High Renaissance of the first decades of the sixteenth century and the re-fashion of aesthetic standards into the baroque styles of the seventeenth, artists generally fell into three categories—all overlapping one another. There were the artists who, predominantly, echoed the masters of the High Renaissance: Florentines who owed their major debt to Raphael and Venetians or northern Italians who flowered, like Titian but less grandly, from the Bellini-Giorgione tradition. At the other end of the scale there were the men who forecast the baroque. Sharing the qualities of both groups (and sharing their own qualities in return) were the mannerists, the most distinctively personal stylists within a century that eludes definition. For the purposes of this book, it seems best to rope off the artists into these three groups in spite of their shared characteristics. We can begin with the more conservative ones who, unfortunately but inevitably, and even quite justly, must be recognized as second-stringers to Leonardo, Raphael, Michelangelo, and Titian.

SECONDARY MASTERS OF THE HIGH RENAISSANCE

The High Renaissance lasted so briefly that only a handful of painters other than its great masters can be called a part of it, and the great masters were so very great that even a very good painter must suffer in their company. This has been the fate of Fra Bartolommeo, who for about ten years was the most respected and influential painter in Florence— a position he occupied largely by default after Leonardo, Raphael, and Michelangelo (the three artists who influenced his style) had left town.

Baccio della Porta, who became Fra Bartolommeo, was born in Florence in 1475, the son of a muleteer. He entered the workshop of Cosimo Roselli at about the same time as another youngster, Mariotto Albertinelli, who, born in 1474, was a year older. They opened a shop together, and were successful in turning out altarpieces in the current mode.

But at just this time the inspired zealot Savonarola was carrying on his revivalistic campaigns for the purification of the Church and, along with it, the correction of the morals of the Florentine citizenry. Albertinelli, who had an impressive reputation as a carouser, was not affected, but Bartolommeo was so moved that in 1497, when he was twenty-two, he burned all his non-religious works. The next year he witnessed Savonarola's execution, and in 1500 he entered the Dominican order with the intention of giving up painting. Albertinelli completed for him a *Last Judgment* for Santa Maria Nuova. Now in the Museo di San Marco, and in ruinous condition, it is thought to have influenced Raphael, just as Raphael's later work influenced Bartolommeo.

Bartolommeo changed his mind and began painting again after four years of retirement, and in 1505, now thirty, he became director of the painters' workshop in the Monastery of San Marco. His life was beyond reproach; his conduct was identifiable with his painting, which was almost monotonously devout. The soundness of Bartolommeo's craft, his command of monumental compositional devices, makes him a painter one admires, without excitement, when one runs across him in a museum, only to forget him until the next time. If his conversion to piety was accompanied by any of the traumatic agonizing that Savonarola inspired in some souls, it does not show through in his painting. Fra Bartolommeo is a remarkably impersonal artist—serene, but spiritless.

He took a trip to Venice in 1508, picked up some ideas there (and left some in exchange), and then, back home, joined forces again with Albertinelli, reopening their shop in 1509. He made a trip to Rome in 1514, where his manner received important infusions from the Vatican paintings of Michelangelo and Raphael, and where he himself contracted malaria, of which he died three years later, in 1517, at the age of forty-two.

His friend and business partner Albertinelli had died rather more spectacularly, if Vasari's story is to be believed, two years before this (in 1515, at the age of forty-one). During the execution of a commission in Viterbo, Albertinelli had acquired a band of sweethearts whom he remembered with such nostalgia that he made a return visit for the sole purpose of renewing old ties and demonstrating that his prowess was undiminished as he entered his fifth decade. This he did with so much enthusiasm that he collapsed and had to be carried back to Florence, where he died within a few days.

Albertinelli, like Fra Bartolommeo, painted only religious subjects. Also like Fra Bartolommeo, he once reached a decision to give up painting in order to follow another way of life. The alternative he chose, however, was not the monastery but the tavern. He operated one for several years.

Bernardino Luini (c. 1481/82-1532) was the most facile and successful vulgarizer of Leonardo's style among the many Milanese painters who sprang up as imitators in the wake of the master's stay in that city. Until he fell under the spell, Luini was a painter of attractive gaiety. Then, sacrificing a healthy superficiality in his effort to plunge more deeply into the realms of spiritual expression, he imitated the rather morbidly soft smile that marks the paintings of Leonardo's Milanese period. Sometimes it is difficult to say whether Luini exemplifies the vast gap between genius and the imitation of genius, or whether his prolific and saccharine confections define (embarrassingly) a certain spiritual flatulence in Leonardo's own late painting. But since the latter view is an aesthetic sacrilege, the former prevails.

The sixty-two years of Sebastiano del Piombo's life must have been enjoyable ones. Born in 1485, he died in 1547 after having known some of the great men of his time, and quite early having secured a sufficiently prestigious position among them to feel justified in quitting his profession and retiring to a life of ease.

He was born Sebastiano Luciani in Venice, but became Sebastiano del Piombo in Rome after Pope Clement VII appointed him Keeper of the Papal Seal, a sinecure at a comfortable stipend. "Why paint any more?" he asked himself, and could not offer a convincing answer. Recognizing that there were men at work—including his good friend Michelangelo—who could put him in the shade with their slightest efforts, he sensibly withdrew from competition, and spent his life in pleasant professional idleness, painting a bit now and then, but giving fuller scope to his talent for quiet social pleasures.

Sebastiano del Piombo, at that time Luciani, was in all likelihood trained under Giovanni Bellini, and without question was strongly influenced by Giorgione. He probably completed some of Giorgione's works when Giorgione died in 1510. (Sebastiano was twenty-five.) Some scholars believe that the *Fête Champêtre,* or *Concert,* in the Louvre, usually given to Giorgione, is entirely Sebastiano's. If so, it is the most gracious of his paintings.

He did not stay long in Venice. In 1511—now twenty-six—he was called to Rome by Agostino Chigi to work in his villa along with Raphael and his circle. It was an elite group, both socially and aesthetically, but Sebastiano quarreled with Raphael and, joining the opposing faction of Michelangelo's admirers, became one of the few people who could call Michelangelo a friend. The great man, who could be unreasonably jealous of other artists, was so fond of Sebastiano that he even gave him drawings to work from. And though thorny and suspicious in most relationships, he made Sebastiano something of a confidant. Sebastiano served as courier between Michelangelo and his Platonic love, Tommaso Cavalieri, in their exchanges of letters and poems.

As an artist, Sebastiano del Piombo managed to combine a Venetian opulence with Roman formal disciplines, and in this way he affected subsequent Roman painting. But the mechanics of his art are always a little too obvious. He was quite successful, nevertheless (his sinecure from the Pope was one of those semipensions that were awarded in recognition to famous men), and ultimately he received an accolade that he could in no way have envisioned: about the year 1869, an unknown thirty-year-old Frenchman named Paul Cézanne saw a reproduction of *Christ in Limbo* (the painting is now in the Prado), which Sebastiano had painted about 1530, and was so attracted that, after his own fashion, he copied it.

Giovanni Antonio (or Giovanantonio) Bazzi, a cobbler's son, was born in 1477. By the time he had reached his early thirties, his conspicuously indulged aberrations had earned for him the nickname by which he is still known, Il Sodoma, "The Sodomite." If he had been a better painter, Sodoma's art might be considered before his personality, but as things are, the order must be reversed. This would not have displeased him. He bore his scandalous nickname with delight, and he continued to provide verifications for it until he died, in 1549, at the age of seventy-two.

Sodoma as a personality runs so true to a homosexual type so familiar in the arts today that he could very nearly serve as its model. He flaunted his aberration as a badge of superiority that freed him from the conventions that bind other men, and in a tolerant society this exploitation of a weakness could be indulged to the limit, although it could probably not hoodwink a whole segment of society in his time as it does in ours.

Like his counterparts in New York or London or other international art centers today, Sodoma subscribed to the formula of snobbery that interprets spectacular trivialities as hyperrefinements beyond the capacities of people limited by normal emotional processes, identifies high fashion with eccentricity, and introduces expensive exotica into the appurtenances of clothing, living quarters, and partners in love. The theatricalism of the formula is attractive to the *jeunesse dorée*, although it may be puzzling to the solider citizens who eventually foot the bill, and if anything like a social critique can be extracted from such thin material, it is a pattern of mockery that simulates an intellectual examination of established institutions.

In 1531, when he was fifty-four, Sodoma summarized the exhibitionistic triviality of his type in, of all things, a tax return. The punch line of this absurd document is a triple flaunting of his nickname: he signed it "Sodoma Sodoma *derivatum* M. Sodoma." In the course of numerous obscene puns he refers to himself as a gelding who has eight horses to "groom," which horses, however, are nicknamed nanny goats. He lists among his possessions an owl that he thinks he had better not say much about because of some curious connections it has with his pet monkey. He concludes with the multiply preposterous statement that he has upward of thirty children and hence is obviously tax exempt, although he wishes the tax collectors well in their work all the same. Any one of several artists working in New York today can be imagined sending a similar return to the Internal Revenue Service and supplying the gossip columnists with photostats in a bid for publicity. In its combination of archness and insolence, Sodoma's tax return could stand as the manifesto of a social attitude.

Sodoma's private life—if a life so flagrantly publicized can be called private—did not disturb his contemporaries. In his case as in others where artists were roustabouts, eccentrics, adulterers, and even felons, the patrons, including the Church, saw no reason to demand a correspondence between an artist's personal habits and his way of painting. (Pope Leo X awarded Sodoma the title of *cavaliere* in 1518.) But his nickname caused much puzzlement and distress to his admirers in the nineteenth century; they could not reconcile it with the sweetness they found so appealing in his Madonnas.

Actually this sweetness, mawkish to the point of morbidity, is sufficiently synthetic to be all that could be expected of an artist whose way of life was entirely lewd but whose facile professionalism was quite naturally devoted to satisfying the market. The market in Sodoma's case was for holy pictures, and he supplied them. It is here that the parallel between him and his counterparts today breaks down. The patron used to dictate subject matter and, in Sodoma's time, this subject matter was predominantly religious. Today the artist chooses his own subjects and they are almost entirely secular, with the result that the present-day Sodomas have found a formerly unavailable outlet in art and have exalted the japery, the viciousness, and the affectations of their way of life into a code of aesthetics. There is plenty to say about all this, but it belongs elsewhere.

As for Sodoma the painter:

He was born in Vercelli, the Piedmont. Trained in the Lombard tradition, he is classifiable as a Lombard painter, but he adopted Siena as his favorite city and did so much work there (he finally died there) that he is also called Sienese. He has no stylistic connection with that school, which in fact was moribund before he gave it his coup de grâce. He was in no way an original painter. He drew upon the most superficial aspects of Perugino, Raphael, and Leonardo in forming his style, with Leonardo's most unfortunate works as his major source. Sodoma worked in Milan in 1498 (he was twenty-one), and there he absorbed the pseudo-Leonardesque sentimentalism of the Milanese Leonardesque school.

Sodoma was first in Siena about 1501, and between 1505 and 1508 he completed a set of frescoes on the life of St. Benedict in Monte Oliveto, twenty miles from Siena, that had been begun by an artist of entirely different stamp, the fiercely vigorous Signorelli. His work was impressive enough so that Agostino Chigi called Sodoma to Rome, where posterity narrowly escaped a disaster: apparently Sodoma was in line to do the frescoes in the Stanza della Segnatura that shortly afterward were turned over to Raphael. Rome did not respond to Sodoma, so he returned to Siena. He also worked in Mantua, Florence, Volterra, and Pisa. At best inconsequential, at worst lamentable, he was an artist who never had difficulty finding work. On the whole, by his own standards, he must have led a most satisfactory life.

Lorenzo Lotto—whose pictures are too easily passed by in a museum when they hang alongside more obviously dramatic ones—is the extreme example of the sixteenth-century artist left in an undetermined position between contrasting ideals: those that he could not attain, and those that, for some reason, he did not recognize as within his reach. Lotto could not attain to the philosophical intellectualism of Leonardo, the balance of Raphael, or the passion of Michelangelo. At the same time, although he was a solitary and restless spirit, he did not express his disturbed and questioning temperament in corresponding pictorial forms, as the mannerist painters were doing. If he has to be classified dogmatically with any one group of painters, that group would be the High Renaissance painters in Venice fathered by Giovanni Bellini (who was perhaps his teacher) and Giorgione. But he would rest uneasily there, seeming sometimes too early a painter (related, even, to Botticelli) for that company, and at other times protomannerist or protobaroque.

But these are only labels. Lotto's special character, which has brought him an increasingly enthusiastic band of supporters within recent years, is that of a spirit unidentifiable with any single aspect of his time, unable to adjust to the practicalities that bring a man to success, sensitive to the currents of change flowing around him, but always involved in a search for an elusive ideal that, for all he knew, may not have existed. In these facets of his personal and painterly character, he is a prototype of the modern artist.

Lotto was a wanderer. Born in Venice about 1480, but never content to stay in one place for long, he may even have gone to Germany in his youth. There is a strong Germanic influence in his painting that could have been stimulated by Dürer's visit to Venice in 1506 (at which time Lotto was there), but suggests a further acquaintance with Holbein and even Grünewald. Lotto's early years are cloudy. By 1509 (he was about twenty-nine) he was in Rome, working in the Vatican apartments, where he could have met Raphael. By

1513 he was in Bergamo, where his family had originated, or was based there while making excursions around and about. Between 1526 and 1529 he was mostly in Venice. Then for ten years he roamed the small cities of the Marches. Now aging, and never having been able to make a decent living, he came to Venice and lodged with a nephew for two years. Then to Treviso for three years, staying with a friend named Giovanni di Saon. From 1545 to 1549, Venice again, where, in 1548—nearing seventy now—he drew up a will, cutting his friend in Treviso out of some previously scheduled bequests, and describing himself as "alone, without loyal help, and quite troubled of mind."

From the age of about sixty-nine for four years he was in Ancona, and in his financial desperation organized a raffle of thirty of his pictures. Only seven were sold. Although he had painted some important altarpieces, he was as forgotten as if he had accomplished nothing at all. Frightened now, and weary, he gained admission to the sanctuary of the Holy House of Loreto, and in 1554 became a lay brother of that order, deeding over to it all such worldly goods as he had, and all his works. He died two years later, aged about seventy-six.

His paintings, seen in retrospect over all the long years, show him again and again on the point of becoming the great and important painter that he is not. As the fascinating and yet never entirely satisfying painter that he is, he demonstrates two qualities fairly consistently, in spite of his chameleon-like changes under a series of influences: there is a restlessness to his art, even when it echoes the serenity of Raphael or Giorgione, and in his portraits there is an acute sensitivity to character, a discernment of psychological values as the specific and intimate characteristics of individuals rather than as generalized characteristics of a type. In his very last years he developed a contrasting manner—austere, and almost monochromatic in contrast with his former bold color. Unsatisfactory in themselves, these last paintings, in a secretive way, provide a final enigma in the case of Lorenzo Lotto.

In 1538, when Lotto was about fifty-eight years old, he started an account book that is a unique document in the history of art. Minutely detailed, it is not only a ledger but, by second nature, a diary. He kept it for eighteen years, almost to the day he died. Begun at the time when he was entering the final severe phase of his troubles, the explicit factual record must have provided for the increasingly insecure man a single and continuing definable thread running through the vagaries of his way of life. But the record, day to week to month to year after year, grew more and more sinister in its facts.

Jacopo Negreti (1480-1528), called **Palma Vecchio**, was a pupil of Giovanni Bellini and much influenced by Giorgione, Titian, and Lotto—but particularly Giorgione. There is much confusion concerning his work, since a great deal of it was uncompleted in his studio at the time of his death and was taken over by other artists. His hallmark is a coloration somewhat more blond than Giorgione's and, as well, a blonde female type, a bit too luxuriantly buxom, that has always passed as typically Venetian, yet must have become extinct. You never see it in Venice today.

Born Giovanni de Lutero, Dosso Dossi was the last painter who by stretching things can be called a member of the school of Ferrara—which he was, geographically. He was either born about 1479 in Ferrara or taken there at an early age (his father was an estate agent for the rulers of Ferrara, the Este family). He became court artist to the Estes after

1516, and a few years earlier is known to have been in Mantua. Nothing is known of his early training.

Whatever predilection he felt for the hard, violent Ferrarese manner, or whatever early training he had in it, was largely negated by the antipodal example of Giorgione, to whom he is most closely related. Poetical, literary (with many pictorial references to Ariosto, who mentions him as well as his younger brother, Battista, in "Orlando Furioso"), Dosso Dossi is an only partially realizable painter who tantalizes by this incompleteness. But his lyrical power and personal style are evident in at least one painting, the one that always comes to mind when his name is mentioned, the *Circe* in the Borghese Gallery in Rome, where the enchantress sits in a landscape surrounded by her lovers transformed into animals. Dosso was at his most inventive in landscape backgrounds like this one, struck here and there with unnatural light. A series of pure landscapes, executed in fresco for the Estes, and conceivably his masterpieces, have disappeared. He died in 1592.

In tandem with Fra Bartolommeo, Andrea del Sarto succeeded to the position of reigning master in Florence after the city had lost Raphael and Michelangelo (and its leadership in Italian painting) to Rome. A most estimable artist but hardly a stimulating one, Andrea was not the man to lead Florence to a new position. He is the perfect example of the artist who just misses greatness. He had neither the independently inventive spirit that could have served him as a catalyst for his talents nor, an occasionally successful substitute, the capacity for assimilation and retention that Raphael possessed to so high a degree.

Andrea del Sarto's capacity for assimilation was less impressive and was also, unfortunately, combined with an incapacity to resist the assimilation of any new trend that attracted him; his art became a kind of passageway through which the ideas of other men flowed in succession without strengthening his potential for individual expression. He was a superb fresco painter, technically. Whatever he painted, in any medium, was always graceful, always tasteful; strong sensuous undercurrents in his work never developed the self-confidence to break through the surface of decorum. As a result his pictures were attractive in a way that demanded no effort and no great sensitivity on the part of the observer, and he was a popular and busy artist. The same easiness and essential meaninglessness made him an idol of the Victorian taste for sweet Madonnas.

The artists who most influenced him, listed in order of appearance, provide a thumbnail review of the fifteenth century. His earliest authenticated works reflect Masaccio and Ghirlandaio. As he matured, there are hints of Botticelli and Filippino Lippi, and then directly recognizable derivations from Leonardo, Raphael (his most successfully assimilated source), and Michelangelo (his least). He also knew and admired the Venetians, and he made a successful (and of course graceful) fusion of Venetian colorism with Florentine-Roman draftsmanship.

Andrea deserves a special award for having introduced Dürer's prints to Italy. He knew them well, owned many, and borrowed from them freely. But in this case he borrowed motifs without being affected by Dürer's style (whose residual Gothicisms turned out to be so fascinating to mannerist painters that Dürer, the humanist, became a source for anti-classical affectations).

Andrea was born in 1486, the son of a tailor—from which "del Sarto," making him "Andrea the Tailor's Boy." Vasari, who knew him well, says that he was apprenticed to a goldsmith when a child. As a youth he worked in the shop of

Piero di Cosimo—one of the few artists who left no conspicuous mark on him. As a man he was convivial and high-
spirited, a gregarious fellow who not only enjoyed but was
greatly enjoyed by large companies of friends—until he made
a notoriously unfortunate marriage.

In 1517, when he was thirty-one, he succumbed to the
charms of a young widow (everyone admitted that she was
beautiful) named Lucrezia di Bartolomeo del Fede. Of low
origin and evil temperament, Lucrezia soon drove Andrea's
family out of his house and installed her own instead—one
instance of the complete dominion she exerted over her husband. In his lengthy biography of Andrea, Vasari belabors
Lucrezia convincingly, although, for some reason not known,
he tempered his judgment in the second edition of his
"Lives."

The rather soft and passive character of Andrea's art is
consistent with a personality that would welcome domination.
In 1519 he had the honor of being called to France by
Francis I, but after less than a year, unable to bear the separation from Lucrezia any longer, he returned to Florence for a
visit and then wrote the King that he had changed his mind
and would not continue in his service. Francis was furious,
and Andrea's erstwhile companions in Italy—for this and
other reasons in cumulation—wrote him off as a lost soul and
poor company. He remained in great demand as an artist.
He died in 1531, shortly after entering a religious order, the
Company of St. Sebastian.

Andrea del Sarto perhaps was born just a little too late
or just a little too early. If he had been somewhat older, he
might have found in the air of Florence before the High
Renaissance a strengthening vigor that went out of it when
the Roman achievements of Raphael and Michelangelo set
an impossible standard for emulation. And if he had been
younger, he might have participated in the movement—or

impulse—called mannerism, which supplied niches for many artists of lonely or dependent temperaments. His pupils included two of the great mannerists, Pontormo and Rosso, as well as our old friend, the minor mannerist and major historian, Vasari.

MANNERISM

"Mannerism" is the newest, or most recently popularized, term adopted to designate a major development in the history of art. Originally useful in the designation and re-evaluation of a group of sixteenth-century Italian painters whose eccentricities of style are "mannered" in what was once a derogatory sense, "mannerism" has lately become a catchall term that, like "classicism" and "romanticism," can be applied very widely, as to definition, as to geography, and as to century.

The term will be most useful to us if it is applied internationally to the anticlassical, individualistic approaches of the sixteenth-century painters, an application flexible enough to include at one extreme the precious artificialities of little men and, at the other, the masterpieces of Tintoretto and El Greco. El Greco may, indeed, be the supreme mannerist painter, exemplifying by his violent eccentricities of style the first mannerist premise, which is the denial of Renaissance realism and classical harmony in favor of any distortion of form or color that will release emotional expression in new harmonies of its own. The expression can be extremely concentrated, personal, and even ingrown, by contrast with the expansive, universally inclusive humanism of the High Renaissance ideal.

This emphasis on personalism and on distortion should suggest immediately a connection between mannerism and such modern artists as Vincent van Gogh and his descendants, the German expressionists, and even the abstract painters who put their faith in the personal impulse above all else. Popular imagination has fastened on Van Gogh as the supertype of the disturbed artist (or mad genius) whose art must flow from him like blood from a wound. This standard image is grossly exaggerated in its emphasis on an emotionalism that ignores the equally strong element of rational calculation that goes into the planning of any work worth considering as a work of art, but it is only a gross exaggeration rather than a total misrepresentation. The re-evaluation of the Italian mannerists, and their renewed popularity, are in great part a reflection of this twentieth-century attitude toward the artist and his means of expression.

The roster of sixteenth-century mannerist artists includes a higher than normal percentage of neurotic personalities, with Jacopo Pontormo as the perfect example. But mannerism was also adaptable to the cold, fashionable, stylistic elegance of a painter like Bronzino, to the decorative affectations of Primaticcio and the School of Fontainebleau, to the violent vulgarisms of Giulio Romano, and—as we have already said —to the intensely mystical spirituality of El Greco.

Jacopo Pontormo, the quintessential figure of Italian mannerism, evokes the trauma suffered by artists lost between two worlds, the assured, defined, and stable one idealized in High Renaissance classicism and the equally assured one of the grandiloquent baroque. Pontormo's art is altogether anti-classical by intention and antigrandiloquent in the natural course of things—an art of uncertainties and retreats, if you wish, but one that can reduce both reason and grandiloquence to inconsequence. For Pontormo the concept of universal truth was untenable and the only defense against anguish was a search for personal compensations. His art is haunted, withdrawn, and inaccessible, and the same adjectives apply to his personality outside his art, if the one can be said to have existed outside the other.

Increasingly eccentric to the point of insanity, Pontormo would probably have been recognized today as a socially benign psychotic, which makes him a prototype of one modern concept of the artist—the artist as an individual divorced from society, subject to special torments and special revelations, who works for himself from within himself, who relinquishes the pleasures and rewards that other men struggle for and in turn must expect to be rejected and misunderstood, but who leaves for the rest of us the record of a spiritual struggle that was his reason for living and becomes his form of immortality.

Pontormo was born Jacopo Carrucci in 1494 in the small town near Empoli from which he later took his name. An orphan and a prodigy, he was apprenticed, by the age of eleven, in Florence, where he might have had a brief contact with Leonardo da Vinci. In his thirties, Pontormo succeeded to the eminence of his teacher, Andrea del Sarto. Accorded public commendation by Michelangelo, he was accepted as the leading Florentine painter. He was the favorite portraitist and mural decorator of the Medici, and might have settled into his still sufficiently conventional style to become, like some other mannerist painters, a workman whose pictorial formula, with its special eccentricities as his trademark, could be depended upon as a standard brand.

But he grew inward, adapting his style not to the taste of patrons but to the demands of his own shy, introspective, and solitary nature. In his forties his popularity declined in favor of other mannerists, especially his pupil Bronzino (whom he virtually adopted as a son), whose stylishness was more easily grasped. Pontormo continued to receive commissions, but his painting became more and more puzzling, filled with ambiguous relationships, with exaggerations and sophisticated refinements of Gothic forms borrowed from Dürer, and with contortions reflecting the anguish but not the positiveness of Michelangelo's late work.

According to Vasari, Pontormo remained temperate and mild-mannered, but would work only for whom he pleased, even if it meant working for low wages. Many of his panel paintings have disappeared; his frescoes are in bad condition, some of them having been painted over, years after his death, because they were never understood. His drawings, to the number of some four hundred (hundreds are lost), are the true Pontormo, the full record of his life from his prodigious youth to his solitary maturity, when (the story has become symbolic of his withdrawal) he would mount to his bedroom and then pull up behind him the only means of access to these quarters—a ladder that operated on a pulley.

Drawings can be the most intimate, immediate, and spontaneous expression of an artist's personality as well as of his skill. Pontormo's drawings amount to a perpetual soliloquy. But the soliloquy never reaches a conclusion. It questions, but the questions are asked without expectation of answers. The ecstatically beautiful bodies of his nudes flow like water or ascend like vapor; they may half rise from reclining positions, turning toward us with unnatural suppleness, twisting around at the waist to gaze at us or beyond us without comprehension of their own being or of ours. They are painfully intimate in their evocations of sensual delight, but they seem removed from sensual experience. The features are often blurred by disturbing reveries—the eyes reduced to smudged sockets, the mouths half opened in a moment before awakening.

As a pure draftsman, in describing the structure of an arm, a leg, a torso, in a few broken lines, Pontormo has his peers only in Raphael and Michelangelo. But he differs from them in that he denies the physical actuality that they capture. His figures have the quality of a mirage; they would elude us by vanishing if we were so foolish as to try to grasp them.

In his closed world, Pontormo kept a diary that is as curious and personal a document as any artist has left us. We might expect it to be filled with mystical ponderings, with the theorizing as to the nature of things—warped to his own peculiarities—that fills the greatest document of them all, Leonardo's notebooks. But Leonardo's notebooks are the ponderings of a philosopher. Pontormo's diary is a day-to-day and sometimes even an hour-to-hour account of a recluse who kept an exact record for himself of what work he did ("the hand and half the arm and the knee and the part of the leg where the hand rests" of a St. Laurence, on one day); of exactly what pains or twinges, probably hypochondriacal, he felt in his body, and of the state of his bowels; of just what treatment he gave himself; of the weather; of the time he arose; of the time he went to bed; of the time of the notations; of his diet, even down to the measurement, in ounces (ten), of the bread that he ate one Saturday night with two eggs and a borage salad. And if this spelling-out of the minutiae of existence seems for a moment paradoxical in a man so unworldly, it is in the end the most poignant revelation of Pontormo's isolation within himself.

Pontormo died in 1556 at the age of sixty-two.

Giovanni Battista Rosso, or Il Rosso, or Rosso Fioren-
tino, owes his name to his red hair—rare enough to set him
apart in Italy even if he had not been in other ways an exceptional character. He was tall and handsome, a cultivated man
and a man of elegant attraction, but he was also a man of
neurotic temperament who may or may not have terminated
his restless, adventurous, and professionally successful life
by suicide. People are still arguing about that.

Rosso was a close friend and exact contemporary, by
year of birth (1494), of Pontormo's, as well as Pontormo's
fellow student under Andrea del Sarto. Between 1513 and
1523—that is, until he was nearly thirty—he was working in
Florence, and in 1521, when he was only twenty-seven, he
painted his key picture, and one of the key pictures of Florentine mannerism, his *Descent from the Cross* now in the
museum in Volterra. It is a haunted picture, filled with a
morbid unease. Eerily, ten figures participate in the lowering
of Christ's body and none seems to comprehend the event—
or to be fully conscious of another's presence. The passion of
the subject, and its religious significance, are lost in a broken
scheme of individual experiences of a nature not made clear
to the observer for the reason, apparently, that the nature
of the experiences is not understood by the individuals who
suffer them.

By the time he was thirty, Rosso was in Rome, and he
stayed there until the city was sacked in 1527. He was captured by the Germans but escaped, and for three years he
wandered in central and northern Italy. Vasari, who was his
friend, reports that on one occasion during this period of
wandering Rosso came to blows with a priest who had repri-
manded him for misbehavior during a Mass, and that to
escape the scandal, and prosecution, Rosso had to flee the city
secretly. But by 1530 he was in Venice, and apparently his
reputation as an artist had not suffered from whatever bizarre

social lesions his conduct had developed, since in that same year he went to France and began a period of most impressive success under the patronage of Francis I.

Rosso became a great favorite with the King. As a theatrically handsome figure in the circle of the court, he lived in Paris like a nobleman, on the proceeds of work the King commissioned as well as on the income from sinecures he was granted—and by borrowing. He designed fetes and spectacles as well as all kinds of ornamental objects, and was awarded the plum of royal commissions, the decoration of the Grande Galerie of Francis' palace-château of Fontainebleau.

The Grande Galerie is the Book of Genesis of that Franco-Italian mannerist hybrid called the Fontainebleau Style. Rosso and his countryman Primaticcio were the dominant Italian figures in the initiation of the style, but its development, after Rosso's death, fell to Primaticcio. The work from Rosso's hand has suffered too severely from repainting to tell us much about the originals. Surely we are safe in assuming that for purely decorative purposes Rosso modified his haunted manner for one more appropriate to the mode of courtly affectation and the glorification of female sexuality that so preoccupied his French patron.

Rosso had come to France at the age of thirty-six; he died there ten years later in 1540, still at the height of his success. His impulsiveness and his short temper (characteristics that need not be at all inconsistent with the charm, cultivation, and talent that made him a favorite of the King's) may have contributed to his death.

Rosso had taken into his house an intimate friend and co-worker, Francesco Pellegrini. He owed Pellegrini a substantial sum of money (one of a number of heavy debts he had accumulated), but when a hundred ducats disappeared, Rosso accused Pellegrini of the theft. Pellegrini was put to torture, yet maintained his innocence, and when released entered suit for libel against his former friend. The rest of the story is in dispute. According to Vasari, who had known Rosso well, and according to the report accepted in Florence, Rosso committed suicide with a poison he obtained by claiming that he needed it for the mixture of a special paint. Recent research has shown, however, that Rosso died after an illness; also, a Mass was held for his soul, which at that time was forbidden to suicides. The story of Rosso's suicide, nowadays, is reluctantly discredited by most scholars, but Rudolf and Margot Wittkower, in their "Born Under Saturn," suggest a solution that makes the best of both versions of Rosso's end: that he did take the poison, that it was mortal, but that its effect was delayed, and that during the interval Rosso confessed and received extreme unction.

In any case, it is not difficult to imagine that Rosso was ready enough to die. He was only forty-six, but forty-six is an age when physical charms of the kind that had helped Rosso along in his career are becoming a bit frayed. He had never married; he had unjustly accused a good friend and as a result was facing a court action that, while not exactly a matter of life and death, was not going to reflect very well on him; he was in debt, and he loved the kind of good living that is impossible without a lot of money; and, finally, he was ill, whether because he had taken a poison or for some other reason. He was not of a temperament to make the demanded adjustments. He must have found death easeful.

A painter, a sculptor, a designer, and an architect, Francesco Primaticcio made up in versatility what he lacked in profundity. As chief organizer and designer of royal projects for Francis I, and then for Henry II and Catherine de Médicis over a period of more than thirty-five years, he decisively influenced French art and also, though not quite so strongly, art in Germany and the Netherlands. Born about 1504, he learned his craft under Giulio Romano, went to France in 1532 (Rosso had arrived two years earlier), and took full charge when Rosso died in 1540. At the time of Rosso's death, Primaticcio was on one of his periodic returns to Italy, which he combined with forays to collect art for the French monarchs. He died in France in 1570 at the age of sixty-five or sixty-six.

Agnolo Bronzino (Agnolo di Cosimo di Mariano) was in his way—an extremely effective way—as dependable a portrait painter as ever lived, but this dependability was the result of a calculation so extreme that his portraits might have been designed by a well-programmed computer and executed by mechanically operated precision instruments. His sitters, uniformly endowed with an impressively aristocratic hauteur, and clothed in rich stuffs, have little to do with flesh and cloth. They might have been cast in steel and then enameled, or carved in tinted ice, except that they have none of the weightiness of steel and nothing of the vulnerability of ice to warmth.

But these frigid, polished effigies, existing only as fastidious surfaces utterly detached from the disruptive forces of life, are exactly what Bronzino and his patrons wanted, and within their limits they are among the most fascinating portraits ever created. They cannot be called the most attractive, since unapproachability is the fetish of their world. The beings, or pseudo-beings, painted by Bronzino are unwilling to concede to the observer any slightest indication that in their private lives they might share passions common to the rest of men. With their glance meeting ours as if by chance, and without interest, they are spiritually as well as physically immobile, apparently congealed within their desired airlessness. They are like impregnable fortresses; their courtly dress is an armor against all intrusion; they are a supercaste without flaws and incapable of defection from the norm they share. One of them is very like another; such individuality as they may have behind their calculated façades is indicated only by secondary clues—a book, a statue, a child, as an accessory appropriate to a profession or an interest particular to the sitter.

Bronzino was born in 1503 near Florence and died there in 1572. Only nine years younger than Pontormo, he was that eccentric master's pupil and adopted son, if not by law, then by affection. He based his style on Pontormo's early work, but developed it in the direction of extreme formality. As a result, he displaced Pontormo as court painter to the Medici when Pontormo's increasingly ingrown and personal vision became incompatible with the supreme impersonality demanded in portraits for a court where an almost ritual formality was the fashion.

As a painter of religious subjects, Bronzino was defeated by his limitation—a lack of interpretative depth and scope, probably inherent in his talent, but also cultivated as a stylistic iciness. In his occasional allegories, notably *Venus, Cupid, Folly, and Time* in the National Gallery in London, he presents charades impeccably organized into mannerist decorations of the extremest artificiality. He is, all told, a perfect example of an artist whose strength lies in the exploitation of his limitations. Perfect within his manner, he is the perfect mannerist of elegance.

Parmigianino, as his name reveals, was born in Parma (in 1503). His real name was Francesco Mazzola or Mazzuoli; his father, Filippo, was also a painter, as were his uncles Pier Ilario and Michele Mazzola, who became his guardians when his father died, only two years after his birth. These relatives amounted to nothing as painters; the boy's first strong influence came from the example of Correggio's work in his home city. The ubiquitous Raphael exerted a stronger influence when Parmigianino went to Rome at the age of twenty-one in 1524. He knew Rosso there, and like Rosso left the city after the sack of 1527—although without sharing Rosso's adventure of being captured by the Germans and then escaping.

Parmigianino's great adventure was with alchemy. He died in 1540 when he was only thirty-seven years old. In that brief span, he managed to create a body of work that reveals him as an artist of great originality. Also, he became transformed from a fastidious and mild-mannered youth into an unkempt, long-bearded savage of irascible disposition. In the end he was giving every appearance of madness, and mad he was on the subject of alchemy, for he bankrupted himself and wore himself out tending his furnaces.

Parmigianino's painting is quite at variance with his second personality. He is the exemplar of the shift away from morbid reflection discernible in Pontormo and Rosso, toward the hyperrefined, hedonistic, artificialized gracefulness of a group of slightly younger mannerists. His Madonnas are the prototype of the long-legged, ostrich-necked mannequin of fashion ads (his *Madonna of the Long Neck,* in the Uffizi, is always cited as his typical painting); the Christ child lies across his Mother's lap with the languid, exhibitionistic air of a naked infant-odalisque. His male saints pose with full consciousness of their alluring bodies, displaying well-turned legs at the most advantageous angles while rolling their eyes heavenward. But elegance these theatricalized scenes do have; Parmigianino's affectations are carried through in high style, and, purely as a painter, he is a creator of luscious surfaces.

After the sack of Rome, Parmigianino settled in Bologna, but early in 1531, when he was twenty-eight, he came back home to Parma. In the same year he was given the most important commission the city had to offer—the decoration of the dome of the Steccata, a Renaissance church, where he might have produced a work in rivalry with Correggio. About six years earlier, just after Parmigianino had left for Rome, Correggio had completed the decoration of the dome of the Cathedral in Parma, and in doing so had created a prophecy of the baroque that should have inspired emulation. Nothing of the kind happened. Virtually nothing of any kind happened. Eight years after the commission was awarded, Parmigianino had made so little progress (being preoccupied with his furnaces) that the commissioners canceled his contract. (The job was next offered to Giulio Romano, who refused it when Parmigianino wrote him a letter complaining that he had been ill-treated.) This was in 1539, and in the next year Parmigianino died in the little town of Casalmaggiore, which, although not far from Parma, was outside Parmesan jurisdiction and thus offered refuge from the various legal troubles that beset him.

Parmigianino requested that he be buried naked, with a cross of cypress wood upright on his chest, and so he was.

Giulio Romano, born Giulio Pippi de' Gianuzzi in 1492 or 1499, died in 1546. He was a mannerist painter and architect who had been chief assistant to Raphael between 1515 and 1520, had finished some of Raphael's work after that artist's death, and then in 1524 had gone to Mantua as court architect and painter to Federigo Gonzaga. An efficient technician, a tactful man of the world, and a success, Giulio Romano is hard to defend as an artist. He exaggerated first Raphael's most faulty manner and then Michelangelo's late style. He had an unerring eye for the worst of any man he imitated, and among mannerists he is the one who justifies a now outmoded view toward mannerism as nothing but a degenerated High Renaissance style. In his best-known work, *The Fall of the Giants,* in the Palazzo del Te in Mantua, he covered an entire room with frescoes in illusionistic perspective that envelop the observer in a scene of cataclysm. Here Michelangelo's forms are so coarsened, and his drama is pushed to such an absurdly melodramatic point, that no terror is engendered; rather, the effect is at once alarming and hilarious, as in the pseudo-perilous Katzenjammer Castles in amusement parks.

Giorgio Vasari (1511-1574), the art historian, whose name has occurred so frequently up to this point in this book, but soon now must disappear, was also a mannerist architect and painter, a younger member of the circle that originated around Andrea del Sarto in Florence. Born in 1511, Vasari was twenty-five years younger than Andrea, seventeen years younger than his colleagues Pontormo and Rosso, and eight years younger than the stars of the second generation, Parmigianino and Bronzino. Born in Arezzo, Vasari was proudly Tuscan—not quite to the point of chauvinism, but sufficiently to believe that Tuscan art (essentially, Florentine art) of the Renaissance was the supreme achievement of the ages.

This thesis, of course, can be defended with very strong arguments. Art history still follows, very largely, the line that Vasari laid down. When he published his book of lives, "Le Vite de' Più Eccellenti Architetti, Pittori, et Scultori Italiani" (usually shortened in English to "Vasari's Lives of the Artists" or simply "Vasari's Lives"), in 1550, the scheme of the book was quite direct: the arts had reached their first apex in the ancient world of Greece and Rome (especially Rome) and then died out during the Middle Ages; they were reborn in medieval Tuscany and reached the climax of grandeur with

Michelangelo—a Tuscan, even though he worked so much in Rome. The very word "Renaissance" (*il rinascimento*) was coined by Vasari. It is a word that is as misleading as the originally derogatory term "Gothic," but "rebirth" carries a connotation so strong that for more than two hundred years it contributed to people's misconception that medieval society and medieval art were (just as Vasari thought of them) a waste of centuries between the fall of Rome and the rise of Florence.

But this bias does not keep "Vasari's Lives" from being the most important single history of art ever written. It was the independent effort of a man busy and successful as a painter and just as busy and successful (and much better) as an architect. An achievement without precedent, "Vasari's Lives" not only collated a great mass of fact that would have been lost, but set the pattern that remains basic to any critical-historical writing on art.

The original "Lives" of 1550 concluded with Michelangelo, the only living artist discussed in it. In 1568 Vasari issued an enlarged and revised version, including other living artists, himself among them. The second version is not quite as clear in its historical scheme, but is the better known, simply because it is the more copious. Numerous editions have followed, keeping up with the work of scholars who have been busy at the job of separating Vasari's facts from the legends and rumors that he sometimes recounted as facts. The complete separation between fact and fancy will never be achieved with certainty, and many artists may suffer (or benefit) as personalities because of Vasari's penchant (always a strong temptation) for deducing a man's character from his art. But no reservations concerning his method can make Vasari anything less than the greatest figure in art history. He was the man, in truth, who conceived of such a thing as art history in the first place. With Vasari, art and artists finally assumed their place in the world as facets of civilization as important as politics and politicians, rulers and realms, philosophers and philosophies.

As a painter, Vasari was an intelligent, even scholarly, practitioner. As an architect he was perhaps no more than that, but an intelligent, scholarly architect has more to offer than a painter with those qualifications. Vasari's best-known building is the Uffizi Palace in Florence. It is gratifyingly appropriate that his building should now be the outstanding museum-storehouse of the work of the great Tuscan artists that he celebrated.

Jacopo Robusti, nicknamed Il Tintoretto, or "The Little Dyer," after his father's calling, was born in Venice in 1518. Giorgione had already been dead for eight years, and Titian was painting vigorously, as he would continue to do —the unchallenged Grand Presence in Venetian art—until his death, when Tintoretto was fifty-eight years old. As if determined to have the scene to himself as the city's most eminent painter, Tintoretto lived for another eighteen years, dying in 1594 at the age of seventy-six.

Tintoretto is a mannerist painter within the first ring of inclusion if the center is assigned to such painters as Pontormo, Rosso, and their colleagues or followers to whom the term is most narrowly applied. He is mannerist in his cultivation of dramatic, expressive distortions, but differs radically from the central Italian mannerists in point of view: he is outside the whole area of neurasthenic suggestion, the evocation of isolated, personal, and often troubled experience, that runs through so much of the best of mannerist painting. He is a painter of tremendous vigor, of a theatricalism at once so violent and so skilled that at his best he shifts from the area of superb operatics into strong and true emotionalism.

Tintoretto was a great showman, in paint. His exploding and flickering lights, the bizarre angles at which his figures fly through the air, his intense darks from which wraithlike figures emerge—all this painted with a brush loaded with braggadocio in celebration of the color and texture that were part of his Venetian heritage—would be a kind of Barnumism if Tintoretto were not in such perfect control of his seeming flashiness, and if he were not always conscious, in the end, of representing a grand tradition.

Or two grand traditions. "The drawing of Michelangelo and the color of Titian," he is said to have inscribed over the entrance to his studio, or on its wall. Perhaps he did. At any rate, he is reported by trustworthy sources to have said that he wanted to make such a combination in his painting. He did not, however, make it. As a draftsman he developed a broken line to describe exaggerated swellings and contractions of the forms of the body that would have appalled the basically classical Michelangelo, and as a colorist he turned Titian's serene lyricism into a stormy dialogue between violent darks and hectic lights. Perhaps what Tintoretto meant was that he wanted to combine the dynamism of Michelangelo with the opulence of Titian, and this, in truth, he did, without sounding the human spirit as deeply as either, in spite of his intensity.

Tintoretto worked briefly in Titian's studio. We are told that he was an unruly student who could not get along with the master, but by the mass of evidence, he seems to have been an even-tempered man, amicable in company although not a great socializer: for this, he was too busy a worker. His very early career is vague, and he emerges in 1548, at thirty, almost as explosively as the figure that hurtles through the air in his first success, *St. Mark Rescuing a Slave* (Venice, Academy).

Tintoretto's life seems to have been as orderly as it was

busy and successful. As his commissions multiplied, his studio grew to the dimensions of Titian's. His happy marriage supplied him with studio foremen—two sons named Domenico and Marco, and a daughter, Marietta—who became proficient in their father's manner and were entrusted with more important work than were the usual shop assistants.

Tintoretto's monument is the Scuola di San Rocco in Venice. He decorated the entire building over a period of many years while working on other commissions, secure with a sensible contract that awarded him an annual stipend. Beginning in 1565, he executed in the great hall of the lower floor a series of paintings 12 feet high of the scenes of the Passion. When these were completed he went on, in 1578, to repeat the performance in the matching upper hall with paintings 16 feet high on the life of Christ; in an adjoining room he painted scenes of the life of the Virgin. The *Crucifixion* from this group may be his masterpiece, if one painting is to be singled out of the lot.

Tintoretto was a painter of such daring and such energy that he seems to have expended the reserve of vital creative force intended to last Venice for the next hundred years. It was not until the eighteenth century, with Tiepolo, that the city produced another painter fully worthy of its tradition—although Tintoretto's somewhat younger contemporary, Veronese, deserves respectful attention as a sumptuous decorator who had his share in the final display of grandeur.

Francesco da Ponte (1470/75-1539/41), who took the name Bassano from his native city on the mainland near Venice, was the patriarch of a three-generation family of painters. A follower of Bellini, he had all the marks of the modest provincial. His son Jacopo, the foremost painter of the dynasty, can in no way be thus dismissed.

Jacopo Bassano (1510/18-1592) was born and died in Bassano (then a flourishing city), but he was frequently in Venice, and was sensitive to the international currents of mannerist painting. If Jacopo can be said to have had a provincial accent of any kind, it was a pleasant one, in the direction of restraint. He often draws upon Florentine and Roman mannerist devices and sometimes suggests the late Tintoretto or even El Greco, but he makes his own sober and thoughtful adaptations as something more than a country cousin. In one respect he stands as a minor pioneer: he employed a pictorial vocabulary of peasants, farm beasts, and other robust rural elements in devotional pictures that forecast later genre painting.

Jacopo's three sons conclude the Bassano dynasty. The eldest, named for his grandfather and called Francesco the Younger (1549-1592), established a Venetian branch of the family workshop in about 1581, with his two brothers. He was a painter of some merit but a man of unstable temperament who committed suicide shortly after his father's death. The middle son Leandro (1557-1622) responded to a *retardataire* vogue and was much honored for his imitations of Giorgione. The youngest, Gerolamo (1566-1621), imitated his father—but not very effectively.

It seems a denial of every reasonable expectation that a young Greek artist who had come to sixteenth-century Italy would choose to abandon Venice and Rome, the great centers, and settle in Toledo, which by comparison was a closed and declining society, and become the earliest of Spain's trinity of great artists—El Greco, Velázquez, and Goya. And it seems downright freakish that the one among them who was Greek by birth and Italian by first adoption should be the most subjectively Spanish of the three—a less grandiloquent way of saying that El Greco summed up the passion and mystery of the Spanish soul. Everything about El Greco is unexpected. We do not know a great deal about him as a person, and we could never know enough to harmonize the enigmatic contradictions of what we do know.

He was born near Candia in Crete in 1541, and was trained as an artist in the Byzantine style still current there. In his early twenties he went to Venice (Crete had been under Venetian dominion for three centuries), where he studied with Titian, according to mentions that have come down to us from his contemporaries, but where he certainly was much more affected by the tempestuous art of Tintoretto. At an unknown date he went, with good introductions, to Rome, where, we may believe in spite of confused and incomplete information, he had a degree of success.

His name was Domenicos Theotocopoulos, and all his life he continued to sign that name, in Greek letters, on his paintings, just as the monkish icon painters signed theirs, although signatures on European paintings at that time were uncommon. This Greek signature, and the fact that Spain tagged him with the sobriquet El Greco, "The Greek," shows that he remained an exotic outsider in a country that he apotheosized in a way, it seems to us, possible only to a man who was born in it and raised in it, acquiring the emotional sensitivities that are planted in childhood and ripen in youth and early manhood.

And yet El Greco could not have developed this style that seems so Spanish if he had not retained so much from his Byzantine training and his Italian experience. "And yet" is a phrase that pops up continually in any effort to explain El Greco. There is hardly a flat, unequivocal statement to be made about him beyond the facts of such dates, fees, and the like, as are recorded in Spanish legal documents.

His fees were high, and an unusual number of the documents have to do with litigations over payment. When he lost a suit over his *Burial of Count Orgaz* (Toledo, Church of Santo Tomé), which did not satisfy the patron but can now be found in any art history, he countered with the pronouncement: "As surely as the rate of payment is inferior to the value of my sublime work, so will my name go down to posterity as one of the greatest geniuses of Spanish painting." Years before, he gave, or is supposed to have given, himself a similar vote of self-confidence when the question came up of retouching Michelangelo's *Last Judgment* in the Sistine Chapel by adding loincloths to the nudes. El Greco suggested that the whole thing might better be torn down, and he offered to do it over again without any offending passages and at a level of excellence equal to Michelangelo's.

You did not say that kind of thing about Michelangelo in Rome—and don't yet. The remark has been offered as an explanation of El Greco's emigration to Spain. Although it seems unlikely that he would have had to leave town because of it, he did go to Madrid about 1576, with letters of introduction to the court. The only valid professional reason for going to Spain would have been to work for Philip II at the Escorial, but if this is what El Greco expected, he was disappointed. He would normally have returned to Italy after such a setback, and we do not know why he did not. He was thirty-six years old when we find him settled in Toledo, and he painted there for thirty-seven years until his death in 1614.

Philip II had removed the court from Toledo to Madrid sixteen years earlier. No longer politically important, the city was still filled with intellectual ecclesiastics, and was in that position where cultivated taste, isolated from the main stream of things, may become highly esoteric. El Greco's style, already eccentric by the provincial standards of Spain, and increasingly individual from year to year, appealed to such a circle, which, moreover, found him exotically attractive as an emissary from a wider and freer world.

El Greco must have been a godsend to men like Fray Felix Hortensio Paravicino, an important scholar and poet who praised his genius in sonnets. El Greco's portrait of Paravicino (now in the Museum of Fine Arts in Boston) is an accolade to the writer in the spirit of the poems. Like the rest of El Greco's portraits, this one is technically Venetian in its parentage, but it is pure El Greco in its emphasis on inner spirit rather than worldly presence. In its expressive exaggerations (it is "out of drawing"), it is a portrait that would satisfy only the exceptional person who belonged to the special circle that El Greco found in Toledo. He could never have become a widely popular portraitist for the very reasons that make him a great one. We know little about his relationships with most of his sitters, but we must be safe in believing that, like Paravicino, they wanted to be painted by El Greco—and he wanted to paint them—because of reciprocal intellectual and aesthetic interests.

The members of this coterie were men of influence, which probably explains how El Greco received some of the large commissions that, once executed, proved unsatisfactory to the commissioning patrons. He remained, always, a special case. For all the influence he exerted on Spanish artists, he might never have left Greece. And here we come to a seeming contradiction—the attempt to explain the exalted emotionalism of his art in terms of the spiritual climate of seventeenth-century Catholicism (which was more intense in Spain than anywhere else) while at the same time explaining the dry, routine productions of his Spanish contemporaries as an expression of the Inquisition. But the contradiction is only apparent. It is merely another indication that El Greco was a rebel and an outsider who painted in accord with his own theories while native Spanish painters followed the pseudo-religious and pseudo-moralistic policies laid down by fiat.

We can visualize El Greco at this time in terms of some presumed self-portraits in his elongated style—distinguished, long-faced, high-foreheaded, with luminous eyes and an air of melancholy sensitivity. The vision may be overpoeticized. El Greco was not a dreamer. He was a man of Crete, where a fierce traditional independence had hardened in the face of foreign oppression. In autocratic Spain, El Greco was conspicuously vehement in his assertion of his rights as a free man. How he ever weathered the Inquisition is a question: the Tribunal tried 1,172 cases between 1577 and 1614, the years of El Greco's arrival and his death, and he served as interpreter for some of the accused Greek refugees. He must have been outraged when barbarous punishments were inflicted in the name of holiness, and could hardly have failed to speak his mind.

Only a man who held a most respected position and who had made influential friends could have remained secure in so precarious a situation. In Toledo, among wealthy men who were effete remnants of a culture, El Greco surely exerted an extraordinary fascination. The Greek language was a fashionable mark of cultivation everywhere in Europe. El Greco had traveled, and his Spanish friends were seldom permitted to leave the country. He brought with him to Spain a splendid library, which included the works of the great men of ancient Greece in the original. He had seen the luxurious way of life of Titian and the Roman artists, and he emulated it. "He earned many ducats but wasted them in ostentatious living," a contemporary observer (Jusepe Martínez) wrote. "He even kept paid musicians in his house so that he might enjoy every pleasure while he ate." The so-called Casa del Greco in Toledo, a tourist attraction, is only a reconstruction of a house in the quarter where El Greco lived, but he can be imagined there among the flowers, the fine furniture, the works of art, the library, and the retainers who surrounded him.

He must also be imagined living in concubinage with a woman named Jerónima de las Cuevas. Her name is just about all we know of her. It was recorded the week before El Greco's death when he gave power of attorney to her son, Jorge Manuel, and recognized him as his own son also. El Greco's unconventional domestic life marks him again as an outsider, since liaisons of this kind, while acceptable enough in Italy, were taboo in half-puritanical Spain. If El Greco's recognition of Jorge Manuel, who was a man of thirty-six, was not merely a gesture of affection to a son his mistress had acquired earlier, it might mean that the liaison had begun shortly after El Greco arrived in Spain—and could explain why he stayed there instead of returning to Italy after a conceivable professional disappointment in Madrid.

Jorge Manuel was himself a painter, sculptor, and architect (El Greco also was all three), although not very talented. He had taken over most of the management of his father's studio at the age of nineteen and was one of several students and assistants who copied and varied the master's paintings to the subsequent wild confusion of scholars. El Greco had a stock repertory of subjects kept on hand in the form of small-scale versions for examination by clients. Any chosen subject could be adapted to required dimensions and modified to include special references. There are as many as eighty versions of some of the subjects, ranging from El Greco's original masterpiece to the stalest kind of hackwork. This assembly-line production would have shocked even Perugino, who approached it in a less open way. But for El Greco it was the normal professional procedure that he had learned from the Byzantine hagiographers who had taught him his craft. As usual, he was simply being El Greco, The Greek—an independent individual who was accepted in a society where the nonconformist was usually hunted down.

The Spanish painter Francisco Pacheco visited El Greco in 1611, three years before his death, and was amazed to hear the old man comment on Michelangelo in a way that would not have amazed anyone who had heard him offer to repaint *The Last Judgment* half a century earlier: Michelangelo "was a good man, but did not know how to paint." "However," Pacheco continued, recalling the incident in his own old age thirty-eight years later, "those who are acquainted with this man will not think it strange that he should have departed from the common sentiment of the rest of the artists, for he was odd in everything as he was in painting."

Pacheco's "those who are acquainted with this man" hints that already El Greco had begun to be forgotten, and that his paintings were not understood. Velázquez, who by then was established as the dominant figure in Spanish painting, is always pointed out as an exception because he admired what El Greco had done. The decline from prominence to obscurity had begun in the last years of El Greco's life. Toledo had been ruined by the wars with the Netherlands and by the Inquisition's successful expulsion of the Jews and the Moors, who had been her finest craftsmen. In his decaying city, El Greco himself might, at last, have been trapped by the intrigues of the enemies he had made during an unconventional lifetime. Pacheco found him as rebellious as ever in spirit, although so broken in health that he could not leave his house to show the visitor around the city—for which he apologized.

But neither the poverty of Toledo, nor the disappearance of his patrons, nor any undercutting by enemies, is a necessary explanation for the neglect that the old El Greco suffered. He could have been merely the victim of a shift in taste. In Spain and in Italy the new trend favored the ordered, balanced, rational art that Velázquez represented in his country. El Greco's style had reached its final stage at the extreme of the opposite virtues—rapturous excitement rather than order, mystical conflict rather than rational balance, fantastic distortion rather than legible realism.

But it was not simply a matter of changing tastes. In spite of the expressive distortions introduced by the mannerists, El Greco's art had become incomprehensible or repellent by any of the standards by which art was judged, and it was to remain so for three hundred years. He seemed to be raving in an unknown tongue; critics and historians would call him mad, or, more ludicrously, would attribute his frenetically distorted forms not to the inspired vision of a lunatic but to the faulty vision of a sane man afflicted with defective eyesight.

El Greco was not babbling. With a clear eye he had invented a new language in painting, a language we have called mystical but that is becoming understandable in psychological terms as the Age of Science tracks down the origins of experiences and actions that the Age of Faith left unexplained and called miraculous. There is hardly a layman today who would wonder what El Greco was trying to do, whether or not he could explain El Greco in words and whether or not he liked what El Greco did.

These phosphorescent worlds of his, where naked bodies are stretched and warped, wavering upward toward some yearned-for bliss; these gestures, so tense yet pervaded by a mortal languor; these eyes that melt and run in rivulets of light; these swelling thighs and chests and constricted ankles and waists; all this adulation of beautiful flesh, flesh denied and enhanced by subjugation to an ascetic ideal—all this is part of what we have codified as passion and sublimation; and it is an expression of ecstatic helplessness in the face of the irrational forces that seem to direct our lives. El Greco

rejected every painterly translation of natural law: true perspective, accurate anatomy, logical illumination are abandoned for twisted and quivering space where bodies that
would be monstrous if they were not superhumanly beautiful
exist like materializations of the spirit within a light that
never existed on earth. The world we see becomes of no
consequence; all vision is inward, or outward from within
through a lens that changes record into revelation. Harmony
means nothing in a realm of rapturous discord, and logic
becomes a distortion rather than a clarification of truth.

None of this could be read, much less accepted, by the
seventeenth or eighteenth century, or by the nineteenth until
its very end. El Greco is hardly mentioned in anything written about art for two centuries after his death, except now
and then as a two-headed calf might be mentioned in a text-
book on veterinary surgery. When a Captain S. Cook (not
the famous explorer) mentioned him in some notes on a
Spanish journey taken in 1829-32, and wrote, "Unfortunately
he adopted an unique and extraordinary tone of color which
destroys all pleasure in examining the greater part of his
work," he was not only exceptional in mentioning El Greco
at all, but was being exceptionally understanding in granting
that El Greco's color was "adopted"—chosen deliberately.
Even Bernard Berenson, as late as 1947, had not accepted the
genius of this anti-Renaissance artist, and could write of "the
Greco admired by culture snobs—who uses pigments to
startle and strike like so much stage thunder."

Pacheco mentions that El Greco had written on art and
philosophy, apparently explaining art as a demonstration of
philosophical principles by which analysis rather than inspiration was defined as the source of an art expressing mystical
passion. But El Greco's manuscripts, which must have been
written in Greek, meant nothing to anyone who handled his
property after his death, and have disappeared. Not even a

secondhand record remains of the correlations he must have made between the most individual style in the history of painting and the thought of the most enigmatic individualist who ever entered the profession.

El Greco is difficult to place in the context of art history. Right now he seems to belong more to the twentieth century than to any other, which means only that we do not yet understand him in relation to his own. There are reasons for calling him a mannerist—the supreme mannerist, even—and there are reasons for connecting him with the antithesis of mannerism, the baroque. He is called the only disciple of Tintoretto, and it is pointed out that his style was fairly well set before he came to Spain. But his spiritual incandescence has little to do with Tintoretto's dramatic flashes of lightning, despite a stylistic relationship too obvious to need pointing out. And if El Greco was not much impressed by Michelangelo's *Last Judgment,* his tapered, wavering figures ascending to heaven have their own cousinship to the bulkier forms of Michelangelo that descend into hell.

Byzantine painting, Italian painting, and something El Greco found in Spain combined to form him. But it is difficult not to imagine that his art, isolated phenomenon that it is, was catalyzed by some final and paramount stimulus that makes negligible the early influence of other painters or whatever subsequent philosophizing El Greco may have done in the rationalization of a compulsion peculiar to himself.

Before El Greco, Spain's most emphatic mannerist was Luis de Morales. His long-necked, long-limbed, emaciated figures hint that he might have been the great man's stylistic ancestor, but such a connection must be rejected upon briefest examination. Morales was, however, an interesting artist, more in the circumstances of his career than in his product.

Morales spent most of his life (1509?-1586) in Badajoz, in the territory of Estremadura, which was hardly a center or even an outpost of the arts. Yet he picked up such progressive devices as Leonardesque *sfumato* and the various Italo-Flemish mannerist affectations. There his modernism stopped, however. He grafted the devices onto a limited set of standard images (Virgin and Child, Ecce Homo, Pietà, Christ Bearing the Cross) and in his stereotypes gave full play to a pseudo-spiritual elevation and intensity combined with a pseudo-aristocratic refinement that added up to the brand of pious sentimentality that has always been able to find a wide public.

Philip II, a true connoisseur, rejected Morales completely, but granted him an old-age pension in response to what amounted to popular demand. Morales was tremendously popular with an uncourtly public. He was also immensely prolific during a long life, but always poor: his provincial patrons did not pay well. They rewarded him, however, with the same epithet that a more demanding public had given to Michelangelo: "The Divine." In the case of Morales, though, the reference was more to the aggressive divinity of his subject matter than to the divinity of his creative gift.

Morales probably had brief instruction under a minor Flemish mannerist, but he was essentially self-taught—and whatever serious reservations may be held about his stylistic devices, there is no denying that he developed an arresting style of his own, whatever sources he found as raw material for its synthesis.

To return to Italy:

Giuseppe Arcimboldo, an entertaining artist of little consequence, has had the double good fortune of enjoying exaggerated popularity during his lifetime—for a moderately legitimate reason—and exaggerated esteem in the twentieth century for fortuitous reasons that have little to do with his merits.

Arcimboldo was a trick painter. He hit upon the idea of constructing fantastic heads (and sometimes landscapes) from masses of fruits, vegetables, or animals to produce a double image. In a profile portrait, for instance, what appears to be a nose turns out to be, from another visual approach, a curled-up rabbit. Or, in another picture, a warty cucumber. We speak of people being "apple-cheeked." In one Arcimboldo head, an allegory of summer, the cheek is actually an apple, combined with the already mentioned cucumber and other fruits in a double image that is a head and shoulders of an allegorical figure, or is just a pile of fruits, vegetables, and grain, depending on how you look at it.

Arcimboldo was a slick craftsman, and these fantasies are both decorative and entertaining. They were popular during his lifetime for these reasons, but his contemporaries could also see them as allegories. Arcimboldo observed traditional analogies when, for instance, he would create a double image of a wolf and a human forehead. The wolf is a cunning animal and the forehead is the seat of human cunning. In Arcimboldo's day, such analogies were closer to science (or what was thought of as science) than is apparent to us today.

Although he was widely admired and even quite seriously written about during his lifetime and shortly after his death, Arcimboldo's engaging tricks were relegated to their proper position, remaining attractive as engaging tricks, until he was claimed as a prophet and brother by the surrealists of Salvador Dali's generation in our century. Dali has been especially deft in the concoction of double images, by which a landscape becomes a collection of Freudian symbols. In surrealism, by contrast with the innocent art of Arcimboldo, the double image becomes an illustration of the psychopathological process of repression and sublimation. It is safe to say that nothing of the kind entered Arcimboldo's head; at most, his double images were superficially moralistic and didactic.

Arcimboldo has also been picked up lately by critics intent on extending the boundaries of mannerism. His stylistic affectations and playfulness give him, perhaps, an acceptable card of membership in this order.

Although we know nothing about Arcimboldo's personality, we have no reason to believe that he was an eccentric. Everything indicates, on the contrary, that he was a lively, vigorous, practical man whose fantasies were created not in the spirit of a visionary, a mystic, or any kind of neurotic, but by the application of an ingenious device happily hit upon. He was born in Milan in 1527, and in 1549, when he was twenty-two, he began to work, with his father Biagio, on designs for the stained-glass windows of Milan Cathedral. These were quite normal, even rather dull. He worked in the Cathedral for nine years, and thereafter had some success as a designer of tapestries.

In 1562, when he was thirty-five, Arcimboldo entered the service of Ferdinand I, and he remained at the court in Prague for twenty-six years, serving as court painter to Ferdinand's successors, Maximilian II and Rudolph II. His bizarre concoctions were created for these Habsburgs; Rudolph II particularly admired them, and made Arcimboldo a count palatine. His duties included the designing of pageants and other festivities (his talent for theatrical invention was entirely applicable in this field), and he was also commissioned to seek out antiquities, curios, and rare or freakish animals for the collections of the Habsburg court.

Arcimboldo died in Florence, still in the imperial service, in 1593, at the age of sixty-six.

A Florentine mannerist primarily remembered as an architect, Bernardo Buontalenti (or Bernardo dalle Girandole) was also a painter and sculptor whose exuberant drawings alone would require his inclusion in a book on artists.

Buontalenti, born about 1536, must have been a delightful person. It is somehow appropriate that his first great success was the design of a villa for the flamboyant courtesan Bianca Cappello. In everything he did—whether it was his elegant villas with gardens, or the fireworks displays that he planned for the Medici court (his nickname Girandole means "Catherine wheels")—there was a spirit of fantasy, ebullient or delicate as the occasion required. His designs of settings and costumes and lighting effects for theatricals and other festivities are entirely delightful—but he also worked as an engineer on the harbor at Leghorn and on a canal from Leghorn to Pisa, and drew an annual retainer as supervisor of the riverworks in Florence. He lived in a fashionable house where he taught arts and crafts to fashionable amateurs, and somehow found time to invent a system for preserving snow for summer use. He received a concession to sell the snow but abandoned the project as unprofitable.

Around 1600, when he was nearing seventy, Bernardo's life changed key. Architectural commissions in general had fallen off, and he was living on a small pension plus an allowance of bread, wine, firewood, and other basic provisions that had been granted him by Grand Duke Ferdinand. He died in 1608 at the age of seventy-two, not quite penniless, but with hardly any money, not as the result of profligacy but because he had supported innumerable relatives and had seen through their rough times so many of the young architects he had trained.

PROTOBAROQUE
IN THE SIXTEENTH CENTURY

Although the sixteenth century belonged to the mannerists after the brief and early climax of the High Renaissance in Italy, there were a few painters there who anticipated the next century's rejection of mannerism by never accepting it —or, more likely, by never becoming aware of its temptations. Veronese, who worked primarily in Venice, is now and then included within the mannerist fold by stretching a point, but his opulent realism and his use of monumental architecture rising illusionistically in perspective ally him more closely with the baroque style, which was in a state of gestation during his lifetime. Even more than Veronese, Correggio, active in Parma, must be regarded as a major prophet of the baroque. With any lesser names that seem necessary, these two may be considered here before we move to the North to follow the mannerist (and related) painters who worked beyond the Alps in the sixteenth century in the wake of Grünewald and Dürer.

When Paolo Caliari, called Veronese, was summoned before the tribunal of the Holy Office of the Inquisition, he was asked, first of all, what his profession was.

"I paint and make pictures," he answered.

This was an extremely accurate answer, and very nearly a complete one. As a painter and maker of pictures, Veronese was superb, but he might have said, "I paint and make pictures as decorations." His pictures are wonderful pictures, but they are not the philosophical or expressive documents that great paintings are.

Veronese was born in Verona about 1528, but by 1553 he was working in Venice. Of all the painters whose art reflects that city as one great pageant, Veronese's reflects it most purely. His vast murals and ceiling decorations, with princely men and opulent women swathed in fine stuffs, posing in palatial architectural settings and attended by hardly less princely and opulent retinues, are the apotheosis of the Venetian spectacle. It makes little difference whether Veronese's nominal subject is religious, historical, or mythological. There is no attempt at interpretation, and if you are interested in the subject, you must deduce it from clues that tend to become submerged beneath the staging.

The Inquisition, however, was interested in the subject of the huge *Last Supper* that Veronese had painted for the refectory of the Friars of Santi Giovanni e Paolo. (It is now in the Academy.) In his customary way, Veronese had used the subject as a skeleton for ornamentation, and the ornamentation included a quantity of profane figures and incidents unrelated to the holy event. He was summoned for examination and required to defend such accessories as a servant whose nose was bleeding ("owing to some accident," he said), some halberdiers dressed in the German fashion, a jester with a parrot on his fist, and assorted dwarfs, drunkards, and supernumeraries.

Veronese's defense, in general, was that a painter, when given a commission, was expected to treat the subject as he thought best. His answers (the text of the examination is preserved) were respectful but entirely self-confident, sometimes almost casual. The probability is that as one of Venice's three great living painters (along with Titian and Tintoretto) Veronese had been assured of protection. He was ordered to change the offending passages, and he did change some of them—the bleeding nose was cured—but found it more convenient to take care of the rest by changing the title from *The Last Supper* to *The Feast in the House of Levi,* by which title the painting is still known.

The incident has received somewhat exaggerated attention as a declaration of the rights of artists to paint as they please. As such, it is not really impressive. The Inquisitors' arguments against the inclusion of the unrelated accessories were at least as valid as Veronese's defenses, and he was effectively rebutted when he tried to call in the nude figures of Michelangelo's *Last Judgment* as witnesses. What is important about this trial is that it shows the changed position of the artist, who, until Veronese's generation, had taken it for granted that the patron dictated, or at least shared in, the preliminary conception of a commissioned work.

Veronese was about forty-five at the time of the inquiry in 1573. He enjoyed another fifteen years of success before he died, in 1588.

Antonio Allegri, called Correggio after the small town where he was born, presents the anomaly of a provincial artist who was ahead of his time—and this in a time when things moved so rapidly that artists in the great centers had to work hard to keep up. But being ahead of his time did not affect Correggio's career one way or the other. No one, apparently not even he himself, recognized his innovations for what they were, and he was kept busy, without becoming famous, in Correggio and in Parma, where his fresco of the *Assumption of the Virgin* in the dome of the Cathedral is his most important single work.

Correggio found valuable patrons in Federigo Gonzaga and Isabella d'Este in Mantua, not very far afield. He was—and is—an oddly isolated artist, in more than a geographical sense. In spite of his local popularity he had no local disciples, and he exerted very little influence for nearly a hundred years. It took the seventeenth-century baroque artists to discover this painter who anticipated their aerial explosions of swirling, floating figures. But even here, Correggio remains isolated. His vast dome in Parma makes him a baroque artist before baroque art was born; his jubilant angels are ranged bank on bank in weightless rings, all gravity is defied, and the material structure of the dome is painted out to open up an infinite, luminous space. Yet these anticipations of the baroque have nothing to do with either the baroque's declamatory insistence or its ecstatic exaltation.

Correggio's art is dedicated to an essentially antibaroque tenderness. It is intimate, poetic, and festive, sensuous but gentle. His whole intention seems to have been to please rather than to impress, and if he was ever conscious of himself as an innovator, which seems doubtful, he made his innovations in the natural course of being pleasing rather than as the result of any preliminary theorizing. His innovational *Adoration of the Shepherds* in Dresden, a night scene where the gathering is illuminated by light that radiates from the Christ child, caused no stir. But when Tintoretto created similar effects fifty years later, they were a sensation.

It is assumed that Correggio knew Leonardo's painting, since his own soft atmospheric effects are more rationally explicable as an exaggeration of Leonardo's *sfumato* than as an independent discovery. But just where he might have seen the Leonardos, nobody can say. Although he was not affected by Raphael's ideal of classical balance, or by Michelangelo's spirit of tragic contemplation, he echoes much of Raphael's grace and Michelangelo's drawing. Biographers have worked hard to give Correggio a trip to Rome, where he could have experienced these influences at first hand, but there is no proof that such a trip was ever made. He could easily have seen Mantegna's paintings and there is an obvious early influence here, but it is brief and superficial. Mantegna's hard-bitten style was unsympathetic to the expression of Correggio's gentle ideal. Correggio leaves us floundering: it is impossible to believe that he developed as a solitary provincial, yet he cannot be lifted out of the small world of Parma and his nearby home town, Correggio.

He is also an altogether frustrating subject as a personality. Vasari, guessing or groping, called him a timid, anxious, and melancholy man who denied himself the normal pleasures of life in continuous labor to support his family. Not a word of this rings true. If it is not refuted by known facts, neither is it supported by any. We know that Correggio was born probably in 1489, but perhaps as late as 1494, and that he died in 1534—a short life by either birth date. He came from a moderately prosperous family, if you want to take the average between one story that makes him the son of aristocrats and another that gives him a simple origin. There are archival records of numerous contracts and payments, of his marriage, of the birth of a son and two daughters, and of his wife's death. (The son, born in 1521, was Pomponio Quirino, who became a minor painter.) But there is no credible contemporary record, not even one based on anecdote, to tell us what kind of man Correggio was. Perhaps he was just a very busy man who was not very interesting. He had some knowledge of architecture, since his name appears as member of a board appointed to study means of remedying structural failures in the Church of the Steccata in Parma, a building for which he had, without success, originally presented some competitive designs.

Who were his friends? One must have been Giovanna

di Piacenza, the abbess of the Convent of San Paolo in Parma, one of the most intelligent and learned women of her day. Correggio's first important commission was for the decoration of her living quarters, and, no doubt working out the subject under her direction, he produced a charming allegory on the pagan theme of Diana, the virgin goddess—a startling choice for the quarters of an abbess, but one that Correggio presented in much the same spirit as he would have presented a more likely religious subject.

Correggio never made much distinction between sacred and profane subjects or between fleshly and spiritual passion, if the word passion can be used to describe the gentle transports of his saints and his pagan deities. His series illustrating erotic encounters from mythology—the loves of the gods, including the famous one, now in Vienna, of Io receiving the embrace of Jupiter metamorphosed as a cloud—are, for all their frank sensuousness, more idyllic than lusty, just as his various Christian paintings are more idyllic than mystical.

In both cases Correggio's sweetness is occasionally cloying, the diffuse softness of his forms sometimes disturbingly cottony. But he pleases. There is, of course, the remark made by an official of the Cathedral in Parma, who was offended by the fringe of young legs that float and wave from the lower rank of angels so far above our heads. The official referred to the *Assumption of the Virgin* as "a frogs' legs stew." Titian, more sympathetically, said that if you turned the dome upside down and filled it with gold pieces they would not equal the worth of Correggio's masterpiece. And Titian was a man with the strongest respect for money.

In the history of sixteenth-century Italian art Giovanni Girolamo Savoldo supplies both a postscript and a prophecy. A postscript, because he was a conservative painter with no interest in manneristic devices, whose style was a modification of the styles of Giorgione and Titian, the painters who most strongly influenced him. A prophet, because he was an early member—and the strongest—of a school of north Italian realists from such towns as Brescia and Verona who anticipated a major direction of painting in the next century.

Savoldo was born in Brescia, probably about 1480, but his dates are usually given only in terms of his known active period. In spite of his northern birth and his long Venetian residence and allegiance, he is first recorded in Florence, where he was a member of the guild in 1508. He died, probably in Venice, after 1548; in that year Aretino mentions him as enfeebled.

Apparently Savoldo was never a very productive artist and always a quiet, unaggressive man. There is nothing obviously dramatic about his revolution. On the contrary, his paintings are serene and contemplative in mood. The north Italian realists transferred even the holiest scenes to humble locales and surrounded their saints with the commonplace objects of daily life—a possible inheritance from late-medieval art. Caravaggio in the next century did the same, but more emphatically. Savoldo was a prophet, too, in his representation of light. Exploring twilight effects and, more important, the action of artificial illumination from a single non-miraculous source (a candle or an oil lamp on a table), he created realistic night effects more than a generation before they were fully dramatized by Caravaggio.

The Italian mannerist artists imported by Francis I to decorate his palace at Fontainebleau—Rosso, Primaticcio, and others—represented a royal effort to raise France overnight from the position of country cousin to full-fledged sisterhood in the arts. But an exquisitely French tradition resisted this Italianization in one case, the portraits of Jean Clouet.

Born about 1485 in the southern Netherlands, Jean (sometimes Janet) Clouet was the son of an artist of the same name who had served the dukes of Burgundy. It is not known when the younger Clouet came to France, but by 1516, when he must have been about thirty-one, we find him mentioned as one of Francis I's painters. He spent his life in the service of the King and the court, attaining eventually the highest professional title—Painter and Valet of the King's Bedchamber. He mingled on equal terms with members of the court and, with studios in Paris and in Tours, must have taken part regularly in those seasonal pilgrimages between the capital and the châteaux along the Loire between which the French court divided its pleasures.

Jean Clouet's panel portraits, in the tight, sharply defined, and detailed technique of the Flemish and German traditions, are like Holbeins imbued with that special variety of feminine sensitivity that can be present in the French male as a desirable additive rather than as a defect in his masculinity. This quality is most pronounced in Clouet's crayon portraits. Usually drawn in black and red chalk, these continued a tradition already established when Clouet arrived in France, but he brought it to its highest point. The drawings were exchanged as souvenirs between members of the court and were collected in albums, much as we keep photographs. We may suppose that the likenesses were more than acceptable: certainly the drawings are convincing projections not only of sets of features but of personalities as well. Clouet managed to individualize his sitters in spite of the necessity of endowing all of them with the air of elegance and cultivation demanded of members of high society.

As the King's chief painter, Clouet was a member of this society and was paid a salary high enough to enable him to live respectably within it. He must have executed hundreds of portrait drawings. About a hundred and thirty are preserved. Their main concentration is in the Musée Condé at Chantilly, where they are beautifully at home in a properly courtly atmosphere. Jean Clouet died at about the age of fifty-five a year or so one side or the other of 1540.

François Clouet, sometimes called Janet like his father, was Jean Clouet's son, but his birth date is unknown. He was active by 1536 and, presumably trained by his father, succeeded him as Francis I's chief painter. After Francis' death he remained at court under Henry II, Francis II, and Charles IX, and died in 1572. His portrait panels follow his father's pattern, as do his crayon drawings, sometimes closely enough to make definitive attribution to one or the other difficult. But in other paintings he adopted an Italianate gloss in the manner of the School of Fontainebleau. It is possible that he made a trip to Italy; his paintings suggest a familiarity with Bronzino's. He had a large shop, and turned out mythological scenes as well as various kinds of decorations.

9

THE
SIXTEENTH CENTURY
IN THE NORTH

After producing its two greatest painters simultaneously, Germany tapered off during the remainder of the sixteenth century. Cranach, Altdorfer, Baldung Grien, and Holbein were certainly not negligible artists, but neither were they deeply concerned with the spiritual passion and intellectual profundity that distinguish the art of Grünewald and Dürer. The Germans who followed Grünewald and Dürer may be thought of—in the order above—as ranging from mannerist to mannerist-by-default, for want of a better term.

As mannerists, the Germans were in the odd position of skipping a century of art history. In Italy the Middle Ages had given way to the Renaissance in the fifteenth century, and then, in the sixteenth, medieval forms had been revived and interbred with antithetical forms perfected by Raphael and Michelangelo. But in Germany no revival of medieval forms was necessary to the mannerist synthesis: the Renaissance forms imported by Dürer singlehanded were grafted directly onto a living Gothic tradition. The result in the art of lesser men than Dürer was an enchanting hybrid, particularly in Cranach and Altdorfer.

The confusion in the sixteenth century, which is nowadays thought of as an aesthetic crisis, was aggravated in the North by the split in the Church. Lutheranism was officially opposed to aestheticism, which so frequently was an expression of Catholic religiosity or pagan sensuousness. But it was also a force in the air that could encourage a quiet, reflective realism even while it could plunge a Dürer into spiritual agony. Untroubled in this way, the French grafted their cult of woman onto Italianate roots at Fontainebleau, while England remained largely content to import German or Netherlandish artists. A single name, Nicholas Hilliard, adequately represents such native English painting as there was.

Before these strange mixtures finally emulsified into the international style called the baroque, the North produced another painter-genius worthy of a place beside Dürer and Grünewald—the Fleming Pieter Bruegel.

Lucas Cranach, called the Elder to distinguish him from his son, Lucas Cranach the Younger, was so productive and in some ways so contradictory, both as an artist and as a person, that he may best be written up under separate headings —Cranach as courtier, the favored companion and favorite artist of a Catholic aristocracy; Cranach as Protestant, the friend and stout supporter of Martin Luther; Cranach as humanist, the associate of classical scholars; Cranach as portraitist; and, finally, Cranach the pictorial industrialist, a term that needs explanation and will get it.

There is also the very young Cranach, whose painting does not quite fit any of the above categories. He was born in Kronach, Bavaria, in 1472, a year after Dürer. In spite of their virtually simultaneous birth dates, Cranach is best thought of as one of the second-generation German Renaissance painters. He outlived Dürer by twenty-five years, dying in 1553 at the age of eighty-one as against Dürer's fifty-seven, and hence he saw German painting into the mannerist phase that Dürer's late work anticipated. Cranach never worked with Dürer, and although Dürerian traces are inevitably decipherable in his work, the gaiety of his art is opposed to Dürer's sobriety.

Cranach's earliest paintings, before the Lutheran revolution and before his introduction to court, indicate that without this double influence he might have developed into a mystical painter along the lines of Grünewald. Passionate or meditative by turns, and sometimes a little macabre, he set his Crucifixions and his Rests on the Flight in landscapes that anticipated Altdorfer's typically Germanic fantasies. He is known to have worked in Vienna at the end of his twenties. In 1505, when he was thirty-three, he was employed in Wittenberg at the court of the elector of Saxony, Frederick the Wise. He was so well liked and so respected that three years after his arrival he was granted a coat of arms, and he adapted for it the winged serpent bearing a ring in its mouth that he had already invented as his signature.

Then there began Cranach's double life. It is hard to reconcile the activities of Cranach the Lutheran with those of Cranach the inventor of the sinuous, often playful or even wiggly and affected, sometimes erotic style that is identified with him. Martin Luther became his close friend, and when they were not seeing each other they were exchanging letters. Cranach held a printer's license as well as a painter's, and during a notably un-Lutheran career as an artist, which made him one of the wealthiest men in Wittenberg, he published and sold Luther's writings, including his translation of the New Testament.

But no traces of Lutheran tenets can be read into Cranach's painting. Conceivably he might have worked out some sort of Lutheran aesthetic if there had been a chance for him to make a living with it, but the men of the Reformation were suspicious of the taint of idolatry in religious paintings. When not hostile to the arts, they were indifferent to them. Dürer had successfully rationalized the difference between a religious image and an idol, saying that the contemplation of paintings of holy subjects was no more likely to make an idolator of a man than the ownership of a weapon was likely to make him an assassin. And like Dürer, Cranach continued to paint religious pictures. But except in a few of his very early ones, he was like the other post-Dürer artists, who either misunderstood or were not interested in the moral and intellectual problems that tormented Dürer. Any hope for a satisfactory pictorial expression of Lutheran ideals died with Dürer.

It is statistically evident that when Cranach was commissioned by the court to do a religious painting, the preferred subjects were those allowing the inclusion of a female nude. For by this time Cranach had developed a type of Venus (who could assume other roles, pagan or Christian) so provocative that against centuries of competition she has retained her position as a supreme coquette within the sisterhood. Slant-eyed, with small, high breasts; long-legged, with mincing ankles and impractical feet terminating in toes that tend to curl with delight even in relaxation; narrow-waisted, with generous belly and hips; and possessing, as her total wardrobe, a vast collection of great feathered hats and one small veil of maximum transparency, she is a provincial temptress who aspires to the role of grand courtesan. Cranach's patrons, understandably, could not get enough of her, and she turns up as Bathsheba, as Eve, and as any one of the upper circle of female Olympians.

Cranach's acquaintance with Olympus was enlarged by his friendship with the humanist scholars on the faculty of the recently established University of Wittenberg, and some of his pictures that are too easily dismissed as mere pleasurable nonsense are actually his effervescent expression of humanist musings. A baby holding an arrow in one hand and removing a gauzy bandage from his eyes with the other, *Cupid Unblindfolding Himself* (Philadelphia Museum of Art), could easily be passed by as nothing more than a bit of cuteness showing Cupid as a mischievous winged child. But the baby stands (on one toe, about to take flight) on a heavy volume stamped with the title "Platonis Opera," a clue that Cupid, whose blindness is a symbol of man's subjection to the passions, is here opening his eyes to the nobler Platonic conception of man as a being capable of seeing—that is, of understanding his own nature, whether or not a form of love is involved. There are probably similar allegories to be discovered—or rediscovered—in others of Cranach's mythological subjects.

As a portraitist Cranach was not a flatterer except indirectly through his talent for creating decorative silhouettes and harmonious lines without great modification of features. Whether he was dealing with a nose or with details of costume, Cranach could discover an attractive line in any contour as part of a strong, rather flattened pattern. Most frequently he played his sitters against a background of a single color, but now and then he introduced a landscape that was factually or psychologically appropriate to the case. His paired portraits were in great demand, and here he was among the first artists to employ the device of a continuous landscape that ran behind the frames, as it were, to unite the two halves. He seems also to have been the inventor of the full-length portrait. Except when he was painting a friend—Luther, for instance, or his great patron Cardinal Albrecht of

Brandenburg—Cranach (apparently) made no great effort to explore personality. But possibly the reason was that the majority of his sitters offered nothing more for exploration than the sedate respectability, ornamentally encased in fine garments, that Cranach's portraits so consistently reflect.

None of these comments should be taken to mean that Cranach was anything less than an artist of great imaginative invention as well as a perfect craftsman. Certainly he is a strong contender for first place in the second generation of German Renaissance painters. A trip through German museums leaves the impression that he was often satisfied with his own second best, but this is because his workshop, headed by his son, turned out hundreds, perhaps thousands, of copies of his most successful pictures. His coat-of-arms signature was often included as a kind of factory trademark. On one occasion Cranach received an order for one hundred and twenty replicas at once, sixty each of the paired portraits of Frederick the Wise and his brother John, who succeeded him as elector of Saxony. His paired portraits of Luther and his wife were also great favorites, and were turned out with as little question as photographs might be printed from a popular negative today. This was true again of his portrait of Melanchthon. And the flirtatious Venuses were reproduced in such quantity that they amounted to pinups at the luxury level. It has even been suggested that Cranach's increasingly linear style was developed in part because sharply defined patterns against flat backgrounds could be most quickly and accurately copied by his assistants. But if that is true, we owe to practical convenience one of the most sparkling decorative manners in the history of the nude.

One son of Cranach's, Hans, died in his youth during a study tour in Italy. He was much praised as an artist in obituaries, although he had not had much time to prove himself. His brother Lucas the Younger, who was born in

1515 and died in 1586, outliving his father by thirty-three years, did have time to prove himself and must be judged less kindly. He became the manager and finally the inheritor of his father's workshop. Along with numerous other assistants he was an adequate copyist of his father's paintings, but in his own work the scintillant Cranach style lost its gloss. Invention became pastiche, and playful eroticism degenerated into a coarse joke. It was not a case of like father, like son.

Albrecht Altdorfer was born about 1480, probably in Regensburg, and died there in 1538. He was one of the town's solidest citizens. A member of the city council, as well as city architect, he would have been mayor, except that when he was elected to the post in 1528, when he was about forty-eight, he begged off because he wanted to work on a painting that had been commissioned by William IV of Bavaria.

Altdorfer no doubt would have made a good mayor, but Regensburg's loss was Duke William's gain and ours too. The painting, which is now in Munich and is sometimes called *The Battle of Issus* but usually *The Battle of Alexander,* is a summary of Altdorfer's genius. It combines wild fantasy with cosmic landscape, endlessly fascinating miniaturistic detail with panoramic vistas. And as an expression of pure movement—virtually an abstract concept within this organization—it was unparalleled anywhere at the time. This is a large order, but no item of it is exaggerated.

Altdorfer was a wonderful painter, whether you want to take the word "wonderful" in its loosest sense of generalized approval or in its strictest sense, as partaking of the miraculous. In its marvelousness, Altdorfer's art could lead us to think of him as a man of hallucinatory imagination—if the strength of his organizational schemes did not equally reflect the sound, steady fellow that we know him to have been from his career as a prosperous and respected citizen. We are surely safe in deducing his character in this way, although we know practically nothing of his life until he was in his late twenties, and have no documentation of his strictly personal life. He was apparently sympathetic to the Reformation, since in his will he renounced Masses for his soul.

Toward the end of his career, Altdorfer occupied himself more with architecture than with painting, probably because the Reformation's terror of idolatry affected commissions in his part of Germany just as it did elsewhere. But his career was not actually cut short, as Grünewald's was, nor is there any record that Altdorfer went through any severe soul-searching, as both Grünewald and Dürer did.

Soul-searching was in truth not much in Altdorfer's line, whether it was a matter of his own soul or man's in general. If he cannot rival Grünewald and Dürer for the title of greatest master of the German Renaissance, it is only because the personal mysticism of the one and the humanistic passion of the other give them the spiritual depth and intellectual range that distinguish the greatest artists from the merely great ones. Altdorfer, as a merely great artist, holds a sufficiently distinguished position.

His art, by description, might seem only an eclectic pastiche. In a single picture he could combine Italianate Renaissance architecture (which he knew only through drawings and engravings), picturesque medieval rusticity, Christian subject matter, and the primeval Nordic forest, which he represented in masses of dense sprays of foliage, twisted and broken limbs, gnarled trunks, and pendent growths strung like long hair from festooned branches. His scenes have the German fairy-tale air of half-spooky fantasy that reached expression at a celestial level in Grünewald's mysticism and at its most popular level in "Hansel and Gretel."

Even in his later work, which seems to have been influenced by Lucas Cranach the Elder and is much broader and smoother in scheme, the fairy-tale fantasy holds its own.

Altdorfer was also a wit, not in the sense of cleverness or japery or raillery, but in the sense of extraordinarily alert perceptions expressed with arresting individuality and good humor. His *Rest on the Flight into Egypt* in Berlin shows the Holy Family taking a moment's repose, picnic fashion, beside a large fountain of Renaissance design, his version of the spring that appeared miraculously when the Holy Family needed water in the wilderness. Its great carved marble basin catches the streams that issue from a towering central sculpture where classical figures surmount one another in flowery complications. It is a very happy scene—not particularly holy in general effect. The Virgin, seated in an elaborate chair drawn up to the side of the basin (where could it have come from, this chair?), is a pretty woman who with one hand selects a berry or two from a container offered by St. Joseph, while in the other arm she supports the naked Child. Perhaps the Child has just had his bath, for he lies on his stomach on some soft, towel-like cloths that protect the Virgin's gown. He dabbles one hand in the water, while seven tiny winged cherubs (in assorted sizes, but none more than a foot tall) disport themselves in the basin or sit chatting on its rim. They are exactly like bright-colored sparrows splashing in a puddle. All this goes on in the very near foreground, which recedes into a collection of peak-roofed Gothic buildings, half in ruins, including a tower where Rapunzel would be an imaginable inhabitant. These merge into a landscape of hills, cliffs, architecture, and vegetation, which rises from a lake or sea. The tone of the picture is at once festive and gentle, fanciful and reverent.

This is Altdorfer at his most charming, and hardly suggests the explosive climax of his *Battle of Alexander*. His great achievement historically was that he gave landscape an unprecedented expressive importance in itself, lifting it from its position as a sometimes more, sometimes less, conspicuous adjunct to the main theme and making it both the muscular structure and the nervous system of pictures where action and mood are inextricable.

The Battle of Alexander shows an awesomely vast landscape with castled mountain peaks rising from plains where armies battle in surging phalanxes. We look across the lakes and seas and islands of a deserted moonlike continent that stretches infinitely to merge with a cloudscape where the sun bursts explosively through the vapors on one side of the picture while the moon glows in an aureole on the other. In this literally cosmic drama the picture's nominal subject, Alexander's victory over Darius, becomes unimportant, although Altdorfer tried to follow descriptions of the battle. The armies become patterns of movement united with the movement of clouds and with the formation of hills; the lances and banners have the same thrust as the rays of the sun; the celestial and earthly dramas are inseparable from one another.

In detail the picture is staggering, whether it describes mountain peaks and the encampments of armies like cities, or the individual warriors and horses. But *The Battle of Alexander* is not one of those pictures that are made up of one detail after another into a final entity, like a mosaic. Rather, it is a picture where the inconceivable vastness of a scene beyond time and place has been materialized and organized for us. The details, however arresting, are subordinated to this coordinated vision. If the picture is a logically ordered cosmic landscape it is also a fantasy, one made even more fantastic by a large engraved tablet that states the historical subject—and is suspended from the sky.

The Battle of Alexander, completed in 1529, was Altdorfer's last signed painting except for two done in 1531.

He was a prolific printmaker as well, and designed the gold coinage for Regensburg. Everything we know about him leaves the satisfying impression of a vigorous, industrious man whose well-regulated life led to the full realization of extraordinary powers of imaginative invention.

Hans Baldung, called Grien, was born in 1484 or 1485 and died in 1545. The now inseparable surname became attached to him perhaps because of the pungency of the greens in his paintings, or perhaps because he liked to dress in that color. He must have been a very stylish dresser: fine clothes worn with pleasure would go with the personality that comes through his paintings with a most engaging sprightliness.

About thirteen years younger than Dürer, he may have served an apprenticeship under the great man, whom he certainly admired. He is supposed to have received a lock of hair —the hair that Dürer painted with such pride in his self-portraits—as a memento after Dürer's death.

Wellborn, of a family including doctors and lawyers, Hans Baldung moved early to Strasbourg, where he spent most of his steadily successful life. With Cranach he leads the second generation of German painters of the Renaissance, following Dürer, who interbred the sinuous sophistications of the German Gothic style with the classical forms that had arrived a bit tardily from Italy. The mannerist hybrid flavor is most piquant in Germany, and in Baldung Grien's style it often has a spiciness divided between humor and fantasy that is all his own.

He was best known during his lifetime for his altarpieces, and can stand as a major imaginative German painter on these alone. His religious paintings have a fine theatrical staginess, exaggerated today by the strangeness of the elaborate sixteenth-century German dress in which his various saints and donors pose with absolute aplomb. But the twentieth century with its eye for artifice and eccentric invention has found Baldung Grien most interesting in his allegories—curious paintings sometimes classical in reference, with such ladies as Venus and Lucretia figuring in them, sometimes depicting a world of superstition and sorcery where witches congregate to control the elements and to spin the threads of the fate of men.

Baldung Grien's witches are not Halloween broomstick hags, but pale-skinned, full-bodied young women of exceptional curvature, with hair flying in every direction in undulating locks like nests of escaping serpents. Cherubs and goats are their attendants, and wild skies and emerald verdure their habitats.

Baldung Grien was a designer of stained glass and woodcuts as well as a painter. In one of his woodcuts, *The Bewitched Groom,* a stableman lying on his back on the floor is shown feet first, in violent foreshortening, with a somehow sinister horse behind him. The scene, filled with an air of the supernatural while offered in terms of literally detailed realism, has become dear to the surrealists as an early application of their theories. In his versions of the favorite German theme of Death and the Maiden and the universal one of the ages of man—turned into the ages of woman, with horrifying explicitness about the vulnerability of the flesh to time—Baldung Grien presents the macabre in such high-styled performance that horror and elegance come into balance.

He was unusual as a portraitist also. He showed his sitters neither objectively nor idealistically, and not always in a way that would have been expected to please them, making his own comments, often wry and a bit teasing, about their appearance and their character. But his comments do not appear ever to have offended the eminent citizens who commissioned his portraits. No doubt there was an odd quirk in

Baldung Grien's personality, yet any hints of morbidity are canceled out by healthy wit. His pleasure as an artist lay not in dark themes for their own sake but in the scope they offered his inventiveness.

German genius birthed five great painters in a starry cluster—Grünewald, Dürer, Cranach, Altdorfer, and Baldung Grien were born within hardly more than a decade, beginning with Dürer's birth in 1471—and then just before the turn of the century produced Hans Holbein the Younger as if to tie things off before a long fallow period. Holbein is the most bland and was the most businesslike of the group, an adequate explanation for his enjoying the widest popularity then and now. He is also the least German, which is not surprising, since first Switzerland and then England became his adopted countries. He did not bother greatly with the intellectual theorizing and was not subject to the mystical convulsions that would have allied him to Dürer and Grünewald; he was apparently not sensitive to those fantasy-breeding emanations of the dark Northern forests that produced magic-struck scenes, eerie or humorous, of painters like Cranach, Altdorfer, and Baldung Grien. Holbein's technically flawless, altogether secular, and usually rather matter-of-fact art seems to reflect a man of solid intelligence, circumspect habits, and a personality so steady as to be rather flat.

But Holbein must have been something more than intelligent, and possibly he was just a touch less than stable. You must be more than merely intelligent to merit the admiration of men like Erasmus and Sir Thomas More. And to be an internationally famous artist, immensely productive and highly paid, yet to die at only forty-six at the height of your success and have nothing to leave for the support of your wife and four legitimate children in Switzerland and your two illegitimate children in London, you must be less than fully dedicated to the conventional virtues.

Hans Holbein the Younger was born in Augsburg in 1497 and died in London in 1543. He and his brother Ambrosius were trained in the large workshop of their father, Hans Holbein the Elder (c. 1465-1524), a prosperous artist of high reputation then as now. The two boys were among their father's last apprentices. He broke up his shop about 1514 and moved to Isenheim, in Alsace, about three years later. Augsburg was a center of international commerce where trade with the South had stimulated a lively receptiveness to Renaissance humanism. The year after his father's shop broke up, that is, in 1515, the younger Hans, now eighteen, went to Basel. An early work done there indicates a wittiness and an interest in humanistic ideas hardly apparent in the rest of his painting.

"Early work" may be too solemn a designation for the item in question: some sprightly drawings made for a humanist schoolmaster in the margins of a copy of Erasmus's "Encomium Moriae." As a result of more formal efforts, Holbein was admitted as a master in the Basel guild in 1519, and in that same year, his twenty-second, he married a girl named Elsbeth Schmid, who, as Elsbeth Holbein, seems not to have had too good a time of it.

Holbein's portrait of Elsbeth with two of their children, painted about ten years later upon one of his periodic returns to Basel from England, shows a rather plain woman with small eyes and a fleshy nose who, nevertheless, might have been shown, without idealization, as a pleasant and attractive person if she had been painted with any of the tenderness or jubilant warmth that might have been expected from a husband reunited with his beloved wife and their offspring. But the husband and father is not present in the picture even by suggestion, as Rubens, for instance, is present in every adoring stroke of the brush in his portrait of Hélène Fourment and their children. Elsbeth sold the picture (which is now in the Basel museum) while Holbein was still alive, probably for the first reason that she needed money, but conceivably for the second that it was not an altogether happy souvenir.

Holbein stayed in Basel for six years after his admittance to the guild and his marriage, but probably interrupted his stay with occasional trips to France and Italy. Religious paintings were still an artist's stock in trade, and in this field Holbein was proficient enough. But there is no point in pretending that his realistic, mundane altarpieces carry any religious effectiveness except by sheer association, even in an example or two where he has drawn on Grünewald. An exception is his *Dead Christ* (Basel) of 1521, which is quite simply an explicit study of a corpse stretched out on a slab, but even here the effectiveness comes primarily from the audacity of representing the body of Christ with an uncompromisingly detailed realism that would be more expectable in a photograph taken in a morgue.

Holbein also made a couple of excursions, exceptional for him, into classical antiquity during these first years in Basel, with portraits (now in the Basel museum) of a woman named Magdalena Offenburg, showing her in one as Venus and in the other as the courtesan Lais of Corinth. This appropriately named Magdalena was a suitable model in both instances. Beautiful, and of noble birth, she was notorious for a sexual career of such flagrant indulgence that she had brushes with the law. Nothing further is known about her connection with Holbein, but perhaps nothing more need be. The paintings, in any case, are among his least interesting.

But during these years Holbein also showed where his greatest talent, or his genius, lay—in portraits. He painted three of Erasmus. The one in the Louvre, painted about 1523, when Holbein was only twenty-six, shows the philosopher in profile, writing at his desk. The long, sharp nose, the thin cheeks, the wide, thin, half-smiling mouth, the slightly knitted brows, and the quiet, lowered gaze, might be no more than a very accurate delineation of a certain man's appearance. But Holbein's genius in portraiture was that he could capture through the delineation of externals the personality that these externals usually reveal only when the living subject talks, moves, listens, gesticulates, changes expressions. As a pictorial structure, the painting can be reduced to half a dozen rather lightly modeled silhouettes in decorative combination. But this is only the surface. As a reflection of a personality, the portrait summarizes the removed, ironic, analytical humanist mind that rejected Luther's painful excesses as restrictions on man's only saving virtue—his capacity for self-knowledge through intellectual freedom.

The Lutheran wariness of the arts began to make Basel an unhappy spot for a painter, and in 1526 Erasmus wrote to Sir Thomas More ("The arts are out in the cold here," he said) to introduce his twenty-nine-year-old friend. By the end of the year Holbein was in London, staying in Chelsea with Sir Thomas, who had written back enthusiastically about him to Erasmus. Holbein stayed in England for two years, then returned to Basel for three or four, buying a large house there. But things had not improved. The city council in 1529 prohibited paintings in churches and ordered those already in the churches to be removed and destroyed. Holbein went back to England.

The situation was full of contradictions. Although he must have shared Erasmus's objections to Luther's God, Holbein became a Protestant in 1530. And in spite of his Protestantism he was taken on by Henry VIII, who loathed Luther on several counts, including the paramount one of politics. Henry had also quarreled with Holbein's first sponsor in England; he put Sir Thomas More to the block in 1535 at just about the time he appointed Holbein court painter.

Holbein was not yet forty, and was internationally famous, the most famous living Northern artist. Dürer had died in 1528, but even if he had lived, Holbein's reputation might have overshadowed his; it was through Holbein rather than through his own works that Dürer's innovations, drastically reduced in depth and intensity, spread across Europe and even to the Near East. Holbein's production was ceaseless and vast. His illustrations and decorations of books alone would have been an impressive lifework in a life longer than his. Aside from paintings, miniatures, drawings, and woodcuts, which number into the hundreds even in a qualitative selection, he executed large mural projects now destroyed, designed and supervised festivals and decorative projects for Henry VIII and other patrons, and designed jewelry and stained glass.

Considering Holbein's eminence, there are surprisingly few firsthand accounts by people who knew him, but we do know that when he made his last visit to Basel in 1538—he was then forty-one—his manner of dress was sumptuous enough to inspire comments on this princely creature in comparison with the young man who, when he first left Basel, could afford to buy wine only by the glass. But if he was prosperous he must also have been profligate; there are numerous records of his emergency requests to patrons for payments in advance to meet current debts. Although he remained a citizen of Basel, and was begged by the city fathers to remain there to add luster to the city, he returned to England in 1541, or earlier, and died there in 1543, probably of the plague. Back in Basel, Elsbeth's inheritance consisted of one trunk. In London, the sale of Holbein's goods (including a horse) paid a few small debts and provided seven shillings and sixpence a month for his two illegitimate children, described as being still "at nurse."

Holbein's self-portrait in the Uffizi in Florence, painted the year of his death, shows a man whose large head, square face, and heavy, compact shoulders suggest a powerful, stocky body. The nose is irregular, wide, and somewhat flattened, like a pugilist's. His whole appearance, in fact, is more a boxer's than an artist's. One eyelid droops very slightly over an intent, rather hard gaze. The mouth is full-lipped but also somehow hard. It is a rather forbidding face without being at all austere.

In his best portraits (especially his best drawings, where the immediate record of his response to the sitter has not been modified by the process of turning out a highly finished, detailed painting), Holbein could reveal a man's character while seeming only to record his appearance. If he did this in his self-portrait as successfully as he did in the portrait of Erasmus, then it is easy to imagine him as a shrewd, aggressive, sensual man who would be as relentless in his dealings with others as he was indulgent with himself. But this is hardly the record that a man would have liked to leave of himself, and it raises confusions in several directions as to just how objectively, from just what point of view, Holbein went about the extraordinary representation of features and the revelation of personality in any of his portraits.

Hardheaded as he doubtless was, Holbein must have been a man with an observant sensitivity to the state of the world. In his *Dance of Death,* a series of woodcuts on the old medieval theme of the universal enemy indiscriminately carrying off kings and beggars, maidens and youths, villains and saintly men, he transposed to a new key the old medieval warning to prepare for judgment, combining satirical comment on the condition of the state and the Church with his century's advice to the living that they gather roses while the roses were gatherable.

All told, Holbein remains a puzzle. Even those who view him more sympathetically than we have managed to do have difficulty in connecting the man with the works. As a man, he led a life that surely must have been eventful in ways that we know nothing of, while his art, for contemporary taste, is marked by a bland eventlessness.

Nicholas Hilliard, or Hillyarde (*c.* 1547-1619), was an English goldsmith who also painted portraits, specializing in the portable miniatures that, in the fashion of the day, were often worn as jewelry. Born four years after the death of Holbein, whom he regarded as his model, and seventeen years before Shakespeare, whom he outlived by three years, he is placed historically in company that rather pathetically reveals his small stature. His art is charming but so slight that his name would hardly be known outside the catalogues of antiquarians except for one circumstance: he remains England's master pictorial artist of native birth in his century. About 1600 he wrote a treatise on painting, "The Arte of Limning," in which he defended linear as against shaded drawing, and recorded conversations with Queen Elizabeth in which they agreed upon this point.

His son Laurence Hilliard (1582-*after* 1640) followed him in his profession.

Jan van Scorel was born in 1495 in Schoorl (of which his name is a variant spelling) in Holland, rather romantically. He was the natural son—the only kind there can be, of course —of a priest. He himself was ordained in his mid-thirties, largely, it seems, as a matter of convenience at the midpoint of a life that had been far from humdrum.

He received a good education, studied painting under respectable masters in Amsterdam, and, about 1518, when he was twenty-three, went to Utrecht (which was later to be his adopted city) for a brief stay with Mabuse (Jan Gossart), who was court painter there. After a few months he set out on travels that took him through Germany (where he is supposed to have met, and possibly had some instruction from, Dürer), Switzerland, and Austria, where he paused to execute his first important commissions. But he was soon on his way again, and in the fall of 1520 he went to Venice, where he met a group of Dutch pilgrims bound for the Holy Land and joined them. He stayed in Jerusalem until Easter, 1521, and then returned, via Rhodes, to Venice, and thence to Rome.

His Roman visit in 1522 was luckily timed. Adrian VI, the Utrecht pope, who lasted only twenty months, accepted his twenty-seven-year-old countryman as a protégé, giving him a studio in the Vatican and commissioning him to do his, the Pope's, portrait. Jan also became Inspector of the Belvedere (he was an adequately qualified architect and engineer as well as a painter and something of a humanist scholar) and Canon of Utrecht during Adrian's brief eminence. (Jan's ordination as a priest was a technical prerequisite.) Adrian died in 1523, to the delight of the Italians, who had loathed his ascetic personality and his attempted reforms of the Curia. Jan returned to Holland, his adventures over. Although he continued to travel now and then, adding France to his list of countries, he settled in Utrecht, and died there in 1562 at the age of sixty-seven.

In Rome, Jan had studied the remains of classical antiquity along with the art of Michelangelo and Raphael, and thus he brought, from firsthand experience, the Renaissance-classical tradition to Holland. His art, at once sober and graceful, is somehow never very memorable. In 1550 he received an important assignment: he was called to Ghent, where, with the painter Lancelot Blondeel, he restored Ghent's proudest possession, the Van Eyck altarpiece. As a good Hollander among Flemings, Jan took the opportunity to make a rather audacious addition to the great monument of Flemish painting. At the center of the landscape of the Adoration of the Lamb he added the soaring tower of Utrecht Cathedral.

Lucas van Leyden died in 1533 before he was forty, but in his few years was astonishingly productive, beginning at a phenomenally early age—so early that his birth date of 1494 is often but not very successfully questioned. According to that date, Lucas's talent as a graphic artist was well developed by the time he was fourteen (he dated work in 1508). He was trained by his father, a painter, Hughe van Leyden, none of whose works are known, and another painter of Leiden, Cornelis Engelbrechtsz, but he learned most from the example of Dürer. Under this guidance, and with the help of what he learned from the painter Mabuse, Lucas achieved for Dutch art something like the transition from medieval to Renaissance standards that Dürer achieved more significantly in Germany and Mabuse more affectedly in Flanders. He shares this distinction with his contemporary Jan van Scorel.

Lucas was born, lived, and died in Leiden, but traveled in Flanders (with Mabuse) and met Dürer in 1521, when that master was feted in Antwerp. Lucas married the daughter of a magistrate of Leiden and was a member of the civil guard. His early biographer, Van Mander, tells of his odd habit of working in bed, of his fear of being poisoned by envious colleagues, and of foppish dilettantism—none of which fits in with the productive energy apparent in both the quantity and the character of Lucas's work. As an engraver and woodcut designer, he is second only to Dürer. As a painter he had a feeling for straightforward, plain-faced realism prophetic of later Dutch painting, but this quality was defeated, in his later work, by the intrusion of Italian mannerist devices.

No artist has a stronger claim to the title of father of still-life painting than Pieter Aertsen if we grant the usual number of grandparents and others on down the line. At a time when still life was serving artists in the way stage props serve a dramatist—that is, as clues to a story or as part of a decorative setting—he painted monumental arrangements of meat, vegetables, fruit, pots, pans, hampers, and anything else that might be found in market stalls or in kitchens, and painted them as self-contained subjects. Or almost. Deep in the background there is often a religious subject—as in the standard example, his *Meat Stall* (Uppsala University, Sweden), where a miniature Flight into Egypt occurs in a miniature landscape, a small vista framed by a huge pig's head, fish, sausages, and the like.

These religious vignettes might have been included to calm the unease of customers who could not quite come around to the idea of total still life. Or perhaps the inversion by which incidentals are magnified and a major theme reduced could have appealed to more sophisticated buyers. Aertsen also painted straightforward religious pictures that alone would have assured him a respectable minor position, and in his inclusion of peasants in his kitchen scenes (and landscapes) he was a forerunner of the next century's genre painting. He had numerous pupils and is even credited with influence on the still life of Caravaggio and Velázquez—an easy possibility, since his work was known and admired by collectors in Rome and Madrid.

Aertsen was born in 1508 in Amsterdam but settled as a citizen in Antwerp in 1535. He married there, became a member of the guild, and prospered. But about 1555, when he was in his late forties, he returned to his birthplace, was repatriated, and died there after another twenty years in 1575. The destruction of numbers of his altarpieces and other religious pictures in the iconoclastic devastations of 1566 might explain his greater concentration on still life after that time—although his *Meat Stall* was painted as early as 1551.

Even more extremely than most great painters, Pieter Bruegel the Elder exists at two levels. At the popular one, his fantastic drolleries and his pictures of rollicking peasants are taken at face value and bought by the thousands in reproduction. At this level Bruegel is certainly as curious and delightful a painter as you could find—but only curious and delightful. At his true level, when these obvious charms are recognized as nothing but a pictorial skin, Bruegel is discoverable as an extraordinarily complex painter-philosopher. He stands with the small company of the greatest artists of any time and place, and in his own century he stands alone as the only genius to appear in Northern art between Dürer and Rubens.

Very little is known about his life. When he died in 1569 he was probably not much beyond the age of forty and perhaps had not even reached it. He materializes for the first time in a document of 1551, when he was accepted as a master in the Antwerp painters' guild. Assuming that he went through the usual mill of apprenticeship, he would have been in his early twenties then; so he was probably born between 1525 and 1530. Several Netherlandish towns claim honor as the locale of that event.

With very few facts available to support wishful conclusions drawn from his art, it is possible but dangerous to reconstruct a personality called Pieter Bruegel. A good beginning is to reject a couple of impostors born of romantic matings between the nominal subjects of his paintings and the popular conviction that all artists must be a little freakish. First there is the picaresque adventurer Bruegel, who loved drinking and dancing with the peasants at their festivals, and then went home to describe village weddings and harvest feasts in genre pictures. At the other extreme there is the Bruegel invented to explain his fantastic subjects, apparently the member of some secret religious cult whose esoteric and even diabolic catechism could be set down only disguised in cabalistic symbols or allegories. (Even Baudelaire, groping in the nineteenth century's bepuzzlement over Bruegel, could speak of his "hallucination" and thought of him as "driven by some unknown force" that, while it did not quite permit him "to see the devil himself in person," did coincide "in the most surprising manner with the notorious and historical epidemic of witchcraft.")

Either of these Bruegels is as false as the other, both are simple-minded, and neither is tolerable. Whatever else he was, the real Bruegel was a man whose interests in common things and fantastic inventions were neither discordant nor contradictory, but were interdependent aspects of reflections upon the nature of man, his relationship to himself and his small world, and to the cosmos as his world turned through its seasons.

So much we can see in the paintings, but all efforts to particularize this man are frustrated. Even his name is variously spelled and misspelled (as "Breughel"); he himself changed Brueghel to Bruegel about 1559, but the *h* was retained by several generations of his descendants. Certainly he was famous and successful, since the Habsburgs were among his patrons, with the result that the finest concentration of Bruegels is now in neither Antwerp nor Brussels (he worked in both cities) but in Vienna. He must have been well educated, since he was part of the liberal humanist circle that included such men as Abraham Ortelius and Plantin—and he was not there as court jester. The single fact we know about his personal life is that in 1563—when he would have been between thirty-three and thirty-eight, with six years to live—he made a respectable marriage to a girl named May-ken, the daughter of the painter Pieter Coecke van Aelst (who may have been his teacher). Their two sons, only babies when their father died, grew up to become prominent artists —as did three grandsons and five great-grandsons, all painters named Brueghel. Marriage and fatherhood do not prove steadiness of character, but in Bruegel's case there is no record or legend to contradict the probability that everything else supports.

Bruegel lived during a time of social, political, and religious upheaval that affected him directly, but his convictions are known only through deduction from his art. In the case of Dürer a little earlier, we can follow in his letters, in his writings, and in the recorded comments of his friends the moral agonies and the aesthetic preoccupations that determined the nature of his art. But we have not one single helpful word from or about Bruegel in this respect; it is impossible to think of him as orthodox in politics or religion at a time when orthodoxy was tainted by bigotry or tyranny, but what deviations he admitted, what loyalties he held, we cannot know.

We must always come back to his paintings, and here at least we can discover three general principles of belief:

Men as individuals are faulty. Their most degrading folly is a materialism whose most crippling symptoms are covetousness and avarice.

But generically man is noble, heroic. In a state close to nature (although Bruegel must not be thought of quite as a proto-Rousseauist) man comes closest to realizing his potential grandeur.

And the proof of man's dignity is that he is worthy of inclusion as an integral part of the rhythm of the cosmos, a rhythm that can play the movement of hunters trudging through the snow against the movement of the wind they lean into, that identifies the tempo of man's life with the majestic succession of night and day and the turn of the seasons, that accepts his presence without question, imposing no obligation and granting him no privilege as part of a complex where everything from the flight of a bird to the circling of the planets is part of an ineffable union. The scheme is too vast to query and so rich that to exist as part of it is the reward of life.

Even in rudimentary summary, Bruegel's premises become his answers to questions that men have always asked themselves. The concept of man as heroic but men as faulty has cousins everywhere. The ancient Greek version of it is the noble being with the tragic flaw, but in Bruegel the flaw is no longer tragic but contemptible, because remediable; no implacable fate declares that there is no way out. In the Book of Genesis innocence in Paradise is lost through original sin, but in Bruegel man need not suffer forever for having yielded to an appetite in a moment of weakness; he is free to enjoy the satisfaction of his appetites so long as he has the strength not to abuse the privilege, and he needs no Redeemer to restore him to bliss, because he finds his own bliss in identification with the cosmos.

Bruegel's cosmos and its rhythm have an even more thickly branched family tree, spreading in one direction as far as India. Some of his landscapes (as we shall see) were extensions of the theologically organized universe of the Middle Ages, in which every single thing and every single activity had its defined place. But the medieval universe was almost too neat, like a tremendous globular filing cabinet surrounded by a void; its minor virtue of tidiness imposed the major flaw of static definition. In Bruegel's universe nothing is static: everything moves, grows, and responds in endless harmonies of action and interaction. Finally, in his more vigorous way, Bruegel anticipated intellectually the nineteenth-century romantics' emotional identification of man with nature, but without falling into the romantic fallacy of endowing nature with emotions corresponding to man's.

The only concept of the nature of things that seems never to have occurred to Bruegel is our objective scientific one by which the cosmos becomes something physically explicable and hence godless. As for Bruegel's God, we have already said that his religious affiliation can only be surmised, and the usual surmise is that he was a deviant Catholic. When he painted biblical subjects he painted them in his own terms, neither manufacturing them according to the formulas that enabled even the most unreligious painters to turn out satisfactory holy pictures nor giving them any Christian-mystical turn of his own.

The Massacre of the Innocents (Vienna), beneath its nominal subject, is a *sub rosa* indictment of the devastation of the Netherlandish populace by Spanish military force. *The Procession to Calvary* (Vienna) becomes an execution scene concerned less with the victim than with exposing the baseness of human beings who can watch his sufferings with callous indifference. *Christ and the Woman Taken in Adultery* (now lost, but reproduced in an engraving), ostensibly a parable pleading for charitable compassion between human beings, is extended to a social allegory of religious intolerance. And *The Numbering at Bethlehem* (Brussels) is at first glance a genre scene, where the protagonists, Joseph and Mary, are all but lost in the crowd as they enter a snowy Netherlandish village where the census takers are busily at work in the midst of the villagers' busy life.

But *The Numbering at Bethlehem* also shows Mary joyously shielding with her cloak the glorious secret that she carries in her womb. Thus she becomes a symbol of the presence of miracle ignored in the petty bustle of nuisancy affairs. Bruegel developed this same subtheme—our blindness or indifference to wonders that surround us—in paintings that have no specifically religious subjects, the landscapes with figures that are the consummate expressions of his beliefs. Just as the villagers are blind to the presence of miracle in *The Numbering at Bethlehem,* so the men who plod across the landscape of *The Hunters in the Snow* (Vienna) are oblivious to everything but the business at hand. We recognize their integration with the cosmic rhythm, but they are too busy even to suspect it.

This "religion" of the cosmos was surely not something that Bruegel thought of as religion. But a man's true religion is whatever he believes most deeply, and by this definition Bruegel was a pantheist. On the evidence of his paintings, his God was not a force that could be isolated as a central personality—was not the biblical God who created the universe in the beginning to rule it forever—but an all-pervading force, the life force if you wish, that is manifested equally in every detail of an autonomous universe.

Fortunately Bruegel was in the habit of dating his paintings, and in chronological succession they show that he reached his conclusions, or at least expressed his beliefs—that man is faulty, that he is potentially noble, that his existence is legitimized not by playing a central role in the scheme of things but by his being an integral part of it—in the order we have listed, although not within such arbitrarily neat compartments. The best way to pull these remarks together is to summarize Bruegel's development with a few examples of his paintings. But it is time just now to insert a reminder that no matter how profound or how complicated the philosophical aspects of his work may be, the popular Bruegel of the colored reproductions shares with the other Bruegel one characteristic vital to both: a tremendous gusto, a full-blooded heartiness, an ebullient curiosity about the visual world, and an irrepressible appreciation of its rich physical satisfactions. Even if he had had nothing else to offer, this gusto would set Bruegel apart, with no rival except his countryman Rubens, who in the next century responded as fully, in his more princely way, to the same stimuli.

In 1552, the year after his acceptance as master in the Antwerp guild, Bruegel made the Italian trip that for Northern painters was becoming almost a required postgraduate apprenticeship. He must have left home with the standard list of things to see, and with introductions to Italian painters. But the drawings he brought back, the only testimony to the trip, indicate that his interests were altogether unconventional. The journey was unusually lengthy, since Bruegel got as far as Sicily, and if along the way he studied classical monuments and the Renaissance paintings that other artists went to see, his responses were not the usual ones. Michelangelo is a perceptible influence in Bruegel's late work, where his peasants in their earthiness have the grandeur, without the grace, of Michelangelo's figures, but they are not, thank heaven, Michelangelesque peasants. If Bruegel studied the Sistine Ceiling, he was not seduced by it into the stylized imitations that sapped the energy of so many talents in his mannerist generation. We would like to think that he was impressed by the monumental simplicities of Giotto, but there are no hints.

Nature, not other men's art, was Bruegel's study on this trip, in all the dramatic variety that Italy offered in contrast to the intimate monotony of his native landscape. He crossed the Alps, and his drawings of mountains—great peaks and ranges seen from above by an artist who had never seen things from a perch higher than a housetop—are comparable only to Leonardo's, but they differ from Leonardo's in a significant way. Leonardo's mountainscapes (or cosmoscapes) are generalized to recall the geological forces that created them; even the cities that appear here and there in Leonardo's valleys are presented as natural growths (which cities are) rather than as accumulations of habitations; they seem unpopulated. Bruegel's mountainscapes are more detailed; their valleys are nooks and crannies sympathetic to human existence, places where men can fulfill their function as recognized parts of a world even so vast.

For the rest of his life, the view from above, even of a flat landscape or even of an interior, became Bruegel's consistent vantage point. The fulfillment of his interest in landscape, however, had to wait. He seems to have returned to the Netherlands in 1553 or 1554; was certainly back in Antwerp by 1555; and in 1556 suddenly began the fantasy-moralities that brought him the sobriquet "Pieter the Droll." "Droll" carried implications that went beyond the merely humorous, edging into the sinister and terrible, and in this field young Bruegel's mentor by example was Hieronymus Bosch—dead since 1516 but still the great master (as he remains today) of moral allegory in the form of diableries. Bruegel's commercial mentor was Hieronymus Cock, an Antwerp print dealer who had commissioned him to do drawings for engravings on such salable subjects as the deadly sins.

Bruegel was known to the mass of his contemporaries only through these prints. As a painter he executed none of those public commissions, such as altarpieces or decorations for civic buildings, that were accessible to everybody. His patrons were diplomats, statesmen, and wealthy intellectuals —art collectors on an international scale, men like Cardinal Antoine Perrenot de Granvella, archbishop of Malines and adviser to Philip II of Spain, or the geographer and humanist Ortelius.

Nearly twenty-five years after Bruegel's death, when the Archduke Ernest became governor of the Netherlands, part of his personal program was to hunt out and acquire as many Bruegels as possible, and when he died these went to his brother, the emperor Rudolph II, king of Bohemia and Austria, a passionate collector who already had a number of Bruegels of his own. A third Austrian, Archduke Leopold William, who died nearly a hundred years after Bruegel, was a third avid collector who helps account for Vienna's unrivaled collection of Bruegels.

Intellectually, if not by high birth, Bruegel certainly shared the aristocratic character of the men who during his life and long after his death were most interested in his painting. The sobriquet "Peasant Bruegel," attached to him in the sense of "the Bruegel who painted peasants," has misled a few romanticizers even in the twentieth century. To his contemporaries outside the limited circle where his paintings were accessible, and even to other artists and most commentators or historians, Bruegel was "Pieter the Droll" on the basis of his drawings for engravings—the moral allegories and diableries that were published by Hieronymus Cock. "Pieter the Droll" was always thought of as a follower of Bosch, which is much less than half the story.

Like Bosch, Bruegel treated things monstrous and deformed as symbols of moral corruption. But where Bosch's visionary intensity is focused on a nightmarish battle between forces of heaven and hell, Bruegel never quite leaves the real world. There is always an admixture of humor with the grotesquerie, and of compassion with the morbidity. Sin for Bruegel was more than a matter of private degradation: his most hellish conceptions are comments on the texture of society as well as moral abstractions. When he shows us maimed beggars dragging themselves along with rough sticks as crutches, the stumps of their legs trailing and their brutalized spirits showing dark and blank behind their eye sockets (*The Beggars* in the Louvre), he shows them to us not only as Bosch showed his monsters, as symbols of the spirit defiled by sin, but also as the victims of human cruelty. At a time when the maimed, the insane, the feebleminded, and the deformed were laughed at, were thought of as animals differing from stray dogs only in being more diverting, Bruegel made them a rebuke to society. Without idealizing them or pretending that they were anything but bestial, he said that they had been born men and that the guilt of their reduction to a bestial state was on the head of a cruel society that degraded itself by degrading them.

Although in his early paintings Bruegel adapted freely whatever served him in the pictorial schemes of his predecessor, the two artists are not much alike in effect. Bosch's greatest work is calculated to induce a paroxysm of spiritual terror by way of an orgy of sexual excitement. Bruegel's horror of sin has less to do with the putrefaction it induces in the immortal soul than with the ignobility it inflicts upon the living man: foolishness becomes a greater sin than lust. Explicitly sexual references are rare in Bruegel's work, and suggestive sexuality does not exist in it.

Bruegel's revulsion against the follies of materialism might in another artist have produced nothing better than cynicism or ivory-tower withdrawal. Bruegel, however, was certain that a saving grace was bound within the scheme of life. He found it in the natural wisdom of the uneducated man, whose closeness to the earth made him all the shrewder as an observer of the world; whose observations were made from a position outside the confusions and petty competitions that wizened the spirit of a mercantile class; who, with only the cloudiest notion, if any, as to the meaning of the word "philosophy," had built up a kind of spontaneous catalogue of philosophical principles in the form of parables and proverbs.

The intellectual discovery of proverbs as statements not only pithy but profound was not unique with Bruegel. Erasmus, among other philosophers, had collected them. But they were the ideal subjects for Bruegel at just this moment. Their imagery was as fantastic as that of any symbols of sin, but their substance was sociological and humanistic rather than theological. Proverbs—whether in their condensed form as catch phrases or extended as parables—have their source in the life of the people, and they endure for the double reason of their solid truth and the vivid originality of their expression. Bruegel collected (in 1559) about a hundred Netherlandish proverbs and showed them all being acted out en masse in a Netherlandish village, thus producing in one picture a phantasmagoria, a compendium, a genre record of dress and physical types, and a kind of satirical ballet on the subject of man's infinite capacity to demean and defraud himself.

If the form of these proverbs is not always familiar to us, the meaning is: "Heads won't break walls" (It's no use butting your head against a stone wall); "He carries a basketful of light outdoors" (Carrying coals to Newcastle); "An eel held by the tail is not yet caught" (Don't count your chickens before they're hatched); and so on.

Bruegel's recognition of human foibles never reduced him to bitterness—or at least never to any bitterness discernible in his work. From the mass of it we can deduce that he regarded misanthropy as a form of self-interest as degrading in its way as avarice or gluttony. He said something of the kind in *The Misanthrope* (Naples), a painting not clearly decipherable (but perhaps based on a lost parable), where a stooped, sour old man plods through a landscape composed (like the world?) in the form of a circle. The old man has isolated himself within this world under a black cloak with a deep hood. We see only his long, drooping nose, his tight, turned-down mouth, and his dangling white beard; everything is hidden from him except the bit of barren path immediately beneath his lowered gaze, where a few thorns are scattered. He is oblivious to the deep landscape stretching beyond him (suggesting, as do so many of Bruegel's landscapes, the swelling curve of the earth), where a shepherd tends a flock of sheep—some black, some white—and a windmill turns. The misanthrope is not aware, either, of a bizarre, ragged little figure encased in a crystal globe who has reached up under the cloak to filch the old man's moneybag. The misanthrope is doubly robbed: wrapped in the false security of his symbolic cloak and hood, he robs himself of the world—but he cannot escape the world even so, for it in turn robs him.

In Bruegel's picturizations of proverbs and parables the Netherlandish peasant is employed only as a pantomimist, but in the paintings of peasant life he comes into his own as Bruegel's symbol of significant man. Rejecting the elegant but now bloodless gods and heroes who continued to preen and posture in Italian mannerist art and its international offshoots, Bruegel could have fallen into the trap of sentimentalizing a lout as the symbol of virtue, making him, in specious opposition to the Olympians, as bloodless as they. But he recognized that the peasant frequently was a lout and often showed him as one, with an open and sometimes ribald humor that was neither jibing nor condescending. Bruegel prettified nothing. As far as detail is concerned, the peasant pictures are accurate genre records. A feast in a granary (*The Peasant Wedding* in Vienna) is an explicit description of the setting, of the paraphernalia (and table manners) of eating and drinking, and even, if you examine the faces individually, of village types.

But all detail is incidental to the generalization of form by which the commonplace becomes monumental: the village feast that begins as a genre scene ends as an expression of the richness of life. *The Wedding Dance* (Detroit), where the heavy-bodied men and women whirl in a mass that in fact must have been sweaty, galumphing, and picturesque, surges with the life force that for Bruegel was the invincible truth that justifies our existence and by its grandeur is the measure of the petty blindness of our follies.

Like Michelangelo, Bruegel created a symbolic colossus from the material of the human figure. But the two artists' colossi resemble one another only in their weight and breadth. Michelangelo idealized man as the supreme intellectual and passionate force. The idealized body in Michelangelo's art expresses man's spiritual nobility, but exists without earthly connections; it could never walk through the streets, and could inhabit only a landscape invented to suit it.

In Bruegel all this is reversed. The symbol's majesty lies not in its beauty but in its plainness. Michelangelo's Adam, the consummate expression of his ideal, may have been created from clay, but the fact is important only because it emphasizes the miracle of his gloriousness. Bruegel's man need not—must not—lose his identification with earth, for earth is not a base material, and the resources of art are not needed to ennoble it. Man himself draws his nobility from nature, his habitat: his passions are reduced to inconsequence when he accords his life with its eternal rhythm. No matter that the body, wrapped in rough garments that belong to it as a pelt belongs to an animal, is clumsy by any standard of idealized form. In any form but its own, it would lose its identity with nature.

But Bruegel's optimistic faith in the sheer vitality of nature is tempered by his recognition of nature's indifference to man. The justification for our existence may be found in our integration with the great scheme, but this integration imposes its own conditions. In his last years Bruegel returned to the celebration of nature in a series of pictures on the subject of the months of the year, recognizing but transcending the medieval formula that had produced hundreds of pictorial variations as different from one another as the illuminations in the *Très Riches Heures du Duc de Berry* and the crudest woodcuts in popular shepherds' calendars.

Bruegel sufficiently observed the conventional subject matter of the occupations assigned to each month, but his true subject was the mood and the feel and the look of nature in its cycle. Men are as natural a part of it as plants and lakes and fields, and like them, men are subject, beyond their will and for better or worse, to the permeating heat and brilliant light of full summer, to the blustery chill and lowering skies of November, to the frozen spareness of deep winter.

Painted about four years before his death, Bruegel's final visions of nature and man in nature are surely unexcelled by any paintings, anywhere, as expressive summaries of the natural life of our planet as it revolves about the sun, and no other paintings have tied man's life so closely within that spinning. But man's almost puppet-like subjection to nature's cycles is too easily interpreted as Bruegel's ultimate conclusion. When he died in his early forties he was still painting peasant and religious subjects; he had barely abandoned the monsters that had earlier filled his work. If he was trying to reach some kind of conclusive statement of his complex philosophy, he had only begun.

Looking at his total work from the arbitrary boundary line of his death, we are confronted by only a partial fulfillment of his potential: for all its greatness, his total work was only work in progress. He had told us in various ways that man is one manifestation of universal force, but only a tiny manifestation; that nature is indifferent to his welfare, being neither malevolent nor benevolent; and that when man breaks from nature, he becomes the victim of his own frailties. But Bruegel never accepted any human condition as proof that the cosmos is an accident—or that man's life within it is meaningless.

Bruegel, who is not called "Pieter the Great" but could be, had two sons, three grandsons, and five great-grandsons, all painters named Brueghel, as well as three granddaughters who married painters and supplied numerous descendants in the craft whose names—we shall forgo carrying the family tree into further generations where artists continued to proliferate on the residue of a great inheritance—were Borrekins, Kessel, and Teniers.

Of the long list, Bruegel's two sons are the most important. The first son, Pieter Brueghel the Younger, nicknamed "Hell" because of his penchant for painting conflagrations, whether in hell or upon earth, was born in 1564 or thereabouts, some five years before his father's death, and remains a moderately interesting artist in the Bosch-Bruegel hellscape tradition. But in his rather washed-out versions the fires seem to have lost their heat. The netherworld, finally divorced from the medieval terror of sin, becomes more picturesque than diabolic. Pieter the Younger died in 1637 or 1638, having produced one son, Pieter III (1589-1638/39), whose perpetuation of the name did it no credit. He was a painter of no consequence.

The great Bruegel's younger son, Jan Brueghel, nicknamed "Velvet," is a really charming painter in his own right, parentage aside. Velvet was born in 1568, and hence was hardly out of swaddling clothes when his father died. He made no effort to continue his father's tradition but became a consummate minor master within the restrictions of his primarily stylish approach to the minutely detailed rendering of plants and animals. His paintings—sometimes still lifes, often poetically contrived landscapes—always have the high gloss of enamels. They are so entrancing that their lack of profundity stirs no regrets. His most ambitious works, repeated many times, are allegories of the five senses and the four elements, but they are ambitious only in terms of sprightly theatrical complication rather than interpretatively.

Enormously successful, popular, full of honors, and fecund both as a parent and as a painter, Jan spent his life in Antwerp with brief excursions to Italy, Prague, and Nuremberg. Rubens was among his admirers. The two artists exchanged professional favors, Jan executing floral accessories for a Rubens Madonna, and Rubens painting the human figures—not Jan's forte—in a Velvet paradise. Jan's paintings were purchased in quantity in all the courts of Europe; in Madrid's Prado alone there are fifty-four.

Jan Brueghel's two sons, Jan II (1601-1678) and Ambrosius (1617-1675), imitated his style. He died in 1625, at the age of fifty-seven. He must have had a very happy life.